Inside Alcatraz

Inside Alcatraz

My Time on the Rock

Jim Quillen

arrow books

1 3 5 7 9 10 8 6 4 2

Arrow Books
20 Vauxhall Bridge Road
London SW1V 2SA

Arrow Books is part of the Penguin Random House group of companies
whose addresses can be found at global.penguinrandomhouse.com.

Penguin
Random House
UK

Historical photographs of Alcatraz Island and the cellhouse are courtesy of
Golden Gate National Recreation Area/Park Archives and Records Centre
and San Francisco Public Library/San Francisco History Centre.
Family and personal photographs and memorabilia
are courtesy of the Estate of Jim Quillen.

First published in Great Britain by Century in 2015

First published in the United States of America in 1991 by
Golden Gate National Parks Conservancy
Bldg. 201 Fort Mason, San Francisco, CA 94123

Golden Gate National Parks Conservancy is the non-profit membership
organization created to preserve the Golden Gate National Parks,
enhance the experiences of park visitors, and build a community
dedicated to preserving the parks for the future.

For more information please visit:
www.parksconservancy.org and www.nps.gov/alcatraz.

www.randomhouse.co.uk

A CIP catalogue record for this book
is available from the British Library.

ISBN 9781784750664

Printed and bound by CPI Group (UK) Ltd, Croydon, CR0 4YY

I wish to dedicate this book to my loving wife, Leone Marie Quillen.

Thank you for your patience, encouragement, and understanding of the mood swings I experienced when recalling the unpleasant memories necessary to write this book. Had you given less, it would never have reached completion.

Contents

Author's Note

This book is an autobiography describing the progressive and insidious nature of involvement in crime. It illustrates how minor infractions of the law, if unchecked, may escalate into major criminal activities. The ensuing consequences may be death or years of incarceration, humiliation, and degradation.

It was only through the grace of our Lord Jesus Christ, and His intercession, that my life of hopeless incarceration was averted. His help and forgiveness permitted me to obtain freedom, family, and a useful and productive place in society.

As gratifying as it was to achieve a presidential pardon and a gubernatorial pardon, it will be more fulfilling if this book deters others from making the mistakes I made.

There is no glamor in prison. There is only loneliness, fear, heartbreak, and sorrow.

While writing this book, I resolved to write what, in my opinion, was truth as best I could determine without exaggeration or distortion. Many conclusions and opinions were based on what I personally saw or heard. In other instances I had to rely on my personal knowledge and observations as well as conversations with reliable guards and inmates. I believe I came to logical, reasonable conclusions. My writing was done without malice and with no intent to defame, malign, or injure any person or persons in the process. My intent was to show Alcatraz, the administration, Bureau of Prisons, guards, and inmates as they really existed.

Alcatraz was always a prison shrouded in secrecy, and many facts and occurrences were hidden from public scrutiny. The public was allowed to know only what the Bureau of Prisons and the administration wanted known. Much of what was disclosed was distorted, exaggerated, or glossed over with misleading statements or untruths.

The inmates were not without blame in many instances and I had no intent to justify their actions. The purpose of prison is to incarcerate the criminal, not to brutalize him physically, mentally, and spiritually until death is preferable to any existence in such a prison.

I will let the reader decide if this is what drove some inmates to atrocious actions.

Jim Quillen
1991

Preface

Alcatraz, 11 p.m., August 28, 1942

With a crash, the steel gate slammed shut, a sound that seemed to bring finality to everything that life had to offer.

I walked into the small six-by-nine-by-seven-foot gray cell that was to be my home for years to come. I saw a steel bed, a straw mattress, and a dirty, lumpy pillow. The cell was lighted only by the large overhead lights outside, which illuminated each cell enough to enable the guards to make their numerous nightly counts.

I noticed the cell contained a toilet with no seat. At the end of the bed, next to the toilet, was a small washbasin with only one tap. Cold water! Above the sink was a single shelf that extended the entire width of the cell. Next to the bed was a small metal table that folded down flat against the wall. This was my home. I realized that, at twenty-two years of age, this was to be my home, my future, for years to come—and possibly the place of my death.

As I looked about me, it was as though the room began to close in, with some strange odor that dominated the air and stifled me. I suddenly realized it was an odor I must learn to live with, the smell of a marking pen that gave me my new identity. It was on my bedding and my clothing, making me into another nonentity in the world of the criminal. I was engulfed with the realization that I was no longer a person, but instead AZ-586, a criminal who had been sentenced to serve forty-five years in the federal penal system.

I then became aware of the men around me. Some were awake, as I could hear low tones of whispering from one cell to another, passing the word that a transfer of "fish" had come in. This stirred hope in the hearts of some, for each time a new "fish" arrived, it usually meant that there was hope that some of the old "long-timers" might be transferred to another institution.

Not only was my cell dark and gloomy, I realized with a shiver, it was also cold and windy. Although I knew I would not sleep, I would at least be reasonably warmer for the remainder of the night if I got into bed.

While making up my bed, I was startled by the sudden flash of light hitting my eyes. It was a guard making his count. He asked why I was not undressed and in bed. I explained I was a new transfer and had just arrived. He warned me that if I wasn't undressed and in bed in the next few minutes, I might find out what the "hole" was at the "Rock." This added great haste to my retiring.

As I lay there, I began reviewing in my mind the various stories I had heard about Alcatraz. As can well be imagined, I did not sleep much that night.

I had lived in and around the Bay Area all my life, thus Alcatraz's reputation was not unfamiliar to me. My thoughts flashed back to the many stories I had had occasion to hear, read, and wholeheartedly believe. I was soon to learn firsthand, however, that while some stories were fabricated, imaginative versions from a creative writer, most indeed were quite true. Much to my dismay, I could not recall ever hearing anything favorable about the prison or its inmates.

"Rehabilitation" was not part of the Alcatraz vocabulary, or ever considered. The institution was there for the purpose of proving to unruly prisoners that they had reached the ultimate termination of their undisciplined way of life. I recalled the prison being referred to as "Hellcatraz" and "Devil's Island of America." Vivid in my mind were stories of brutality and regimentation. Among the many facts I had read or heard about while in San Quentin (a tough prison in itself) was the lack of privileges allowed the inmates at Alcatraz.

I began to think about my past. How had I, in a few short years, progressed from a state reformatory to the United States' toughest and most notorious federal prison?

I could vividly recall how I had been warned over and over again: "If you don't change your ways, you will some day end up in prison for life!" It was true. The roads to crime and self-destruction are easy to locate in the journey of life, but once embarked upon, very difficult to abandon.

1 Growing Up Fast

I was born in San Fransisco, California, on September 16, 1919. My father was a man who did not know how to outwardly show affection and love. His whole life was devoted to being a good employee for the company where he worked. He was a quiet, nonverbal man and a strict disciplinarian who was inclined to use physical punishment.

My mother was a very lovely woman, with one very large problem: alcoholism. I have no idea how long she had this before my birth, and I did not have the opportunity to learn much about her or to know her very well, as by the time I was seven, she had deserted us. I do know my father had tried in many ways to help her, but to no avail.

Now, working in the medical field, I realize that alcoholism is a disease; but I have often wondered, as I have grown older, what underlying factor drove her to this point. I am sure that, in her own way, she loved her children—my younger sister Kay and me—but I am also sure the only thing she seemed to need more was alcohol. Thus her priorities in life were alcohol, husband, and then children. My sister and I were not bad children. In fact, I would say we were normal, average children and most generally well behaved. But for my part, that would soon change.

My memories of childhood during the time we were together as a family are mostly of a violent or sad nature. Today I have only three prominent memories of my mother, and each is associated with violence and sadness.

The first memory is that of my father, my mother, and myself sitting in front of the fireplace one evening just prior to Easter. We were fixing an Easter basket for my sister, who was asleep in another room. We were laughing and having a good time. My mother had been drinking but was not causing any problem. She was sitting in front of the fireplace. My father was sitting with his back to the door that opened into a hallway that led to the bathroom and my parents' bedroom.

My mother excused herself to go to the bathroom. I was looking toward my father when I heard her returning. She opened the door, hesitated a few seconds, then reached down into the woodbin beside my father and picked up a large piece of firewood. My father didn't pay any special attention when she returned, as he was fixing the basket for Kay. Instead of coming into the room and sitting down, my mother suddenly brought the piece of wood crashing down on my father's head. It made a terrible sound that I can remember to this day.

I do not understand why it didn't kill him. I am sure that was my mother's intention. It did cause a terrible laceration to his head, but he did not lose consciousness. He had the presence of mind to roll away so that my mother could not hit him again. When he got to his feet, she dropped the wood and ran into the bathroom, locking the door behind her.

My father took my sister and me with him when he went to get medical attention. After the doctor closed the wound, he advised my father to go home and rest. When we arrived home, my mother was gone. She was gone for several days. When she returned, my father was forgiving and took her back. Our lives settled back into the same old routine.

Whenever my mother could find a way to buy some liquor, she would. My father was very tolerant of her behavior but he also could become very violent if she managed to start an argument. This, at times, was not too hard to do, especially if my father was tired. Often this lack of tolerance was detrimental to all of us.

Some time after the incident when she'd hit my father with the wood, and when everything had been going reasonably well, my mother went on another drunk. When my father came home from work he was disturbed but patient with her. He asked her not to drink anymore and she agreed. During the course of the evening she found a way to sneak a few more drinks and became very abusive to my father. He finally told her that he was going to find her booze and dump it out because she was getting loud and mean.

To find her hiding places was not a simple matter as she

was ingenious when it came to hiding her supply. But my father was a stubborn and determined man and, after much hunting, he found her supply and dumped it down the drain. This infuriated my mother to the point that she became violent. My father calmed her down and convinced her to go to bed. She agreed but told him he could not sleep in the same room with her.

Our home was a small one-bedroom house and my sister and I slept on a davenport that opened up into a bed. On many occasions when my mother was drunk, my father would be forced to sleep with us. The second memory of my mother relates to a night when my sister and I had been in bed and asleep for some time. I was awakened by my mother shouting and swearing and my father tearing things up, looking for her liquor. I was frightened by all the commotion and afraid that my father would be injured again, but because I was so sleepy I soon went back to sleep until I was awakened by my father getting into the bed with us.

At this time in my life I had a small brown-and-white fox terrier named Spotty who always slept on the foot of our bed. I can remember my father asking the dog to move over because he was taking up all the foot room on my father's side.

I guess the three of us had drifted off to sleep for some time before we were awakened by the dog barking and whining fiercely. My father told the dog to shut up. I believe he thought the dog was barking at something outside, but the dog wouldn't stop. This was unusual because he always obeyed my father. My father then decided the dog needed to be let out, so he got up, walked the few steps to the front door, and opened it. When the fresh air hit him, he realized he was feeling ill and dizzy, but it passed after a few breaths.

Suddenly he realized the house was full of gas. He ran back to the bed, picked up my sister, and yelled for me to follow him. He ran out on the porch with Kay and then came back to help me out. When I got to the porch, I saw that my little sister's coloring was blue, and I am sure that in a short while she would have been dead.

My father left us on the porch and went back into the house looking for my mother. As he went, he opened all the windows so he wouldn't pass out. He looked through the house but my mother was gone. Apparently, some time after we were all asleep, she had gotten up, gone out the back door, walked around to the front door, and plugged the crack at the bottom of the door with rags. She then came back into the house, turned on all the gas jets, including some old wall outlets. She then went out the back door, locking it after her. She stopped to plug the crack under the back door with rags. I'm sure she had made arrangements to be picked up by someone, as we lived too far from town for her to walk.

She never returned.

My father took my sister and me to the doctor to be examined. We were all right and were sent home and put to bed. It was this incident that made my father realize she was never going to be a wife and mother. He tried to keep the three of us close together for a while by boarding us with a family who lived a couple of blocks away. This didn't work out, as I would just leave and go home. He then decided to let me live at home with him.

He would wake me in the morning as he left to go to work and tell me to get ready for school. I would get up, make the bed, fix breakfast, dress, and go to school. At noon, I would run home (about three blocks), make a sandwich, and return to school. After school I would return home, wash the dishes, set the table, peel the potatoes, and wait for my dad to get home to make supper. This worked out well and even though I missed my mother, I was happier at home than I would have been living in someone else's home. I could also walk the short distance to see my sister every day.

Things went well until my dad decided to start night school. He would come home from work, cook dinner, eat, and then leave to attend night classes. This would leave me alone from about 6 p.m. until 11 p.m., or even later, every night. At first I would go see my sister each night, but I got into a fist fight with the son of the family she was boarded with and wasn't allowed to visit unless my father brought me, which only occurred on weekends.

I soon began running with a gang of guys that were several years older than myself. We would go to the waterfront and run through the boxcars and even, on occasion, break a seal on a car to see what was inside. I ran with this gang for a long time, until they were caught breaking into a boxcar and were sent to Juvenile Hall. Fortunately for me, I had not gone with them that night. I don't recall the reason why, but it kept me from being locked up with them.

I was allowed to run wild and totally unsupervised during the formative years of my character and I believe that, by associating with this gang that was so much older than myself, I found, or believed, that I was as tough and as able to handle myself as they were. I also believe this gave me the feeling I could challenge authority and was smart or clever enough to do whatever I chose to do. This reasoning was faulty, of course, as I found out years later when I was in prison.

My third memory of my mother was also the last time I ever saw her. I had gone to school as usual. About 11 a.m. I received a call to go to the principal's office. I was told to go home immediately, change into my best clothes, and wait for my father to pick me up. I had been home an hour when my dad got home. He changed his clothes and told me to get into the car because we were going to San Francisco. As we were driving to Point Richmond to catch the ferry, my father told me that my mother was dying. He had received a phone call at work and the caller told him that my mother wished to see me before she passed away. He spoke to me about being brave and unafraid. This helped, but I was still frightened.

We caught the ferry to San Francisco and, after much searching, found the address my father had been given over the phone. It was a rather poor area of the city.

My father told me to stay in the car while he determined if we were at the right house. I watched as he climbed some stairs and knocked on the door of this dirty-looking house. He waited a couple of minutes, then knocked again. This time the door opened and I heard my father talking to someone in a very angry voice. He suddenly turned and walked rapidly away, toward the car. Immediately there was another person running after my father. It was my mother. She was very drunk, dirty, and loud. My father got into the car and started driving. As we pulled away, I looked out the back window and saw my mother running after us and yelling that she wanted to see me. My father did not slow down or look back. It was obvious he was very disturbed.

As we drove back home, we both realized my mother would never change and that we would never be together again as a family. It seemed to me that from that day forward there was a change in his attitude toward me, and a very noticeable change in my father's outlook on the world.

He had never been a drinker but, at times, if I was awake when he came home from night school, I could tell he had been drinking. The time of his arrival home also later became and later and the frequency of his not coming home at all became more regular. The relationship between us became very strained and I felt I had become a tremendous burden to him. I don't know if this was his feeling or not, but when I reflect back on what he tried to do for me, I realize that I owe him much more than I ever gave him credit for in my younger years. I am sure that not many men would have done as much or tried as hard as he did.

This strained relationship continued for a time, then he decided to put me in another boarding home. I was boarded with people who lived several miles from my father's house. I did very well there for a time; the family was good to me and I liked them. It was also too far away from my father's house to run home. I don't know why, but much to my surprise, my father decided to board my sister Kay with the same family. At that time, my sister was three or slightly older. For some strange reason, I had the feeling this family didn't like my sister. I felt they were always picking on her and, as a consequence, I would stick up for her and we would both end up in trouble.

I can remember the last day we spent there. It was in the summer and I was out of school. The lady of the house was doing her summer cleaning and made the children, including her own son, go outside. Apparently she had washed and waxed the floors. While we were waiting for the floors to dry, she stayed outside with us. The problem started when Kay complained she had to go to the bathroom, but the lady would not let her go inside. As a result of not being allowed to go inside, my sister wet her underpants. This made the woman very angry and she swatted her on the bottom a couple of times.

I was watching what was going on without saying anything until the lady told Kay she was going to punish her by washing her face with her wet pants. I thought she was only threatening her until she actually took her pants off and grabbed my sister. She was kneeling on the ground trying to hold her when I yelled at her to stop and to leave my sister alone. She ignored me and started to wash Kay's face with the pants. I ran over, pulled Kay away, then hit the lady in the face as hard as I could. I then grabbed my sister and started running down the block as fast as I could. I looked back once and saw the lady sitting on the ground holding her face and her son yelling that he was going to call the police. This frightened me and I continued running. I didn't know where we were going but I was convinced that if I went back, I would go to jail.

When I finally decided that I wasn't in immediate danger of being caught, I sat down on the curb and tried to figure out what I should do. I decided that we had to go home to my father's house. We started walking and I finally found a street I recognized and then knew we could make it home if we could just keep walking and not get caught. When my sister couldn't walk any further and would cry, I would pick her up and carry her. It was suppertime when we arrived at my father's house and we were both hot, hungry, and tired.

We never thought about knocking, but walked right in the back door of the house. We were both startled and surprised to see a very pretty young lady cooking dinner in our kitchen. At first I was frightened, but I knew my dad had to be there and he would make it all right. The girl asked who we were and what we were doing there. I told her I lived there and wanted to see my father. She left the kitchen and I could hear her telling my father that there were two children in the kitchen looking for their father.

My dad came to the kitchen and asked what we were doing home. I told him the story and I could tell he was angry at both me and the lady with whom we were boarded. I could hear the girl in the other part of the house crying. My father got us a glass of milk and told us to sit down. He went back into the bedroom to talk to the young lady, but she wouldn't listen to him and apparently jumped up, ran into the bathroom, and locked the door. We could hear my father talking to her and pleading with her to unlock the door, but she refused.

My father finally threatened to break the door down if she didn't open it. We then heard her tell him that she was going to kill herself. This must have frightened him because he did begin to kick in the door. The young lady suddenly unlocked the door and ran past my father to the bedroom. He went into the bathroom and we heard him say, "Oh, my God!" We then heard him on the phone, telling the doctor she had swallowed a full bottle of iodine. The doctor told my father to bring her to the hospital immediately. By this time, the lady had become violently ill and was retching and vomiting continuously. My father told my sister and me not to move and he would be right back. He went into the bedroom, picked up the lady, and carried her to the car to drive to the hospital.

We never saw the young lady again.

At that time, I really didn't understand all that had

happened, but as the years have gone by, I have reflected on this incident many times and realize that my father had asked this young lady to live with him without telling her that he was married and had two children. When we walked into the house, we upset the whole apple cart. My dad again decided we would go back to the old arrangement we had before we made the trip to San Francisco to see my mother. It seems that during this period my life started to take a very downward trend.

I began doing poorly in school and became somewhat of a school bully. I was constantly picking a fight with someone. I took pride in the fact that I would fight anyone, no matter how big. As a consequence, I was not permitted to play with many of the children who lived in our neighborhood.

I do recall making friends with a boy named Ernest Rassmussen. I would go to his house quite often. He had so many brothers that I don't think I ever knew all their names or how many there were. I soon found out that if you went there at suppertime, you could just walk into the kitchen, sit down, and someone would feed you. They didn't eat fancy foods but if you liked beans, stew, spaghetti, and things of this kind, there was always plenty to eat. His mother must have loved kids and cooking, as it really was a happy home.

I also met another boy whom I took a terrible dislike to. His name was James Pichlesimer. Even though fifty years have passed, I can still remember a couple of incidents related to this boy.

I recall one day we were playing together and for some reason a disagreement arose. I hit him, he fell, hit his head, and was unconscious. After I hit him, I ran home and left him lying there. I was scared but was also pleased with myself for knocking him unconscious with one punch. This brought about my first encounter with the law.

The fight occurred in the early afternoon and by the time my father got home from work, I had forgotten about it. My father and I were eating dinner when there was a knock on the door. He answered the door and there were two officers from the Richmond Police Department. As soon as I saw them, I remembered the fight and thought that James must have died. It was instant terror for me. When they asked my father if I lived there, I knew I was going to jail.

My father called me into the front room and the police said they wanted to talk to me about a complaint they had received. They asked me to relate what had occurred and if I had hit young James Pichlesimer. I admitted that I had. They then went on to imply that I had used a rock or other type of weapon on him. Of course this was not true and I told them so. After more questions, they apparently believed that it was a simple fight between boys and nothing more. I was given a stern lecture and the officers left. My father was very angry with me and insisted that I go over to this boy's house the next day and apologize for my actions.

I really didn't want to do this, but my father stated that if I hadn't done it by the time he came home from work, I would be in big trouble. He said he was going to call the boy's parents to check if I had done as he told me.

So, after school the next day, I worked up enough courage to go to the boy's house. I knocked on the door and both James and his mother answered. I told them I was sorry for what I had done the previous day and that I had come to apologize. Mrs. Pichlesimer was very gracious and said she did understand how these things could happen. She said I was forgiven but she would appreciate it if I didn't come to their home or associate with James anymore. This was fine with me, as I thought he was a real wimp.

After his mother left the door, James opened it enough to stick his head out and tell me that it might be over as far as she was concerned, but it wasn't over with him and he was going to get even. I passed this off as just talk and went home. When my dad came home, he asked if I had apologized as he had ordered me to do. I told him I had, and just as he had said he would, he called the family to check it out. I was glad I had done as I was told. This whole incident was soon forgotten by me for a month or so.

One day, I went to the home of a boy who lived two houses away from James. While we were playing, I noticed that the Pichlesimers were getting ready to go on a trip. We could see them carrying clothes and suitcases to the car. I never gave it much thought except to think it must be nice to go on a trip with your family for the weekend. Before the Pichlesimers left, I had to go home. I was home that entire weekend. It was also one of the few times my father was home on a Friday night and spent the whole weekend without going out to see his "war buddies," as he often called his dates. My father could vouch for my time the entire weekend.

On Sunday evening there was a knock at the front door and my father answered it. It was the same two Richmond police officers. They wanted to see me. I was truly in the dark about what they wanted. My father asked the reason and the police explained they had received a call from the Pichlesimer family complaining that they thought I had flooded their home with a garden hose during their absence.

My father explained that I had been with him all weekend and that it could not have been me. The police said they believed him but they would still have to take me to the station to get it straightened out. My father then explained that I had apologized for the previous incident and had not played or associated with the boy since that day. I then told the police about the threat James had made about getting even with me.

To make a long story short, the police began to believe my father and me and went back to talk to James again. What happened, we found out later that night, was that James had gone to the back of the house while his folks were packing the car, opened a bedroom window, slipped a garden hose in, then turned on the water. He then rejoined his parents and they left for the weekend. When they came home and opened the door, the water rushed out to meet them like a river. It ruined much of their home and furnishings. It was James who pointed suspicion at me. It was his way of getting even for the trouble we'd had. I am sure it would have worked except the police either tricked him or he gave himself away in some manner when the police questioned him the second time.

A short time after this episode, my father decided to divorce my mother. I don't know why, but Kay and I were made wards of the court. She was taken from the home my father boarded her in and I was taken away from my father. We were taken to the small town of Martinez, where we were placed in a detention home.

We were the only two children in that detention home, to my knowledge. It was the first time in my life that I can remember when I could not come and go as I pleased. There were heavy mesh screens on the window where I was locked up for the night and in the dayroom, where we were kept during the day. I don't know where they housed Kay at night but, because of her age, it was where she could be observed and cared for at all times.

I guess she must have been about four and I was about ten or eleven. At night I was locked in a special little room off to the side of the dayroom.

I was not isolated, because people were always coming and going, but still, I was lonely. I can remember looking out the window through the heavy screen, wishing I was home and that somehow everything could be made okay so that my mother and father were back together and we were a family again. I had a very lonely feeling in my heart for my mother even though I knew she had not been either a good wife or mother. I also wondered if I would ever get out of that detention home, as I felt caged, lonely, and forgotten. This same thought would be on my mind constantly in later years.

During the day it was not bad, as my sister and I were together. Our father came to see us two or three times during the weeks we were there; I looked forward to these visits, and they kept me going.

I can remember one time when he came. It was after visiting hours and they would not let him in. Somehow he found the window of my room and came around to talk to me for a couple of minutes. I'll never forget how I felt when he left. I spent a great deal of that night crying, until I finally fell asleep.

My father was granted his divorce and was given custody of my sister and me. I think the court had insisted that he make better arrangements for our care, because we all went together to live in the home of a Mrs. Julio. I assume my father paid room and board for the three of us. He and I shared a room together and Kay shared a room with Mrs. Julio's grown daughter, Alma. We all had our meals together, family style, and it seemed like a normal home with Mrs. Julio as the mother. My life settled down into a very happy existence. I liked Mrs. Julio and she in turn liked each of us and made it known that she did. She was always ready with a word of praise when you did something well, but would also scold you if you misbehaved.

This happy home life lasted for about a year. Reflecting back over my life, it is ironic to think that during the happiest year of my childhood, I accidentally became a thief, and the person I cared for the most, aside from my family, was the victim.

It was an episode in my life that to this very day makes me feel ashamed. As I said, the first incident was an accident, but after that, it was just plain stealing. Mrs. Julio would often have me go to the store for her to get groceries. She would give me a list of things she wanted and I would get them for her. On some occasions she would give me the money to pay for them and other times she would have me put them on her charge account at the small neighborhood store.

One day, she sent me to the store having given me the money necessary to pay for the items. I tucked it into my watch pocket so I would not lose it. But instead of paying for the purchase with the money, I had the man charge the items, which I took home to her. I did not do it with the intention of stealing the money. I just somehow forgot she had given it to me to pay with. It wasn't until a couple of days later when changing clothes that I found it tucked away in my pocket. At first I was surprised, but then remembered where the money had come from. Instead of telling Mrs. Julio, I decided to keep it. It was not a large sum, just some change, but the act was the same. I stole it.

I had never before stolen anything, but soon realized that I had an easy source of money if I wanted to take the chance. I had broken the seals on those boxcars with that gang of kids, but I had never personally profited from those pranks. This was a new experience and certainly a new temptation that I found hard to resist. I did not want to lose this source and became very cautious in my dealings. Now if there was something special I wanted, I could just steal the money when she gave it to me for groceries. As I said, Mrs. Julio was a very good woman. Fortunately, she never caught me, as I am sure it would have broken her heart.

The sad part of this episode is that a seed was sown in my head, in that I now believed stealing was easier than working for what one wanted.

During the time I lived with Mrs. Julio, I made one very close friend. His name was Alroy Williams. In a very short time, we became quite inseparable. I suppose it was because we seemed to have a lot in common and understood each other's problems so well. He, like me, was somewhat of a loner and not really acceptable to the families in our neighborhood.

Alroy always seemed to have money, so one day I asked him where he got it. He told me he would show me if I promised never to tell. We went into the front room of his house, where he pulled back the rug. Under the rug were rows of bills. His mother told him to get it from there whenever he needed money to eat. With my newfound interest in money, I was quite impressed, but I did keep my promise. His mother was a divorcee and was often gone all day and far into the night. She was an exceptionally beautiful young lady. Al lived a very similar existence with his mother as I had when I lived alone with my father. Years later, I realized that his mother's income was the result of prostitution and that was why he was not accepted by so many of the people in our neighborhood.

The so-called good people of our society punished him for his mother's sins. Mrs. Julio, however, was a fine Christian lady and she firmly believed the sins of the parent should not be taken out on the child. She never objected to my playing with Al and he was free to come to our house anytime he wanted. Mrs. Julio even invited him to many meals at our home. I am sure that the good Lord rewarded Mrs. Julio for her kindness to him.

I can still remember the day Al told me he was going to move. It came out of a clear blue sky. Thinking about the incident later, I surmised his mother had been forced out of town, given a choice between being arrested for prostitution or leaving the area. I remember how broken up I was about losing my best friend. I can only hope that his early life turned out better than mine.

Not long after Al left town, my life once again started changing. My father began staying out late, spending whole weekends away from home, chasing around and drinking again. He was never a heavy drinker and I can't recall ever seeing him really drunk. He would just get to feeling happy, and Lord knows he had few happy occasions prior to my mother's leaving.

None of these things did much to please Mrs. Julio,

however. I am sure that for some time she had entertained the prospect of marrying my father. I think during this period she realized that, whatever my father was looking for, she was not it. She finally told us we were going to have to move. During the last part of our stay with Mrs. Julio, my father had been going with a woman named Alice, and when we moved from Mrs. Julio's he rented an apartment in Berkeley and the four of us moved in.

For the first few months everything went well. Alice was good to us, cooking, cleaning, and making a home we all enjoyed. She really did seem to care for all of us, but there was one thing lacking in her life. She wanted to be married to my father. He, on the other hand, was very gun-shy whenever marriage was mentioned. He said he had had one marriage that put him through hell and there would never be another. Alice's method to help my father change his mind was to have us children continually ask Dad when he was going to marry her. This went on for about two years. I guess we all just finally wore him down, as he decided to get married.

2 The Beginning of Trouble

Within a very short time after their marriage, my relationship with Alice started to deteriorate. I was continually in trouble with her and my father about one thing or another. There was no peace between Alice and me; in fact, it became open war.

I am sure that I contributed more than my share to this poor relationship. As I have grown older, and especially since I became a parent, I have become more sympathetic with what she had to put up with. I was doing poorly in school, cutting classes, and not really trying to learn.

I eventually became a habitual runaway. I would run away from home at the first sign of a quarrel with my stepmother—not give any warning, just take off. I might be gone for two days, two weeks, or two months. Whenever I did come home, I was taken back in and somehow my absences from school were squared away so that I didn't get into trouble with the authorities.

Of course, it was never forgotten that I did these "bad

things," as my parents called them, and I was never allowed to forget how much I had hurt and worried them.

The fourth time I ran away from home, I went with a fellow habitual runaway named Dwight. He and I caught freight trains and traveled from Berkeley, California, to a small town in Wyoming where Dwight's folks had homesteaded 160 acres of land years before. We had big visions of going there to live in the cabin on the property and making our fortunes.

It started out badly from the very beginning. It was March and, although it had been raining, the weather cleared. We were at school when we decided to run away, because we were both in trouble in school as well as at home. We decided we would go to Wyoming, even though neither of us had ever been out of California, to get away from the people who we thought were against us. We walked from Berkeley to the railroad yards in Oakland, where we caught a freight train pulling out. We didn't have the faintest idea where it was going but it seemed to be headed in the direction we wanted.

We ended up in a small town called Roseville, which was the division point of the railroad. We realized when we got into the railroad yards that the train we were riding was going to be broken up and cars from it sent to various sections of the country. We got off and made our way out of the yards to an area where many transients were congregated around little fires. This trip was during the time when there were many, many men on the road. People were traveling over the entire country on freight trains in an effort to find work.

Apparently the railroad was sympathetic to the fact that times were hard and that these people, for the most part, were trying desperately to improve their situations in life. No one was ever hassled. In fact, the train crew, if asked, would give information on the destination of their train and where empty boxcars were in order to get out of the cold. If their train was not headed in the right direction, they would give information on the one that was: where it was "making up," which track it would be on, its time of depart- ure, and the best place to catch it before it got rolling too fast. They were really, as a whole, good men who had a love in their hearts for their fellow man.

We talked to some of the men waiting for trains and learned we wanted to catch a train headed for Sparks, Nevada, the next division point. Sparks had no special significance to us. We thought all we had to do was catch the train headed there and everything would be fine. If we had known what was in store for us when we caught that train, I am sure we would have turned around and gone home. I have had some close calls with death in my life, but I am sure the only thing that spared our lives that time was the intervention of our Savior.

We located the train we wanted to take, but it was dark and the train was moving, so we caught the first car we could. It was an oil tank car and certainly not the ideal car to ride. An oil tank car is nothing more than a large cylinder that sits on wheels and has a handrail around it. It also has a narrow platform or walkway that goes entirely around the car. This walkway is used by the crew to walk from one end of the train to the other. We thought this would be a fine place to ride, so we moved to the front of the car, which was following a boxcar. The height of the boxcar broke the flow of wind and made holding on to the handrail much easier. What we were not aware of when we caught that car was that we were committed to riding it through the Sierra Nevada mountains in the month of March.

When we left Oakland, the weather had cleared, but when we started climbing into the mountains toward Sparks, stormy weather converged upon us again. The higher we climbed into the mountains, the harder the snow and cold hit us. We were having a very difficult time hanging on. In addition, we started passing through the mountain snow sheds.

These are large and long (often half a mile) wooden sheds built to cover the railroad tracks in areas where large snow-slides occurred frequently. Before they were built, slides would block the tracks and bring all movement to an end.

When our train passed into these sheds we would be freezing, but once inside, the heat from the large locomotive (or locomotives, if the train was long enough) would suddenly warm us up. Unfortunately, the accumulated smoke in the shed would almost choke us to death. At times it seemed there was no air, only smoke. Several times we thought we were going to be forced to jump before suffocating, but just before jumping, we would again come out into the cold, snowy, fresh air.

First we would freeze, then we would choke. This went on mile after mile. We both finally came to the realization that we had to do something, as we were both fast becoming tired and could not stay awake. We debated taking turns holding each other as the other slept, but we both realized if the one holding passed out or fell asleep, we would both fall to our deaths beneath the train wheels. I am sure this gave us additional strength to hang on.

We debated jumping from the train, but this was equally bad because we were miles into the mountains and the snow was very deep. We would have frozen in a very short time. We finally took our belts off and hooked them over the handrail around the car in the hope that if we passed out, they would support us until we woke up, or would wake us when they tightened around our waists. It wasn't much to go on, but it worked. When the train reached the summit, it stopped for a brake check before starting down the other side. The brakeman found Dwight and I hanging by our belts, unconscious.

After much slapping, shaking, and yelling, the brakeman got us awake and able to move again. Fortunately for us, during the summit check, the train brakeman walks the entire length of the train, checking to make sure everything is okay. He checks all the boxes at the end of the wheel axles, which hold the lubricant that keeps the wheels from overheating. He also checks the train in general, to ensure against any accidents on the downgrade. I don't know if we were unconscious or just asleep when he found us, but after we started moving around again, we were fine except for being so cold. The brakeman was very angry, but I suspect somewhat relieved that we were not dead. He told us to walk to the front of the train and climb up on the oil tender, which carries all the oil the train uses as fuel.

The brakeman assured us we would be warm there and would make it into Sparks without freezing. He said he'd see if we were awake when we arrived in Sparks. We found the tender, climbed up on top, and soon were warm. The heat from the locomotive passed over the top of the tender, but the smoke drifted back without dropping down on us. It was a real blessing lying up there, warm and comfortable, after such a cold and almost fatal ride. We must have fallen asleep in just a matter of minutes, because neither of us remembered leaving the summit or the ride down the mountain.

It was early the next morning when the train pulled into the yards at Sparks. The brakeman, true to his word, woke us. He explained that the train was going to break up and we'd have to locate another train. When we sat up, we realized that our clothes were saturated with oil. We were both terrible messes. Apparently when we first lay down on the tender, we were so cold that we did not realize we picked a place where some oil had spilled the last time they had filled the tender. The brakeman began to laugh, but to us it was very serious, because these were all the clothes we had.

We heard about a transient camp located near town where we could clean our clothes. We were told it was best to go after lunch, because that way we would get supper and breakfast the next day, before being sent on our way. We went down to the jungle (the place where men riding the freights congregate) to see if we could get a cup of coffee.

It was still cold, but the weather had cleared and it was not snowing. We met some boys close to our own age and they invited us for coffee and to share some stale breakfast rolls. Some of these boys had been to the camp and were waiting for trains to "make up" and pull out so they could be on their way to other towns.

As well as I can recall, this camp was supported and operated by local people, with money contributed by the state and federal governments. It was clean, and although the food was plain, it was hot and plentiful. A cot and bedding were furnished for the night, breakfast was served early in the morning, and then we were asked to help clean up the sleeping quarters before we left. We were given a dollar in cash if our destination was outside the state of Nevada.

After we were cleaned up, the people in charge of the camp assigned us a cot and informed us of the rules and of the consequences of breaking them. We were properly impressed and spent a most comfortable night there.

Early the next morning, we were back at the railroad yards, where we met a couple of boys who seemed to know the ropes. We asked them where we should look to catch a train headed for Salt Lake City or Ogden, Utah. They told us where to catch it and also suggested catching a "reefer car." This is the name given to a refrigerator car used to ship perishable produce across the country. Next to an empty boxcar, an empty reefer car was the best car to ride, with one exception: there was a certain amount of risk in riding one—falling asleep in the "ice compartment." When the ice compartment car reached the destination where it was to be "iced," there was a risk of being crushed to death.

The reefer car was constructed with ice compartments at each end. The car was usually loaded with fruit or vegetables being shipped to the East Coast. The ice compartment was divided off from the rest of the car by a heavy mesh screen and steel bars. The compartment was as wide and deep as the car, but only about three feet in length. The bottom of the compartment was covered with heavy wood slats that allowed the water from the melting ice to drain out the bottom of the car. These cars could retain cold inside for hundreds of miles because they were so well insulated.

When these cars were iced, they were pulled into an ice plant under a large chute; the hatch cover and insulating pad were pulled up and huge blocks of ice were sent down the chute into the compartment. These blocks often weighed two hundred or more pounds. When the compartment was full, the train was pulled forward and the rear compartment was filled. The insulating pad was dropped back in and the hatch was closed. When opening these compartments, the train crew never checked inside, because they were required to work hard and fast to ice many cars before the produce became too warm. A couple of pieces of cardboard laid over the slats in the bottom and a blanket could make riding in the ice compartment of an empty reefer a very warm, comfortable, pleasurable ride, well protected and insulated from the bitter cold outside.

Dwight and I located where our train was making up, but being new to this business of riding freight trains, we decided to wait and catch it on the fly, as the train began to move. It is really not as dangerous as it sounds, provided the car is moving slowly in the yard, before the train has gotten up to steam or speed. The disadvantage is that it is difficult to look the cars over to see if they are empty.

It is also extremely difficult to get into an empty boxcar on the run; thus, since we caught her on the fly, we decided to walk the top to find an empty reefer. We soon found one without ice and, after opening the hatch, we climbed down inside to check it out. It looked okay, so we settled down and were enjoying a nice comfortable ride when we began to suspect the car we'd picked was not empty. We could smell fruit. We peeked through the heavy mesh wire screen and could see boxes. Where this fruit was coming from in the month of March I have no idea, but it was there. It also made us realize that we had done just what we had been warned against doing.

We decided we would ride where we were until we felt the train slow down, then get out in a hurry. Fortunately, we both stayed awake and had no problems. We rode inside until we felt the train slow down for a small town and, when the train jerked as the brakes were applied, we came scrambling out of that compartment scared half to death. It frightened us enough that even after the train had passed through town, and there was nothing in sight for miles and miles, we still did not return to our warm little shelter. We rode the remainder of the way into Ogden atop that very car. When we arrived, we again found that our train was to be broken up and its cargo dispatched to various locations throughout the country.

We went into town, got something to eat, and acquired a couple of blankets for a bedroll. We returned to the jungle where we met some others in our age group (thirteen to seventeen) and sat around talking to them until we decided to sleep for a while. We had inquired about where a train would be making up that was headed for Cheyenne, Wyoming, and with this information we were all set for the next leg of our trip. We decided we would board the next train before it began to move.

After waking in the morning, we were invited to have coffee and stale sweet rolls with our companions of the night before. They had several large paper bags containing doughnuts and various breakfast rolls. We inquired where they had gotten them and were told that if we went to this huge bakery, several blocks from the jungle, we could get a large bag just like theirs for ten cents. We decided to get some so we would have something to eat once we got settled on the train headed to Ogden. We hurried to the bakery where we purchased a huge bag of day-olds. Then we hurried back to the yard to make certain not to miss the train, but when we returned, there was no activity in the area. There would be no train headed in our direction that day, so we stayed in the jungle. We went to bed early in the evening to be ready for the train, which we had heard would be pulling out very early the next morning.

We arose early as planned, caught our train, and, after a couple of uneventful days, found ourselves in the small town we hoped was to become our new home and future. Looking back, I know now that it was only through the grace of God that we did finally arrive there safely.

As we set out to find the homestead, we had visions and fantastic plans and ideas. We were not only feeling relieved, knowing we had made it, but also feeling rather excited knowing we were about to embark upon our long-awaited, new, trouble-free future. All too soon this glorious feeling came to a sudden halt, as our world crumbled before us when we finally reached the homestead.

The place was a total wreck, run-down, deserted, and in ruins. The cabin had fallen apart many years before and there was no possibility of making it suitable to live in. We soon realized that from the very beginning this trip had been totally foolish, had almost cost us our lives, and now left us completely devastated. In dead silence, we turned and began tracing our steps back, away from what was to have been a promising new life.

It was freezing cold and there was lots of snow on the

ground. We had to have a sheltered place to sleep. We came upon a farm that had a large barn. Wearily, we climbed up into the loft and made a bed in the hay with our blankets. We spent the next three nights there. During the day we would do odd jobs in town and at night we would sleep in the barn. This way we managed to keep going. The nights were cold in the barn, but it was warm enough that we made out reasonably well. On the fourth morning, we were caught coming out of the barn and told not to come back. Both Dwight and I, by this time, had just about had enough and decided we were going to return to warm California. We caught a ride with a farmer into the small town of Gillett. Here we caught a train we thought was headed for Ogden, but ended up in Butte, Montana. We finally got our directions straight and caught trains that took us into Salt Lake City. During the days it had taken us to get from Gillett to Salt Lake City, we had had very little to eat, and by the time we arrived we were both feeling ill.

We decided to try our luck going door to door, offering to work for a couple of sandwiches or wages, in the hope we would get our stomachs full and accumulate enough food or money to see us through until we got back home. We soon learned that if we asked at homes where there were children, we would always get something and seldom were asked to earn it. The weather was cold but we had learned that we could always find a place to sleep by locating a reefer or empty boxcar on a siding and spending the night inside. After two days in Salt Lake, we decided it was time to be on our way home. We caught a train and retraced our route back to California. Our trip east had taught us a lesson; when we left Sparks, Nevada, to go over the Sierra Nevada mountains, we were warm and secure in a boxcar.

When we arrived in Oakland, Dwight headed home to whatever punishment he would receive for running away. I too went home but after peeking into the kitchen window and seeing my family at the dinner table, I decided to postpone facing the consequences until the following day. We had a shed out behind our garage where I made a bed and spent the night. The next morning after I heard my father leave for work, I went into the house to face my stepmother. She was furious and I am not sure to this day if it was because I ran away, or because I came back. If it was the latter, I can now understand, because I am sure in her mind it meant the start of more trouble.

After I had faced my father that night and listened to the usual lecture about the shame and humiliation I had brought on them, I was allowed to rejoin the family. I can still remember thinking how they had twisted things to make it appear that they were wronged and not me. Possibly this type of logic is natural at that age, but I realize now that I was using their honest and loving discipline as a means to justify my own rotten behavior. I'm not sure how my father managed to keep me out of trouble for this escapade, but he got me back into school without too much fuss being raised. Things again settled down into a routine. I fought with my stepmother about anything and everything.

My next episode of misconduct occurred when I was caught off the school grounds smoking. At this particular school, when a student was in trouble, he was given a choice of two punishments: either taking a notice home to his parents describing his misconduct or taking a strapping from the principal.

I was called to the principal's office, where I admitted to smoking and elected to be strapped. Just the week before this incident occurred, however, I had had a minor surgical procedure done and it was still not completely healed. I asked if the punishment could be postponed for a week until I was well. The principal stated that I had made my choice and it was going to be administered then and there. This led to a confrontation, as I had made the decision that I was not going to let it happen then and there.

The principal and I argued back and forth as he attempted to get me cornered, wherein he could get in some whacks. I, in turn, was trying to find a way to get past him and out of the office. He finally cornered me and gave me a couple of swats. I became infuriated at this and reached over to his desk and picked up a large, heavy glass paperweight. I was no longer intent on trying to escape, but instead wholeheartedly determined to do him considerable bodily harm.

It must have become very evident on my face, for he suddenly turned and started to bolt from his office. I saw he was going to get away and, beside myself with anger, threw the paperweight at his head as hard as I could. It missed him, passed through the glass of his office door with a tremendous crash, sailed over the heads of several girls typing and filing just outside his door in the outer office, hit the glass in the door on the other side of the room, and came to rest in the corridor.

You can imagine the commotion that took place, with the principal hightailing it out of there, the girls screaming and running for the corridor, and my cussing a blue streak, threatening unbelievable torture to the principal if I ever caught up with him. By the time I got to the corridor there was a large congregation of people. I pushed my way through them and went to my next class. Just before my class ended, however, two large policemen came into the classroom and asked the teacher to point me out. They handcuffed me and took me to the Oakland Juvenile Hall.

Upon arriving there I was stripped, searched, and given jail clothing and put into a cell. I began to realize that I was in serious trouble and would in all probability end up in Preston School of Industry, the state reformatory. I was locked in the hall for three days before I had a visitor. I don't understand how the mix-up occurred, but my parents were not notified of the incident at school, nor that I had been taken to Oakland Juvenile Hall. When I didn't come home from school, my family just assumed that I had run away. They were finally informed of my incarceration when the probation department came to our house to tell them they were expected to appear in Juvenile Court for my hearing. My father came to the hall for two reasons: first, to see me;

and second, to raise a commotion because the procedure for informing him of my arrest had been handled so poorly.

I went to court and was sentenced to Preston School of Industry; however, the sentence was suspended and I was given five years' probation. I returned home, but the situation was even worse. I went back to school with the understanding that if I had to appear before the principal for any reason, my father must appear with me. If my father could not appear, I was to be suspended until such time as he could appear. This was for the protection of the principal as well as myself.

This episode had a very unfavorable impact upon my life. Up until this time, I had not been anything special at school, either as a person or as a student. This incident seemed to make me stand out as something of a celebrity because I had been to jail and because I had chased the principal out of his own office. At Mrs. Julio's, I had settled down, stopped fighting, and got along reasonably well with my schoolmates and those who were permitted to associate and play with me after school. Now I seemed to revert back to the same type of character I had become when I lived alone with my father.

I am sure the conclusion I came to was that if you were tough and people thought you were mean or violent, they would respect you, even if they didn't like you. It was a totally erroneous assumption and one that caused me untold grief in years to come. I am also sure that it alienated many people who otherwise might have helped me straighten out my life. This attitude was entirely false and not what I truly wanted to be, but because I gained some feeling of prestige and security from it, it became the way I adopted for my life.

It wasn't long until I was in trouble again. Prior to this time I had not been a thief, except when I'd stolen change from Mrs. Julio. I had always been a hard worker and did any job that I was given or hired to do, to the best of my ability; however, this would all change in short order.

I started associating with a tougher and more hardened element at school. I would break into stores and steal anything I could sell. I even took an order from one of the boys whose family was influential in town to steal a speed-boat, motor, trailer, and other marine equipment that he wanted.

When the equipment was located, the boy let me know and I broke into the store and filled his order. I then drove to the back lot of the store, broke the lock on the gate where new boats, motors, and trailers were stored, hooked the new boat and trailer onto his car, and drove ten miles back to Berkeley, where I hid it in a garage he had rented. For my efforts, I was to be paid three hundred and fifty dollars.

The next day, when I went to arrange a meeting place to be paid, he never showed up. That night he was arrested while driving with the boat to a nearby lake. As quickly as he was arrested, he informed the authorities he had obtained the items from me and had no knowledge they were stolen. Because his father was a very well-to-do, prominent businessman, he was released. The police came to my house that night to arrest me.

When they arrived I was in the bathroom, and heard the police introduce themselves, then ask for me. I heard Alice reply that I was home, then ask, "What has he done this time?" That was enough for me. I grabbed a jacket and went out the bedroom window.

It was dark, but I knew my way around our neighborhood quite well. I had no problem in putting distance between me and the police. I ran about three blocks from home, then ducked into a large vacant lot. I lay in the tall grass for several hours and watched police cars cruising the area looking for me. When I thought the coast was clear, I took off for the home of a friend.

When I arrived at his house, I talked him into getting me his father's gun, a .38 pistol. He asked what I intended to do and I told him I was going to steal a car, get some money from a holdup, and get out of town. I told him about the trouble I was already in because of the boat. I don't know why Eddie decided to come with me, as did his girlfriend Lorraine, but they both joined in my escapade.

I had spotted several cars on my way to Eddie's house that would be easy to steal, as they had keys in the ignition. We chose the first one we came upon, which was parked in a driveway. We pushed it down the street a short distance before we got in and started it. We were on our way. The car was a 1929 Model A Ford Coupe and was an exact duplicate of my father's car. This duplication caused considerable problems for my father and almost resulted in my sister being shot by a policeman.

We committed several crimes that night, then drove to a small town down the coast from Berkeley. We spent a couple of days there and Eddie decided this type of life was not for him. He wanted to go home. We drove back to Berkeley and dropped Eddie off, but Lorraine decided to stay with me. When Eddie got home, his parents broke him down and he told the whole story. Lorraine and I stayed in Berkeley that day because we did not believe Eddie would tell where we were, but he did. Lorraine and I were apprehended that night. I don't know what became of Lorraine, but I was once again locked up in Juvenile Hall, where I was charged with several crimes, including robbery, burglary, and grand theft auto.

As previously stated, the car I had stolen almost resulted in my sister being shot. Before I was apprehended that night, the police had been watching my parents' house. Upon seeing my father's car, which matched the description of the one I had stolen, parked in front of my parents' home, they jumped to the conclusion that I was inside. They also knew that I was armed, because Eddie's parents had related the entire story, as told by Eddie. In their haste to catch me, they neglected to check the license plates on the car.

When my stepmother answered the door, they charged into the house with drawn guns and made quite a racket as they shouted for me to come out. This scared my sister, who was in another room, and she ran to the back bedroom.

This is the same room I had used to escape through during their previous attempt to arrest me. They heard her running and thought it was me. They ran into the bedroom and might have shot my sister, had my stepmother not rushed after them, yelling that it was not me. They searched the house and found that my stepmother was correct. They warned my parents that if I did return, they were to disarm me and call them, because I would surely be shot if I pulled the gun on a policeman.

Crime is easy to get into, but it can be very difficult to change one's direction once those first few steps have been taken. It is also sad but true that we often involve others in situations that never would have occurred in their lives if we, in one way or another, had not drawn them in. Eddie was a fine boy who had never been in trouble, but, because he admired me and my self-styled macho image, he became involved in a situation that could have cost him his freedom for life. As it turned out, Eddie was permitted to stay at home in his parents' custody. He was given a modest probation sentence and was never again involved with the law.

3 The Reformatory

I was sentenced to Preston School of Industry, the state reformatory. The school operated under a military formula and the toughest boys in the company were cadet officers, which entitled them to special privileges. It was customary, and often desirable, to challenge these officers to fight. It broke up the routine and enhanced one's reputation. And if one gave a good account, the cadet officer would tend to avoid picking him out for discipline in the future. It wasn't too often, though, that a cadet from the ranks whipped an officer, as they were generally older and bigger boys who, if not chosen as cadet officer, would have been in another company of their own age group. When fighting a cadet officer, a prisoner was always at a disadvantage because the cadet officer had to hit first. Be assured that they always picked the most opportune time, for themselves, to do so. A prisoner could never really win, because if he managed to emerge the victor of the first fight, the next-ranking officer would immediately challenge him. They always fought hard and dirty and it was very seldom that anyone from the

48

ranks even won the first fight. If he did, the officers would win the second or third, just because of their numbers.

One correctional officer, with the aid of four cadet officers, ran the company of sixty whenever they were in quarters. They were the authority, and their word was law. They determined punishment for any infractions of the rules and could, for instance, put prisoners on guard line (where, on a weekend, they would stand at attention for hours on end without moving). It may be hard to believe this form of punishment is agonizing, but it truly is. I have seen many, many tough and very masculine young men fall into a faint because they were unable to stand it any longer.

I worked in the woodshop the entire time I was in the institution. Aside from a few fights and smoking, I had no great difficulties. The punishment for smoking was a baldy haircut, and I had my share. After thirteen months, I had acquired the necessary credits for my release on parole. On August 2, 1937, I was released to return home to my parents.

Nothing had really changed at home, other than it had become worse than before. I still could not, or would not, get along with my stepmother. I returned to school and was making a real effort but because of my conflicts at home, I soon gave up on schoolwork and fell back into the same pattern. I was now more knowledgeable and dangerous because of the sophisticated education I had had while institutionalized. I stole a car and took off, committing more crimes in order to eat and keep moving. Again I returned to Berkeley and was apprehended. I was tried and recommitted to Preston after an absence of only three months. I felt I had failed in my latest venture because I had not utilized what I had learned while incarcerated. I vowed to do it better in the future.

When I returned to Preston, I had no intention of serving my sentence. Because I was a second-timer and parole violator, I was assigned to a company that did only hard manual labor. Whenever we were at work, we were guarded by correctional officers mounted on horses; the officers would knock a prisoner down if he made a break for the fence. It took me several months to find the opportunity for which I was looking.

We were working about one hundred yards from the fence when I noticed one officer would turn away from our crew and run his horse for a number of yards every few minutes. I reasoned that if I started for the fence just as he turned to run his horse, I would have a fair chance of getting over the fence before he could react and run me down or catch me. The other horse and officer at the head of the crew were too far away to give me much trouble. When I felt ready, I waited and watched for the officer to make his move, but it didn't appear that he was going to do it again. I was contemplating trying it without his turning away, when suddenly he turned. I was off and running as fast as I could.

One of the detail boys spotted me running, yelled, and started chasing me. Any inmate who caught another inmate in an escape attempt was given thirty days' good-time credits. Most inmates would not even consider trying to stop another inmate from escaping, but there was always one who would. If an inmate was successful in catching an escapee, he often paid a price for it, because other inmates would, if the opportunity presented itself, get revenge. Still, some would try to earn those extra credits at your expense. When an inmate escaped or attempted to escape, all his earned credits were forfeited and he started doing time over from day one.

I could hear both the horse and the detail boy running after me, but I made the fence and dropped to the other side before they could catch me. The nearest gate was a considerable distance away. There was a road where I had gone over the fence and across the road was still another barbed-wire fence. I crossed the road, climbed the second fence, and was free of pursuit from the horse and its rider. There was no way he could get the horse inside the second fence, which was on private property. He was also limited in how far he might venture away from the remainder of the crew, because there were others who would run if given a reasonable chance.

It was late in the afternoon and raining very hard. I had thrown my jacket away when I raced for the fence. Soon I was very cold, wet, hungry, and very lost in the hills that surrounded the institution.

I walked and ran a great part of the night, often falling from stepping on rocks or into holes. I ran into a barbed-wire fence or two that I did not see until I was tangled up in them, and discovered that, when you are cold, wet, and miserable, this is a traumatic experience to say the least. It seems as though that wire reaches out to deliberately snare you. It cuts deeply and quickly, and is very painful.

When I was completely exhausted and just couldn't walk anymore, I found a tree that gave a little shelter from the rain and went to sleep. I slept an hour or so, and when I awoke decided I'd better put more distance between the institution and me. I realized I was down in a little valley, thus it seemed to my benefit to climb to the top of the small hill, regain my bearings, and decide which direction to take. I discovered that it would not be to my advantage to travel down the other side as, in amazement, I found myself gazing upon the very institution I had escaped from. I had walked in a large circle around the institution, ending up about a half-mile from where I had started. I could look down from the hill and see the entire place coming to life at the start of a new day.

I again started working my way across the foothills, away from the institution. The rain was coming down as if large tubs of water were being emptied. I had been cold and wet since I first began to run, but now I was completely soaked. Every step I took I could hear water sloshing inside my shoes. I didn't know how much longer I could continue, but I was determined to keep moving as long as I could. I kept hoping to find a road to follow that would lead to habitation or a town. I was totally lost in the hills. Toward evening, I eventually did come to a road, but I knew that if I tried to walk on it I would soon be picked up. I stayed off the road, walking parallel to it.

Just as it started to get dark, I spotted a house about a mile away on the opposite side of the road. I desperately hoped I might find a car to steal. When I was even with the house, I could see two cars sitting in the yard. I sat down behind some bushes and watched. I was beginning to give out both mentally and physically and knew that I had to make my move very soon. After watching the house long enough to convince myself that it wasn't a trap, I carefully crossed the road, then waited several minutes before starting into the yard toward the cars. I was approximately halfway to the first car when a dog I hadn't seen heard me and started barking. He must have been chained, as he did not come at me, but he raised such a racket that he alerted the people inside the house. The porch light came on and a man came out of the house, carrying what I believe was a rifle. I didn't wait to find out, but instead started running. I heard someone yell for me to stop but I just kept running. I don't believe he could have seen me in the dark and rain. There were no shots fired and I got away from the area.

I again crossed the road and headed back into the foothills. I realized it would only be a short time before a patrol car from the institution would be at the scene. People along the roads leading to the institution were alerted when an inmate was on the loose and they in turn would notify the institution or search patrols of anything unusual happening in the area. I knew it was impossible for the patrol to search a very large area, especially at night, so I wasn't too concerned about being caught, but I was concerned that I would stumble into a stakeout they might have set for me.

I walked back a considerable distance from the road, found a large clump of bushes, crawled into them, and went to sleep in the rain and cold. I was physically exhausted and slept through the entire night. The next morning I again carefully made my way back toward the road. I found a little knoll off the road covered with brush, where I would be hidden and could still watch the traffic. I often saw patrol vehicles and other cars from the institution pass by.

I stayed there all day, and at dark came out of hiding. I walked parallel to the road about one hundred yards away. It was still raining and I began to have serious doubts about making good my escape. One thought that kept my hopes up was that the weather was so terrible, they might give up before I did. I walked until about 3 a.m., when I came to a large clearing that extended back from the road. There was a large grove of trees that someone had been clearing and cutting up for firewood. I had a very uncomfortable feeling inside when I reached the edge of that opening. I felt I should backtrack and circle around it, but I was so tired that I decided to sit down and watch to see if I could detect anything that would indicate a stakeout before I started to cross. It was a large area and I knew if I got far enough into the clearing I would not be able to get back to cover before I ran out of steam. I finally decided it was safe and started across. It was just as I feared: they were there, waiting for me. When I heard them yell for me to freeze, I just gave up. I could not have run another step if my very life had depended on it.

I was taken in a patrol car back to the institution, where I was given a hot shower and clean clothing, and then taken to the hospital where I was given an examination. I was not injured, except for numerous small cuts and abrasions caused by crashing through brush, falling down, and running into barbed-wire fences in the dark. I was given something to eat to hold me until breakfast, and taken to A Company for the remainder of the night and then to the detail grounds to receive my punishment.

At court, held on the detail grounds, I was told that I had forfeited all my earned credits and was sent to serve three months in G Company. G Company was the tough disciplinary unit. Inmates were required to work eight hours each day at hard manual labor and then locked up in a cell for the remaining hours of the day. Inmates were allowed out of their cells for meals and showers only. Total silence was required and any breaking of the rules was reason for further disciplinary action. Reading was permitted and one book a week was picked up by someone else. If the book was good, it was great, and if not, it was just tough luck. If an inmate got into trouble in G Company, the usual punishment was to be stripped down naked and placed in a special cell and tear-gassed. Tear gas is not only painful to the eyes but burns and irritates the skin. It was a punishment that I can't recall anyone receiving more than once. It scared everyone, including myself.

We did heavy, hard, manual labor, which was usually pointless work that served no purpose other than to make you work and sweat. We would dig a large deep ditch, move all the dirt to another location, then move it back again and refill the ditch. Often we would work on a hill that stood between the farm and the main institution grounds. We would pick at what remained of the hill for several days until there were tons of dirt to be moved. The crew would then be divided up, three-quarters assigned to wheelbarrows and the remainder to fill them. There was heavy equipment available to do this work, but that would have defeated the whole purpose of G Company.

I served my three months and was once again sent back on the hill to join the rest of the inmate population. I was assigned to A Company, a hardcore company made up of incorrigibles and escapees who had served their time in G Company, but who were still considered troublemakers and potential escape risks. I was assigned to the wood mill to work under one of the most feared men in the institution. I never understood why he was hated and feared, because I got along with him fine during the few short months I worked there.

After three months in the mill, I decided I was going to try to escape again. I can only remember that it was a very short-lived attempt and I was again captured, this time just a short distance from the institution. Once again I was taken to Institution Court and forfeited all my earned credits. I was sent back to G Company, where I spent the next sixteen months. I remained in G Company until a week before my discharge.

Again, I was discharged home to my parents. This, of course, was the usual disastrous situation as before, with Alice and I having nothing in common, but now I had also managed to alienate my sister and father. My father still felt that he had to try to make me do right, as I am sure he would not have allowed me to return otherwise. I tried going back to school and, as a result, was not making any progress.

I finally quit school and got a job driving a taxicab. I was a good driver and managed to acquire a chauffeur's license under an assumed name. I stayed at my parents' home until I had enough money to rent a room of my own and then moved out, after another quarrel with my parents. I did quite well on this job for several months. No one bothered me and I stayed out of trouble. My parole officer was aware of what was going on but made no effort to stop me. He realized, as I did, that my next stop would be the state prison at San Quentin rather than Preston School of Industry if I violated my parole. He was a good man and had no desire to see me in prison.

I continued to do fine for some time but then I started to drink. At first it was just after work and on my days off, then at work as well. Finally, I had enough sense to speak to my parole officer about my problem, telling him I realized that I was headed for serious trouble that could result in being sent to San Quentin or becoming an alcoholic. My parole officer suggested that I enlist in the service. I asked how that was possible since I had been in Preston twice and my record would soon be detected. He told me to enlist under the assumed name I had acquired since leaving home.

4 United States Marine Corps

I went to my stepmother and enlisted her help in joining the U.S. Marines. I needed her signature on my enlistment papers. I am sure she sincerely thought it was best for me and also best for the family. In signing the permission papers in the presence of the notary public, she broke the law for swearing under oath to statements she knew were false.

I left Berkeley on October 12, 1939, to go to San Diego, California, for my basic training as a Marine. After joining, I felt my life was going to make an about-face and I was going to make something of my future. I was truly proud to have been accepted into the Marines and was looking forward to making a career of it. I went through basic training with very few problems, except on one occasion when I foolishly challenged a drill instructor to a fight. This ridiculous, futile challenge resulted in my receiving a tremendous whipping, which was expertly applied to my person without ever putting a cut or bruise on me. Other than this incident, I did rather well with the drills, as I had learned a great deal while at Preston.

My life was going well and I had met some great guys in "boot camp" and was working hard and succeeding in every respect in becoming a good Marine. This success continued until my last day as a "boot." On this day, the training platoon is broken up and each man is transferred to the particular assignment he had chosen. The entire platoon was lined up when the assignments were read, and then given instructions as to where to report before being dismissed. I had a very nervous feeling that I was in trouble again, but didn't understand why. After everyone was dismissed, there were two of us remaining on the parade ground. We were called to attention and marched off the field to the "brig," where we were locked up. When we arrived, we were taken inside and asked to take off our uniforms and put on brig clothing. We were then locked in a large room with ten or twelve other men under sentence by military court martial.

I was really confused by the sudden turn of events that brought me to the brig. During the day, I was not given one word or reason as to why I had been arrested. The next day, I was called from the brig and taken before the base commander. He told me that I had been arrested and jailed because I had fraudulently enlisted in the service. I was told I would be provided with pen and paper to make a statement of my past convictions and arrests. If I refused, my stepmother would be prosecuted for signing the false permission statement she had given under oath. I was upset and at first refused to cooperate with them.

I realized they had acquired my entire criminal record through my fingerprints and felt this was just a means to humiliate and degrade me even further. I was taken to the brig to think it over and told that if I didn't change my mind, they would go after Alice, my stepmother. Back in the brig, I did give some serious thought to the consequences this incident might manifest if I did not comply with their wishes. True, I did not get along with Alice, nor her with me, but I knew deep in my heart that she had more than ample justification for her feelings about me. I felt that in many ways she had, possibly unintentionally, contributed to the problems I had become involved in since she had married my father. However, I did not want to do Alice, or anyone else, any harm. I asked to be taken back to the officer who requested my statement. In his and another officer's presence, I wrote my confession or whatever they elected to call it, and submitted it. It was signed and witnessed, with the usual ritual to ensure everything was legally included in my records. I was then dismissed and returned to the brig.

At this point, I fell into the depths of depression. I had found a new world that I loved and where I felt I belonged; then, within minutes, it was gone. I was back where I had started when I had come home from Preston. I did not have the slightest idea what I would do. I worried that being discharged would be considered a violation of my parole and if it meant that they would lodge charges against Alice.

Back in the brig I sat in despair, attempting to evaluate the outcome of my new dilemma. On the eighth day, early in the morning, three of us were taken to the office of the base commander, where we each were read our discharge. I was given an undesirable discharge, along with the other men, whose assignments were also deferred. We were told we would be officially discharged the following day. The next day we were taken to a San Diego police station, where we were fingerprinted and had mug shots taken. After this we were taken into a room where a high official of the police department gave us four hours to get out of town. We were told we would be arrested for vagrancy and given a jail sentence if we did not comply. We were then taken to a highway near the edge of town and told to be on our way.

5 Armed Robbery

I had been in the service for eight weeks and had received no pay upon being discharged. I had absolutely no money, was six hundred miles from home, and in very great danger of being jailed if I did not put some distance between San Diego and myself. One of the other men who had been discharged with me was in the same predicament. He decided he would head north to Los Angeles. I intended to go back to Berkeley in the hope of getting straightened out. We decided to hitchhike together until we hit Los Angeles, at which time we would part company.

I knew very little about this man, as he was not part of the group I had been closely associated with during our training. He was familiar to me as we were in the same platoon but that was the extent of it. In turn, he knew as much about me.

We began hitchhiking toward Los Angeles. The car that stopped to offer us a ride was a big black, polished Buick with New York license plates. In it were two men, one about twenty-seven years of age and the other in his mid-forties.

They were both fairly well dressed and seemed to be anything but broke. We had ridden with them for possibly an hour when we were asked where we had been and where we were going. Neither Frank, my companion, nor I wanted to explain our circumstances, so we just said we were Marines on leave, and headed for Los Angeles for some fun. George, the older of the two men, introduced himself and his partner, explaining they were salesmen from the East Coast. According to George, his partner, James, was just learning the ropes as a salesman, under his guidance and supervision.

None of this was at all suspicious to me. In fact, I felt extremely lucky to have been picked up by this pair, as they explained they were headed for San Francisco and that I was welcome to ride all the way. I thought the day was going to have a bright side after all, even though I had been feeling totally depressed and humiliated at the prospect of going home and telling my parents and friends I had been kicked out of the Marines. I was sure no one would believe my story, although it certainly was the truth.

I soon found out, however, that what I thought was to be a lucky break was instead the worst luck I could have asked for. Just as we hit the outskirts of Los Angeles, George, the driver, turned and asked Frank and me if we wanted to kick in some money for gas. We had to tell them we were broke. George then pulled the car over to the side of the road and began asking many questions about how Marines on leave and headed to Los Angeles for fun could do so being broke.

After a couple of minutes of questioning, I got fed up with him and told him it was really none of his business but that we had been kicked out of the Marine Corps. I decided to simply get out of the car and leave them sitting there rather than answer any more questions, when George reached under his seat and came up with a .45-caliber automatic pistol. Instantly, I thought they had not believed our story about being broke and were going to rob us, thinking we were really Marines on leave and with enough money to make the robbery worthwhile. I debated whether to sit still or try to make a break for it, when James suddenly turned around with a .45. My decision was quite obvious and clear: I had better sit still. I envisioned how angry they were going to be when they shook us down and couldn't find one red cent between us.

To our amazement, instead of robbing us, George asked if we were interested in making ourselves some money. I'm not sure whether I was more relieved or worried at that moment. In my state of mind, I was game to participate in anything rather than face my family. Frank was more cautious about the situation, but finally agreed to just one job, then he would split and go his own way. Thus it was agreed to by all four of us. We decided to wait until dark and then rob the first liquor store we came to.

When it was dark, we drove into Los Angeles proper and started looking for a place to hit. It was agreed that I would take one gun and the other would remain in the car with the driver, just in case we got trapped. I felt more comfortable handling the gun, as I felt I would not panic. Frank was to tap the till and get the money after I got the drop on the clerks. James was to watch the door and be sure no one walked in and surprised us during the course of the holdup. While George parked the car a couple of stores away from the liquor store, the three of us proceeded as planned.

In order to ensure our safety, we first wandered around, surveying the surroundings. There were two clerks in the store and they made the entire situation very easy, as one went to the back storeroom, leaving his co-worker quite vulnerable. I got the drop on the remaining clerk and ordered him to lie on the floor. Just at that time the second clerk appeared and, with no trouble whatever, he cooperated and joined his co-worker on the floor. Frank did what he had to do and soon had all the money.

James picked up a couple of bottles of liquor and started to leave. I knew I had to march the two clerks to the back of the store before leaving, or we would not have a chance to get away without them seeing the car and getting our license number. I yelled for James to keep the door covered while I escorted the clerks to the back. I made them lie on the floor once again and told them I would shoot them if I saw either of them before I left the store. As I returned to the main store, I realized that I was alone. James and Frank had split for the car while I was in back. I had no choice but to run out of the store, leaving my back exposed, or take a chance of being left behind by my partners in crime.

Just as I ran out of the store, I saw our car starting to pull out from the curb. If we hadn't been on a very busy street, I would have been stranded. To say the least, I was hopping mad and I did not believe their explanation that they were just going to start out slow, but wait for me to reach the car. I knew this was a lie and resolved to get away from them that night, if possible.

We drove away with no problem and it was decided we would find a motel, where we could split the money and get the car out of sight in case it had been observed during the robbery. Just a few miles away we found them what we were looking for. We were able to obtain adjoining rooms and, after paying for the rooms with the stolen money, we gathered in one of the rooms to split the remainder. We each pocketed a little over one hundred dollars.

James broke out the liquor. As we sat drinking and talking, we decided we would pull off one more job around the area before Frank split and then the other two and myself would head for San Francisco. The prospect of putting more money in my pocket outweighed my original plan of parting company with this group after the money split.

We drove to Ventura and checked into a motel where we planned to stay the day. George put another set of New York plates on the car and went out to find our next hit and the best road to take for our getaway. He returned around 4 p.m., but by then Frank was too drunk to be of any help, so we decided to spend the night in the motel. Although we all managed to get quite drunk that night, I was still able to realize that I was associated with two men who appeared to have no true loyalty to each other, let alone to me, and who would desert Frank and me if it came down to a tight squeeze. I was also convinced that George and James were actually not above robbing Frank and me for our cut, if we made a good hit. These thoughts resulted in my sobering up enough to realize I had best take certain precautions. I managed to get one of the two guns we had used in the robbery and decided to keep it on me at all times. At that point, the .45 was my best and most trusted friend.

George told us he had lined up a good score for us, a large wholesale and retail liquor outlet, just on the outskirts of Ventura. He said there were several thousand dollars to be taken with little or no effort. He told us he had run the roads so that if something went wrong, we still had a reasonable chance to get away from the scene, get rid of the car, and split up.

I had never been very long on patience or planning and since everything seemed in line, I wanted to get the job over with for more than one reason. I had made a definite decision I would part company with this pair immediately after splitting the loot. I figured the sooner the better, in all respects.

Frank, on the other hand, was more cautious, even drunk, and asked George and James to wait awhile before he made his decision. He and I went for a drink and he told me he was very skeptical of the other two. He felt, as I did, that if given the chance they would dump us for our share of the loot.

I then told Frank I had taken one of their guns and was keeping it on me at all times for added insurance in the event they were scheming against us. George had not as yet discovered the .45 missing from under the seat of the car, but I knew when he did there would probably be a confrontation between us. I didn't think he would push matters too far, as long as he knew I had the gun. I also felt it might make them have second thoughts about any double-cross, if they thought I didn't trust them. We decided to stay the night in Ventura, then knock over the place George had picked as soon as it was dark the following night. George and James decided to go into Ventura that night, but Frank and I stayed at the motel and kept away from them as much as possible, without being too obvious that we didn't trust them.

Frank and I were in our room talking when they came storming up to our door. I knew they had missed the gun. Frank let them into the room and George started asking about the missing gun. I told him I had it and intended to keep it until we finished the job, split the loot, and parted company. George became quite angry and upset, insisting that I return the gun. I told him I felt that he and James had intended to leave me stranded in Los Angeles and if it happened again, I would have something to get by with until I got home. I did not tell him that both Frank and I felt they might double-cross us.

They finally calmed down and agreed that it was fair that I kept the gun. Neither of them liked it because now Frank and I were on equal terms with them and there was little they could do about it. We agreed to meet for breakfast in the morning, check out of the motel, then drive into Ventura, where we would all split up for the rest of the day, until it was time for the caper. After the robbery, we planned to drive back toward Los Angeles, split the money, and go on our way. Frank and I spent the day wandering around town, having a couple of drinks in various bars, then eating dinner before it was time to meet the other two.

At about 7:30 p.m. we met as planned. It was dark and a bit windy and cold. George told us he would drive by the place we were going to rob, so we could all get a look at it. Having been alone when he picked it out, George was, in fact, the only one who had seen the place thus far. We drove by and looked it over. It was a very large building with a store in front and a large warehouse in the rear. It was very busy at that time and we decided to wait awhile before we attempted it, as we felt we could run into a great deal of trouble if we were not careful.

I have always hated putting things off, and by 10 p.m. I couldn't stand it any longer. It was either do it now, or forget it. Everyone had become uptight and nervous because of the delay. The risk was great enough without the added tension that was building up; someone could easily be killed, or cause someone else to be killed. All agreed, now was the time. We drove back and, as planned, Frank, James, and I headed into the store while George waited in the car with the motor running.

There was one man in the store when we entered. We did as we had on our previous job in Los Angeles, circulating around throughout the store until we were sure it was all right. Feeling everything was okay, I went up to the clerk and presented the .45. To my surprise, instead of being coopera- tive as I thought he would be, he began yelling for us to get out and grabbed for a quart bottle of liquor that was on the counter, as though he was going to hit me with it. In that split second, I racked the slide back and kicked a shell into the chamber of the gun and told him I would drop him in his tracks if he so much as touched that bottle. My threat and the noise of the shell going into the chamber appeared to change his mind, as he became very cooperative and proceeded to lie down on the floor, as I had ordered.

By then I was a bit shaken and bewildered, not only by the clerk's actions but by mine as well. I had always debated in my own mind just what I would do if I were confronted with a situation in which it boiled down to shoot or be caught. I now had the answer. I had decided, in that split second, that if he attempted to apprehend me I would shoot him without hesitation. It was a terrible feeling, realizing that I would jeopardize the life of another individual for money or to keep from getting caught, when I was the one doing something criminal and wrong in the first place. Once I came to this conclusion, I also decided that whatever the consequences, I would take my punishment, if caught, without blaming anyone but myself. I have always lived and served my time with the idea in mind that I was in trouble because I had asked, by my own actions, to be there.

We tied up the clerk, emptied the safe and cash drawer of the register, and left. We were feeling very confident that we had pulled it off, especially after the bad start with the clerk, when the whole thing collapsed on top of us. As we reached an area on the outskirts of Ventura called the Forks, we were suddenly surrounded by police cars. We had driven right into a trap.

We found out later that the reason the clerk had raised such a fuss at the start of the robbery was to alert his wife, who was in their living quarters in back of the store. She heard what was going on and slipped out the back door, ran past George in the car and into a service station where she called the police. There were only two ways we could leave town from where we were, so the police set up the necessary trap and waited for us to drive into it.

6 The Big House

For this caper, I was sentenced to San Quentin, California, for robbery, first degree. On January 9, 1940, I became number 64452. This was the start of approximately eighteen years in three different prisons.

San Quentin was a tough prison, but it was also a place where I could do time without any hassle, if I minded my own business. I was first assigned to work in the mess hall, which was considered a "bad job" but one that all "fish" (newcomers) had to do for a certain stretch of time before going on to the "better jobs." There was only one job in the prison that was considered worse than the mess hall, and that was the jute mill. Newcomers had to work a thirteen-month period in one or the other.

I served my thirteen months in the mess hall and then requested a transfer to the bake shop. This was a good job because the bakers had their own cook and were not required to eat "mainline" food. The work was hard but it was work that I really enjoyed. I had no problems in the bakery except for one fight, which didn't amount to much.

I was assigned to work on the ovens where the bread was baked. It was hot, hard work, but our crew was a good crew and life as a whole was not too difficult. We worked the night shift, and when we had baked the required bread for the day we could clean up the shop and our ovens and then go to our cells to sleep. We would usually get into our cells about 6 a.m. and then sleep until noon. At noon, we would come out, go to the bakery for lunch, and then go into the kitchen yard to sun, play handball, or lift weights. At 4:30 p.m. we would go to the bakery again, have supper, and then return with the mainline to our cells for the evening count at 6 p.m. After count, we would read, sleep, or listen to the radio until lights out. At twelve midnight, we would be released from our cells to go into the bakery to bake the bread for the following day. This was our routine, seven days a week.

The only exception to this routine occurred if we started to get too far ahead on the amount of bread baked. On these occasions, we would skip a shift and not make bread and could either stay in our cells for that period of time or turn out to the bakery just to sit and shoot the bull all night. The bakery was located just off the kitchen and we were very seldom ever bothered by the guards, except for the nightly count.

I had been in San Quentin about eighteen months when I decided I would write my parents a letter. The last time I had written them was when I was still in boot camp in San Diego, and I didn't know if they were aware that I had been kicked out of the Corps. I knew that if they didn't know about my discharge, my letter would be a real shock to them, because they had been very pleased with my progress in the Marines. In my letter I told them the circumstances of my discharge and what I had done. I was very lonely and really missed them and looked forward to getting a return letter.

I was totally unprepared, however, for the response I received. My father, in his return letter, stated that I was not his son. He said that when I was conceived he had been overseas in World War I for nine months and, therefore, I was not his child. He went on to say that even though I had his name, he had disowned me and adopted a boy to take my place. He had removed me from his will and as far as the family was concerned, I was dead and they wanted it to stay that way. I was told never to come to their home, write, or in any way contact them, because they wanted nothing further to do with me. I was hurt more than I thought it was possible to be, but I also knew that there was no way I could deny the shame and humiliation I had brought to them. I knew they didn't deserve what I had done to them. I made up my mind that I would respect their wishes and never again try to make contact. It was a promise that I kept, until the day they contacted me approximately eight and one-half years later.

I don't know what change took place in me at that point, but along with my decision not to contact my family again came the decision that I would not try to straighten out my life. I decided that if my first parole hearing was denied, I would apply for a road camp and escape at the very first opportunity available. I sincerely do not know if I used the letter as an excuse to continue on as I had in the past, or if I was so hurt that I really didn't care what happened to me.

Anyone convicted of first-degree robbery could apply for release after having served two years. Upon completion of the required two years, I submitted my application to the parole board for release. My case went up before the Adult Authority for hearing and my term was set at fifty years, with parole granted after three calendar years served. This required me to serve one more full year before I could leave the institution on parole.

7 Escape

One year somehow sounded like an eternity and I decided that even though I had been granted a parole, I was not going to serve one day more than necessary. I applied for a prison road camp and in another month I was transferred to a camp outside Escondido, California. It was located fifteen miles back in the hills in a very isolated area.

The opportunity for escape was far better than it had been in the institution. At camp I went out to work on the construction of state highways. Although I was closely supervised while at work (making any chance to get a reasonable head start before being missed very limited), the possibility of making it out of the camp complex at night was better than in the prison proper. But even this posed some problems.

First of all, there was no way I could cover the fifteen miles into town before being missed. Second, there was the problem of getting over the fence in the dark without being detected by the yard patrols, and as though this was not enough, the third problem was in getting out of my cabin after lockup without being detected by some of the stool pigeons who were in every unit. They, like the kids in the reformatory, would be given extra days off their sentences if they snitched.

I had asked to be assigned to this particular camp, as this was where a friend of mine, Jack, was assigned. I knew he was also interested in escaping, as he had no intention of going straight when he got out either. I thought he and I could join forces and work together. When I arrived at camp, I had been assigned to the very same barracks as him and we both agreed to make a break at the first opportunity. A third man, Renaldo, a friend of Jack's, also wanted to be included in our attempt. We agreed, and Renaldo became a member of our group.

Although Jack and I were in the same barracks, Renaldo was in another. We enlisted the help of a man in our cabin, who agreed to trade cabins with Renaldo. Once we were all together, it was just a matter of waiting for the right night.

Our plan was simple. We would wait until the two snitches in our cabin were asleep, pry open the window at the end of the barracks, then head for the fence together and hope we could get over it without too much racket, which would bring the patrols down on us before we were clear. We knew we would only have an hour's start, at best, because we would be missed on the next count.

The problem with the fence was that the patrols had no precise routine upon which we could time our break. There were two inside and two outside patrols. All four patrols worked independently of each other and never traveled together. There was no way to predict or detect where they were or where they would be. We decided that if we hit the fence together, we would either all make it together (if we were lucky) or none of us would make it (if we failed). If caught, we would all be sent back inside the walls and lose our parole dates, plus receive additional sentences for attempted escape.

The night finally arrived when everything seemed just right. There was very little moonlight, the two stool pigeons were asleep, and we were more than ready to go. We pried the window open and dropped to the ground outside. We waited a couple of minutes to allow our hearts to quiet down before we ran out into the light and started over the fence. Everything was quiet. No patrols were in sight and there was no noise from inside the barracks. Someone whispered, "Let's go," and we took off.

The fence was eight feet high with an additional two-foot section at the top that sloped inward. This was intended to make it difficult to get over. It really did its job well. The first eight feet were easy, but that two-foot barbed-wire section made life miserable for a short while. All you could do was to throw a leg up on it and then force your way over it; it cut and scratched as you went. We all had a difficult time getting by this section, but after much struggling and fighting, we all made it and dropped to the outside.

Once there, it was just a few feet to darkness and lots of

brush in which to hide. We lay at the base of the fence in the darkness long enough to see if we had been detected. When convinced it was safe, we made a dash for the protection of the brush and darkness. We were free.

Free, provided we could stay out of the patrol's reach during the time it would take us to make it into town. We knew we had an hour at the very most to put distance between us and camp. I knew from my previous escape attempts that I was no outdoorsman—and neither were Jack or Renaldo. To ensure our not going astray, we decided we would stay far enough from the road to keep out of sight and away from any stakeout they might set up, yet close enough that we would be able to see the movement of traffic and not lose our direction and wander off at an angle. We knew the road would take us into Escondido.

We walked several miles that night and on various occasions debated the wisdom of walking closer to the road. It was difficult to walk in the dark at a distance parallel to the road, as we had to climb over the top of each hill and up and down each rise in the terrain.

When it started to get light, we decided we would get back further away from the road and lay low during the daylight hours. We found an area where there was some very tall grass and trees and went to sleep for several hours. When we awoke, it was early afternoon and we were cautious not to move out of the safe area.

We lay there complaining because we had not used enough good judgment to bring a few candy bars with us.

Also, in the excitement of going over the fence and getting away from camp, no one had paid much attention to what the barbed wire had actually done to his hands and legs. We all had severe, long, deep cuts but had not even noticed the pain until we woke up. We were dirty and bloody, but even the pain from our cuts and lacerations could not dull the excitement of being free.

We stayed in our grass area until dark and again started out following the road from a good distance. After walking several more hours, we could see the lights of town off in the distance. We knew then, if we took our time and didn't get careless, we were going to make it. We sat down and discussed what we wanted to do and made our plans accordingly. We decided to get as close to town as possible, but not go in. We would wait one more day before making our move to get a car and then head for Los Angeles. It was a difficult decision to make, but we felt if we waited until the next night, the heat would be off Escondido and we would be able to pick up a car and be on our way without attracting too much attention.

We worked our way into the outskirts of town, and there found another field with high grass next to an orange grove, where we could stay out of sight during the day. We immediately went into the orange grove and picked lots of oranges, as we had not eaten since we left camp and were extremely hungry. After we had eaten our fill of oranges, we settled down to pass the long hours we had to wait before we could make another move toward freedom. Those were some of the longest, slowest-passing hours I have ever spent. It was almost impossible to wait when freedom seemed so near. The time finally passed and it was dark again. We had decided during our wait that we would take turns going out to find a car. We realized three of us as a group would attract attention, but one person would not be especially noticeable since they would expect us to stick together.

Jack was the first to go. We set an approximate time limit of one hour, at which time he was to return. If he had not located a car in that length of time, then the next one would go. After what seemed an eternity, Jack returned only to reveal that he had found nothing. Renaldo went next, heading in a different direction. An hour later he too returned, again with no luck! Although I went in the same direction Renaldo had taken, I covered a different area than he had, and I finally located a car with the keys in the ignition. It was impossible to get to it with all the activity that was going on in that vicinity, however, so I went back and told Jack and Renaldo I had located a car but that we would have to wait until everything quieted down.

The idea did not sit well with either one of them, but it was a case of waiting it out or keep walking around looking for still another car, which in turn would increase the chances of one, if not all, of us getting caught. I have no idea how long it took, but we waited what we considered to be a reasonable length of time before deciding to give it a try. All three of us went back to the spot in which I had spotted the car and no one was around. We pushed the car several hundred yards from the owner's house, then Renaldo got in under the wheel and started it up. It was really a beautiful sound to hear that car running.

8 On the Run

Jack and I climbed into the car and we were off to Los
Angeles. We had decided on Los Angeles as Jack had a friend
living there from whom he could get a gun and some money.
We needed both, as we were all wearing prison blues with
our numbers stamped on them. We'd certainly be caught if
someone saw the back of our shirts or pants. We were almost
into Los Angeles when the car started to cough, as it was
running out of gas. We knew we would be in trouble if we
didn't get enough gas to get into Los Angeles. We also needed
to get another set of plates on the car before it got light. We
were in a residential area of some small town, so we decided
we would get the plates first, then worry about gas.

We started looking for some tools in the car, and under
the back seat found an old sweatshirt and a small toolbox. I
opened the toolbox and all the tools we needed were there,
plus an envelope that contained $15. We couldn't believe
our luck. We located another car, stole the plates, and put
them on our car. We were now in good shape, if we could
just get gas before the car stalled.

We drove back to the main highway and just a couple of blocks down the road found a gas station. Renaldo put on the old sweatshirt to hide the numbers on his shirt and Jack and I got out of the car, for fear there was an alert out for three men dressed in blues. Renaldo drove to the gas station, had the attendant fill it up, and then drove back to pick up Jack and me. We were all set. We had a full tank of gas, new plates on the car, and some extra money to buy food. Because of our clothing, we could not go into a restaurant, so instead decided we would get some grease and oil off the car motor and try to cover the numbers on Renaldo's pants. This worked relatively well and, with the sweatshirt being old, it more or less gave the impression that Renaldo had been working on something greasy.

We found a doughnut shop and Renaldo went in and bought eighteen doughnuts and three large cups of coffee. Words alone could not begin to describe how good those doughnuts and that hot steaming coffee tasted. Except for the oranges, it was the first thing we had eaten since leaving camp.

After we ate, we headed into Los Angeles to locate Jack's friend. He knew the address, but because Jack hadn't been there for several years we had considerable trouble finding it. We finally located the place just before noon. Jack said he wanted to talk to the guy while Renaldo and I waited in the car. We were there possibly thirty minutes when Jack suddenly came hurrying out of the house. As he got near we could see he was very upset. He yelled to start the car and to get out of there as quickly as possible. I was driving and as soon as he was in, we were on our way. Jack had me drive to a park several miles from his friend's house. At first he wouldn't tell us what had happened, but I figured that things hadn't worked out very well. When we got to the park, we pulled into an area where we would not be conspicuous and Jack told us the story.

When Jack got there, his friend had been glad to see him and invited him inside. They were sitting having coffee when there was a news release on the radio about the three of us escapees, giving our names. This upset Jack's friend and made him very nervous. The newscast said we might all be armed and to approach us with caution.

I didn't know it before, but Jack had been arrested for two previous assaults in which people had been shot. He was never tried for them, but in the police files he was considered to be very dangerous, if armed. All three of us had been convicted of armed robbery, first degree, and if we were all armed, as the newscast intimated, we would be shot down if we offered any resistance of any kind.

Jack's friend had given him one hundred dollars and asked him to leave because he said we were too hot and he did not want to get involved. He also told Jack that he did not have a gun or know where he could get one. He wanted Jack to leave, as he was afraid that he would be in trouble if he didn't. Jack felt that as soon as we left this guy would call the cops, thus the reason he was in a hurry to get away immediately. We felt safe as far as the car was concerned, because we had parked a few doors from his house and there was no way he could have seen the car. We were headed away from the house when we left and he did not come outside.

With the one hundred dollars, we had to get a motel room and some clothing so we could clean up and change. We finally found a little motel where we could get out without anyone seeing our clothing. After we got in the room, it was decided that Renaldo would go to a store and get us all some pants and shirts so that we could move around.

Renaldo drove to a small, cheap clothing store where he got us each a pair of pants, a shirt, socks, and a handker-chief. He also bought a razor and some toiletry articles. After we were all cleaned up and dressed, we sat down and had a couple of drinks from a bottle that Renaldo had brought back. We were feeling quite elated, yet at the same time, a worried. Elated in that we were in Los Angeles and free, but worried because we had counted on getting a gun from Jack's friend.

We were now faced with the problem of what to do next. Someone suggested we go into a store and just take a gun by muscle, but we decided that wouldn't work. We then thought about the prospect of just jumping a policeman, taking his gun, and splitting. After much debating, we finally decided on the latter idea and left the room in search of a policeman.

We soon found this idea would not be feasible, as they all

seemed to be working in pairs. We knew we would have difficulty in disarming two at the same time, yet we were getting desperate. We had to get a gun in order to rob a place and get out of Los Angeles, as we had heard a newscast stating that we had been seen in this area. We surmised this could be the reason all the policemen were working in pairs. I still believe the newscast was a result of Jack's friend reporting us to the police.

As we were driving around looking for a policeman to jump, we had passed a small gun shop on a side street, not too far from our motel. We decided to go back and take a look, to see if there was a way we could break into it after dark. When we got back we saw the entire store was covered by an alarm system, but just inside, standing up against the built-in window display counter, were several double-barreled shotguns. We thought that if we smashed the large plate-glass window we would have time to grab the guns, even though it would set off the alarm, and still make it to the car and leave before the police could arrive. We knew there would be a terrible racket when that alarm sounded and it would arouse anyone living in the apartments above. Everything taken into consideration, we all agreed to give it a try. It was too early in the evening, so we decided we would eat and then come back to pull off the job.

After eating and paying for the motel for another night, we were broke again. We had to get those guns. We drove back about 11 p.m. Everything was quiet and traffic was light on the street. Jack and Renaldo got out of the car, but

I remained, as I was driving. Jack took the large rock we had picked up previously and threw it through the large six-by-six-foot window. Immediately, as the glass broke, the alarm went off. Between the glass falling from the window and breaking as it crashed on the sidewalk and the loud, shrill sound of the alarm ringing, it seemed as though people in San Francisco should have surely heard the noise.

In addition to the alarm and breaking glass, there was also a watchdog loose in the store who contributed to the noise. I think the alarm and breaking glass intimidated him because instead of attacking when Jack reached in to get the guns, he just barked louder. Jack grabbed the guns and gave them to Renaldo, who ran to the car and passed them to me. Renaldo jumped into the car, but Jack ran back to get one more gun. Even with this added unexpected delay, we were able to drive away without any problems. The next day, we cut the guns down so they were easy to conceal. After buying some shells in a sporting goods store, we were in business.

During the next week we took off three nice scores. We purchased new clothes and could go anywhere without looking out of place. But, because we also indulged in a great deal of partying, the money did not last long. When three men armed with sawed-off shotguns start taking off good scores, it is not long before the police soon have a make on whoever is doing the jobs. We were sitting in our room one night, having a drink, when a newscast came on describing a robbery we had pulled off the previous night.

We were positively identified as having committed this one, and a reward was offered for any information that might lead to our arrest. It also stated that it was known we were still in the Southern California area and an arrest was anticipated within the next few hours.

We were not sure how to handle that news. It could mean a couple of things. First, that we had been actually spotted in the area where we were staying and that they were trying to locate us, or it was just a ruse to force us to make a break for the state line, where we might be apprehended. We decided that we would lay low for the next couple of days and not take a chance on anything. We knew that it would be difficult for anyone to recognize us, as no pictures had shown up in any of the area papers. We decided that when, or if, our pictures appeared, then we would have to worry about someone recognizing us; but until then, if we stayed out of sight, we would be okay.

Our luck held out until the following night, when there was a front-page story about three escaped convicts running around Los Angeles. We knew then we had to move, as very accurate descriptions had been given of each of us. Renaldo and I might have passed, but Jack had some outstanding features from his career as a fighter that were a dead give-away. We decided that we would head to Las Vegas, Nevada, that same night. We also decided we had to have another car, as the one we were driving might have been spotted.

Jack knew a very exclusive hotel where cars were parked, sometimes for a week or more, while people attended various functions around Los Angeles. Rather than take their cars out, they would use city cabs. To secure a car here, we would have to walk through the hotel, go to the elevator down to the parking lot area, pick out a car with the keys in it, and, hopefully, drive it out through the manned security exit. Jack said no questions would be asked, as we were well dressed and most people stealing a car would just pick it up off the street rather than take a chance something would go wrong while driving out through a security exit.

We decided this would be the best way to do it, as it was almost certain that we would have a car that would not be missed that night (or possibly even for several days, if we were lucky) and we were sure to get across the state line with no problems. We weren't taking too much of a risk, as we were all armed and could just take the security attendant hostage, if necessary.

We walked into the hotel, went to the bar, had a drink, and then took the elevator to the garage. The physical design of the garage was excellent for our needs because we could not be seen by the security guard at the gate and could take our pick of the cars. We soon found what we needed. It was a Packard sedan, about a year old, and it seemed to be in excellent condition. We got in, started it, and headed for the security gate exit.

When we got to the gate, the security guard was talking on the telephone, so we had to wait a few minutes. As you might imagine, many thoughts went through our heads. We were almost certain he suspected something and that we were going to end up having a problem. When he hung up the telephone he looked us over, told us to enjoy ourselves, and opened the gate so we could leave. He would never know how close he came to going for a ride with us that night.

As soon as we were out of the garage, we headed for an area where we could get another set of plates to put on the car. We found a large parking lot and, while Jack and Renaldo watched, I got two sets of plates for our new car. We changed one set immediately, just to be on the safe side, and hid the other set under the back seat. We were now all set to leave town. The drive to Las Vegas took us most of the night, but it was totally without any excitement. After we arrived and checked into a motel, we again started to feel very confident that we had made it. We each had several hundred dollars, and having money, and the availability of gambling, almost caused us to get caught.

I was sitting drinking at a bar in one of the casinos uptown when a casino security guard approached me and asked my age. I had no identification of any kind on me and, in addition, had no card indicating my draft status, which one was required to carry at that time (this occurred during the first part of World War II, when the United States was at war with Japan). I told him I was twenty-one and gave him the year of my birth. He asked several questions and I was just waiting for him to ask me to show some identification, but luck was with me, as he didn't. This saved the day because I could not have produced a driver's license, draft card, or any I.D.

The guard left me, but I had a very uncomfortable feeling that he was not one hundred percent convinced and just might be tempted to investigate further if I didn't make myself scarce. It occurred to me later that this could have turned into a disaster had the circumstances been different. Although I did not have a gun on me, Jack did. Had Jack been present when this incident occurred and had he become apprehensive, or had the guard decided to arrest me, I know Jack would not have hesitated to take him down on the spot. All this worried me, so I set out to find Jack or Renaldo and tell them what had taken place. I found Jack at one of the crap games and tried to talk to him, but he was on a hot streak and talking to him was a lost cause. I told him I was going back to the motel and left.

Once outside and away from the casino I felt better, but soon began to realize that Las Vegas was just about the worst place in the world we could have picked to go. Any kind of action or activity one could possibly want to find was offered here, to attract and suit various types of people from all walks of life, from the best of people right down to the most unsavory elements from all over the world. Drifters, gamblers, criminals, and even fugitives like us could be found here, offset with the largest assortment of police and security personnel (population-wise) that could be found anywhere. I just hoped Jack and Renaldo would get back to the room without getting into trouble of some sort or, worse, busted. To boil it down, it was probably the most dangerous place three escaped convicts on the run could go.

Little did we know the good times were just about over. We were going on the run. We left Las Vegas and were on our way to Salt Lake City, as we wanted to put a couple of states between California and us. We were doing fine when, for no apparent reason, the great car we had picked out began to give us trouble.

I have never been much of a mechanic, but it didn't take one to know the car was finished when there was a tremendous crash and a large hole was poked in the side of the motor by some internal part. We were just outside the very small town of Beaver, Utah, when this occurred.

We were in a real spot now, because we were without transportation and stuck in the middle of nowhere. We knew we couldn't just steal another car in Beaver, as it would soon be missed, and there were too many miles between us and the next large city, which was Provo, Utah.

We decided our best bet would be to walk into Beaver and hope there was a bus station there where we could catch a bus into Provo. When we arrived, we found a small store with a bench in front, which served as the local bus station. We purchased our tickets to Provo and were told we had a six-hour wait. We proceeded to find a restaurant in which we could get a decent meal, eat, and then walk around the small business area of the town.

We were really feeling uptight because we had no place to go, other than that bench to wait for the bus. We realized the possibility of the stolen car being discovered outside of town, raising suspicion, and being connected to us; we hoped against hope that we would be on the bus and gone before this happened. One thing in our favor now, however, was that it had turned dark, so the possibility of it being discovered and investigated before morning was not as great as it had been earlier, when we had walked into town.

Also troubling us was the possibility that the local town constable might become suspicious of our sudden presence in this little town and begin questioning us. We couldn't very well tell him the car we had stolen had broken down, thus we were waiting for a bus. How would we explain our sudden appearance in this town, out in the middle of nowhere, miles and miles from another town?

We finally went back to the bus stop and were sitting on the bench when lo and behold, as we had hoped would not happen, the local constable himself approached us. Jack and Renaldo saw him coming and went inside the store. I stayed on the bench in hope that if he questioned me, I could get by without arousing his suspicions. He very politely asked where I was from and where I was headed. I told him I was from Las Vegas and was headed for Provo, Utah. I even showed him my ticket. Although he said nothing more and simply walked away, I could not help but feel he was not entirely convinced. I was certainly on edge, as we still had better than an hour to wait before the bus pulled in. Jack and Renaldo stayed in the store to avoid further suspicion. I sat there, worrying whether or not the constable had gone to do some more checking up on me. All I could do was sit on that bench and wait.

After an eternity, the bus pulled in and as I was getting aboard, I noticed the constable watching, I suppose to see that I really did get on the bus. When I was seated, he suddenly turned and walked away. I never did understand the entire situation, as it was quite obvious that he had his suspicions, yet he never asked for any identification. He seemed totally unaware that there had been three of us, so apparently he had not actually seen us all together at one time. His main concern appeared to be that I got out of town.

I wondered, sitting there on the bus, if perhaps this was a set-up and somewhere up the line the bus would be stopped and we would be captured. We all sat in different areas of the bus so we could keep an eye out to protect one another. We figured that unless we were stopped out in the middle of nowhere by more than two men, we still had a chance to get away. As it turned out, all our fears were unfounded and we pulled safely into Provo the next morning without the slightest problem. We decided to get a room for the night and take it from there. We had to have transportation and wanted to make another good score. We checked into our rooms for a short sleep and a chance to shower and clean up before eating.

Over breakfast the next day, we decided to steal another car and drive into Salt Lake City, where we would try to find a decent score to take off. We waited until that night and picked up a car with no difficulty. We switched plates with another car located nearby, then drove into Salt Lake City and got a nice motel room, where we intended to stay until we found the right place to rob. Once we had enough money to keep us without worrying, we were going to drive to New York, where Jack was born and his family still lived. For the first few hours we were in Salt Lake City everything was fine, but it was soon to fall apart. We had gone out to dinner and when we returned to the motel room, I bought the local paper at a newsstand.

I didn't look at it until we were in our room and when I did, I almost fainted. On the front page of the paper was a large picture of me and under the picture were the words, "WANTED FOR MURDER." It threw me for a total loss. The story went on to tell that our stolen car had been found in Beaver, and I had been identified by the constable as having been there. The murder was said to have taken place in Salt Lake City, where I supposedly attacked a local merchant who died as a result of my assault on him.

The incident took place in a large parking lot of a shopping center and a fingerprint from my right hand was said to have been found on his car. A picture of the fingerprint was also shown and when I looked at it, and then my own finger, I had to admit they had reasonable cause to believe it was my print. Both prints had a scar in the same exact area and, to the eye, looked identical. Of course, I knew beyond any doubt that they were not the same, as I certainly had not committed murder, nor was I in Salt Lake City at the time of that incident. I was in Provo, Utah, with Jack and Renaldo at the hotel.

This whole incident was later to be acknowledged as a mistake, as it was discovered that the fingerprints on the car were actually very different from mine in several aspects, according to the FBI. But the incident certainly created a lot of heat and pressure for the three of us at that time. Again, the following day, there was another long story and more pictures of the three escaped convicts that were still believed to be in the area. Flyers had been posted, stating that we were to be taken dead or alive, as we were now wanted by the Feds for interstate flight to avoid prosecution and for the transportation of stolen guns and an auto from California. We had also been identified as the ones who pulled one of the robberies in Los Angeles.

We were really in trouble now. Renaldo was getting very nervous and had even suggested, in a kidding way, that we turn ourselves in. Neither Jack nor myself had taken him seriously. Renaldo was soon to be very instrumental in bringing about our downfall in order to protect himself.

We decided that we would no longer go anywhere in a group of three. Two of us would go together and the third would stay separated and away so that we could each come to the aid of the others, if one of us was caught. We were in a hurry to try to pull off one more good robbery that would clear enough money to take us across the states to New York without needing to obtain any further funds. Actually, we had enough money between us, but being somewhat greedy, we wanted more.

We finally found a score that would provide us with the money we needed. Jack and I were all for doing it the next night, but Renaldo objected. He said that he wanted to pull out of our arrangement and go back to California by himself. We finally persuaded him that if we took this score off together, we would split the money and he could go wherever he wanted. The next day we stayed in the motel all day, except for going out to eat. Renaldo was nervous all that day and Jack and I were concerned he would split before we took off our score. Toward evening, however, Renaldo finally seemed to settle down and Jack and I were convinced that everything was okay. Finally, we decided that it was time to go. We checked out of the motel and drove to Ogden, where we were going to rob the railroad depot. When we got there, Renaldo asked us to wait a few minutes while he went to the men's restroom. It was the last time I ever saw Renaldo.

Jack and I waited for about twenty minutes before we really became suspicious and went to check the bathroom. Renaldo was gone and we realized that he had split on us. We knew we couldn't handle the job by ourselves, so we walked out.

We had only walked about a block when we became aware of police cars coming from every direction and all converging upon the depot. We then understood Renaldo had not headed for California, but instead had turned himself in and told where we were.

Jack and I separated and each headed for the car from

different directions. We made it to the car and, after checking to make sure it wasn't staked out, got in and drove away. We were real hot and could not go back to our motel in Salt Lake City. We also knew we had to dump the car as soon as we got far enough away from all the police activity. We pulled into a commercial parking area and paid for twenty-four-hour parking in the hope that the car would not be found, thus leading the police to believe we were still driving it. We each checked into a different room at a hotel, knowing the attention of the police force was focused on us as a pair.

We knew we had to use extreme caution not to attract attention, as it would be the end for us. In desperate straits now, we were in a strange town and were sure that Renaldo was cooperating to the fullest with the police in an effort to better his own situation. We had to get out of town, but we knew there would be little chance that night. Our only hope was to wait it out for at least forty-eight hours, allowing the heat to subside a bit, giving us better odds at making it.

Our luck did not hold out that long. The next morning when we met for breakfast, the papers gave us the story. Renaldo was talking his head off, telling everything he knew. In addition, he portrayed us as being extremely dangerous and well armed, and said he felt we would not be taken without a fight, if we were given the opportunity. We did not want to die, yet I am sure we would have fought if there was a possibility of getting away. He made it appear that we were in favor of such a confrontation, and this was not so.

We decided we would try to make our move that night, provided we could find a car. None of the papers said anything about the car being found and everything indicated they thought we were still driving it. This was a break for us, if it would only hold up through the night. We stayed inside all day and when it was dark, went to the hotel cafe to eat. The evening edition of the paper again carried our pictures and a front-page story with large headlines reading, "ARMED ESCAPED CONVICTS IN AREA." It also revived the story of the so-called killing.

I noticed an elderly couple watching us very intently. I told Jack and he also observed them watching us. They made no move to call the police or manager, but both Jack and I were convinced they had recognized us. We waited until they left and hurriedly paid our bill and left the dining room through a different exit from the couple. They went out into the street, so we went back through the lobby of the hotel and out another door, which opened onto a street opposite from their exit point. We had walked only about a block when we heard police cars converging on the hotel. We were out of sight but knew they would fan out and encircle a larger area as soon as they realized they had missed us at the restaurant. We had to have a car, and in the next few minutes, or we were going to be captured or killed.

We were about four blocks from the hotel when we spotted a large sign that advertised an automobile club. It had a large garage, hotel, and recreation area. This seemed to fill the bill for us perfectly. The weather was bad and it was starting to snow. There was practically no one on the streets, and I'm sure we would have stood out like bright lights to any police car that came cruising by. We decided we would try to pick off a car from the club garage. We had just stepped inside the office of the club when a police car came down the street. They had fanned out and were now searching the entire area.

There was no one in the office but we could hear voices and laughter coming from a room posted "Recreation Area." We could not see inside the recreation area, but could see into the large garage parking facility. There was no one around. We left the office and went out into the garage where we found a car with keys in it. I had just started it up when someone asked what I was doing. I looked up to see two men standing beside the car.

I knew I couldn't con my way out of it, so I just sat there, waiting. Jack had not gotten into the car, he had ducked behind another car out of sight, in the event just such a situation would develop. He stepped up behind them and told them to freeze. When they saw Jack and the sawed-off, double-barreled shotgun, they almost collapsed. I got out, patted them down and then we loaded them into the car. We had no choice. If we let them go, we were hot in two minutes and the car was no good to us. If we took them as hostages, we might get out of the area without being detected, and even if we were stopped, the police would not start shooting while they were in the car. It increased our chances of getting away considerably. Also, four people in the car would lessen the possibility that we would be stopped for a routine check.

We drove out of the garage, we thought unobserved. We were mistaken. Just as we pulled out across the sidewalk to enter the street, two men were entering the club office. We noticed them, but didn't think they noticed us. Unfortunately, there was just enough light for them to recognize not only the car we were driving, but also the older man we had taken hostage. He was the president of the auto club. We decided that we would head for Idaho because Renaldo had spilled our plans about heading for New York. To reach the highway we wanted, we had to pass the hotel where we had been recognized.

As we drove by, we could see two police cars still on the scene. It was a very uncomfortable feeling, passing by one's pursuer so closely. We started out of town as it began to snow harder. Being from California, I had never driven in the snow; I was being especially careful not to make any driving errors, and it was miserable going. The two hostages kept asking to be let out so they could return home. They told us they wouldn't press charges or tell where we were going, or anything about us. I really felt sorry for them and kept reassuring them that we would not hurt them if they just behaved and did as we asked.

After a while, the older man got himself under control and told us that we would not get by the border station between Utah and Idaho. We would be spotted as soon as we arrived. He was so sincere in what he was saying that we decided we would listen to the radio to see if there was anything being broadcast about the situation. We found the local radio station and in a few minutes picked up a local newscast that told of the whole incident. It stated the police knew about the hostages, but were not sure of our exact location. The report went on to say it was believed we were headed for Idaho and alerted people to be on the watch for us, but warned them not to try to apprehend us.

We decided we would double back over the same road we had just traveled and head for Nevada. We thought if they were concentrating on us going into Idaho, we could get by with this maneuver. Everything went fine until we started out of Ogden toward Salt Lake City and realized there had been a roadblock set up. We knew we would never get through. We were able to turn around without attracting any special attention and drove back into Ogden.

There was only one other option open and that was to go into Wyoming. For some reason there was no roadblock set up at that point, allowing us to drive right out of Utah and into Wyoming with no trouble. We continued on toward Cheyenne, Wyoming. The weather was terrible, but we were able to keep going. Our hostages by then had given up asking to be released and just rode along in silence. We drove for the entire night and everything indicated that we were free, at least for the moment.

What Jack and I were not aware of, however, was that we

had been spotted when we turned back to Ogden and had been followed for ninety miles by the FBI. They decided, rather than take a chance on being observed, they would let us keep going as long as we had the hostages. Once we released them, they would make their move. They were willing to take a chance we might slip away after the hostages were released, just to protect them. They knew we were in a very poor region of country in which to hide and if we did give them the slip, it wouldn't be for long, as they knew the area well and we did not.

They had established observation points at intervals between Ogden and Cheyenne, Wyoming. Each time we passed an observation point, they would check to see if we still had the hostages and, if we did, we were allowed to proceed with no interference. We drove until we were on the outskirts of Cheyenne, and decided we would free the hostages far enough away from town so that we could find a place to get holed up before they had the police on our trail. It was snowing very hard when we let the hostages go. We had not seen another car for a long time and felt that it would be a considerable amount of time before they got into town or found a place to call the police. Jack and I had deliberately discussed the possibility of grabbing another car, taking somebody else hostage, and heading for Denver, in the hope we would confuse the police when they were told this story by our first hostages.

Jack and I really did not know what we were going to do. We were just about worn out from the tension and stress of the past few days and needed to sleep and relax for a couple of hours. After letting the hostages out, we decided to ditch the car on the streets of Cheyenne and hope the police would find it and, after talking to the hostages, assume we had already taken someone else hostage and were heading for Denver.

I don't know how we managed to get into Cheyenne, but we did. Somehow the last stakeout had missed us. After waiting beyond the time they felt we should have passed through their checkpoint, they thought we had had an accident and went back the way we had come, looking for us. I later learned there were some serious repercussions for those agents as a result of our slipping by them.

We drove through the main part of town and on through to the outskirts on the other side. There, we parked the car by a bus station and took a cab back to the very heart of Cheyenne, where we checked into the best hotel in town. We went to our room and cleaned up, went into the hotel restaurant for a nice meal and a few drinks at the bar, then headed for bed. We slept until early evening, got up, ate, bought the newspaper, and went back to the room to avoid being seen any more than necessary.

There was absolutely nothing in the paper to indicate Jack and I were even alive. There was no mention of us at all. This should have made us suspicious, but instead we believed that we had convinced the police that we had gone to Denver. We assumed we were being looked for there. We really felt smart, confident, and quite comfortable.

We again went to bed and slept soundly. This was to be our last night of freedom for eighteen years.

When we awoke in the morning, Jack said he was going to the coffee shop to get coffee and a newspaper, then to the hotel barber shop for a shave. I decided to sleep for a while longer. I told Jack to wake me when he came back.

I was in for a far ruder awakening than I had anticipated.

9 Capture

I had been sleeping soundly, when suddenly I realized something was pressing hard and painfully against the side of my head. A voice said, "Don't move, or you're dead."

I opened my eyes and looked around the room to see several nervous uniformed and plain-clothes law enforcement officers, all with drawn, cocked guns. I had a sawed-off shotgun under the mattress but it would have meant certain death if I even attempted to reach for it.

Their relentless search for us had finally come to an end. We had been outsmarted. The long run was over, as was party time, booze, and all the things we enjoyed. It was time to pay the piper.

We were taken to the Cheyenne jail and lodged in the federal high-power tank, a very special section of jail reserved for those who are potential troublemakers, escape artists, and cases that will undoubtedly be given long terms in prison. Without question, we very definitely belonged in this section.

Jack and I were split up and placed in different isolation

sections of the tank. We were questioned separately for hours on end about every crime we had committed in either Utah or Nevada during the time we were on the run.

The purpose of separating Jack and me was to use leverage on us, implying that one had talked and was lying to place blame on the other, in the hope of receiving a lighter sentence. This police tactic often works on "partners in crime," as one or both will eventually become convinced the other is singing his head off to save his own skin. It didn't work with Jack and me, however, as I knew Jack was too stubborn to talk, and I knew he believed I would never betray him. After three days of interrogation, with no success on their part, we were asked to sign extradition papers that would allow the Utah officials to come to Wyoming and return us to the area in which our crime had occurred.

Realizing we would never have a chance to escape from our present location, we decided to go back to Utah, with the faint hope that we might get a chance to run again. It turned out to be a lost cause, as we were taken back in a special harness that had been made especially for us. It was designed in such a way that one could not so much as use a handkerchief, let alone get his hands free.

In addition to the arm and wrist harness, we were shackled together and hooked to a long chain that was handcuffed to a U.S. Marshal. We were taken out of Cheyenne jail during the early hours of the morning and loaded into an unmarked car with a special wire cage in the back seat. This was locked from the outside. There were only two marshals in the car with us, but there were three in the car in front and three in the car that followed, to escort us from Cheyenne, Wyoming, to Salt Lake City, Utah.

We were well treated by the group of federal agents, but once we were turned over to the authorities at the Salt Lake City jail, it was a different story. The federal government had a special arrangement to house prisoners in their jail (we were considered federal prisoners since we had been charged with a violation of the Lindbergh Law, the transporting of a person across a state line against his will).

Being a federal prisoner in a city jail is no picnic. We were put into what was termed the high-pressure tank, under "deadlock." When "deadlocked," only one person has a key with which to unlock the chain that is used on the cell door, which ensures that it is not opened accidentally. Thus, we could not bathe, walk the corridor, or even eat our meals with the rest of the prisoners. The other prisoners were not even allowed to talk to us, for if caught, they were either sent to the hole or restricted to their cells.

We were very angry about these conditions for several reasons. For one thing, there was no possibility of a chance for escape, and we felt we were being singled out for special punishment in an institution where we had not committed any violations. We also felt this caused us to become a source of gossip and conversation for other inmates, thus lessening

our chances of ever being able to associate with or participate in any of the activities allowed the other prisoners in
the same tank.

About the second or third day in jail, we heard rumblings
about how lousy the food was and that someone should do
something about it. This went on every night for a week,
but no one made any effort to change the situation. Finally,
after having heard enough, Jack shouted at the group to
either go on a food strike or throw the food on the floor and
refuse to clean it up—or just eat it and stop complaining, if
they didn't have enough guts to try to change the situation.
This angered some of the others, but it was decided that at
the moment they would not complain, but just eat the food.
Jack and I then made a rather stupid commitment, stating
that when they were ready to riot over the food, rather than
just sit and gripe about it, we would join them.

For the next two nights, we heard the others discussing
plan upon plan of what they would, should, or could do.
It was finally decided to send the sheriff a petition signed
by every inmate on high-pressure row. It said that if the
food didn't improve in two days, we were going to wreck
the cells and go on a hunger strike. This petition was sent
to Jack and me for our approval and signature. I had great
misgivings about how well the others would follow through
after the petition was submitted, but still signed my name
at the very top of the list. This was not a smart move and
I then sent it back to Jack, who signed right under my
name, before sending it on to the others. Of course,

because Jack and I signed the petition first, the Sheriff's reaction would be that we had been the instigators of the entire situation.

This was not true and this serious error in judgment resulted in great pain and suffering for Jack and me. It also drove me deeper into the depths of distrust of my fellow man, a distrust I carried for years and years. It also created in me an almost overwhelming desire for revenge. I had never been one to harbor ill will for long, but the petition resulted in a situation where I ate, slept, and dreamed constantly of deliberate, cold-blooded murder.

The petition had been placed on the food cart with the dirty breakfast dishes and sent back to the kitchen, where it was discovered and turned over to the sheriff. When the sheriff received the petition, he decided he would take immediate action and bring the entire situation to a head then and there.

He assembled what is termed the "goon squad." It is usually composed of the biggest, meanest guys from the jail crew and police force, who enjoy working over inmates. It was a real pleasure for some of those men. One in particular, the captain of police, George, had a reputation for thoroughly enjoying putting the "boots" to an obstreperous inmate.

Unfortunately, having been the first to sign the petition, I was first on the list for the "goon squad." They assembled at my cell door and the high-pressure tier was unlocked. My door could now be opened from the control box at the end of the block. I knew I was in big trouble, because George himself was leading the squad.

Jack and I had talked to the other inmates of the tier and asked them to fight if they were to be taken to the hole for punishment. George signaled for the jailer to open my door. When my door opened, I had a decision to make. Was it fight then and there or was it walk out of the cell, go to the hole, and, in all probability, get a beating there, just as I would have if I refused to leave my cell? I decided I would face the consequences of my actions then and there. It was a typical bad decision on my part.

George asked me to step out of my cell. I refused and invited him to "Come in and get me, if you have the guts." This was total rebellion.

As I mentioned before, George was a man who truly enjoyed his worldly power, authority, and respectability. He was used to being obeyed when he spoke. He tolerated no hesitation and was totally devoid of any sympathy, compassion, or fairness when dealing with others in positions inferior to his—peers and inmates alike. He was not deserving of the respectability that his position afforded him because he enjoyed using his power in a very brutal, physical way against those he felt could not fight back. I was soon to be the recipient of his brutal nature.

George came in to get me. When he stepped through the door, I hit him as hard as I could in the mouth. He went down like he had been clubbed with a baseball bat. For that action, I was to receive a beating that very nearly cost me my life.

It only took the other squad members a minute to over-power me and hold me helpless in readiness for George's recovery, at which time he gave me the worst beating I have ever received in my entire life. He punched me over and over, while I was held by two officers of the squad. When I collapsed and fell to the floor, he then did the number he was so well known for, "putting the boots to an inmate." After he had worn himself out kicking me, he ordered some members of the squad to throw me down the stairs. They refused, saying I had been beaten enough and to throw me down the iron stairs might kill me. They knew every other inmate on the row was aware of what had taken place and there would be no possible way to cover up my death. This did not please or satisfy George, so he gave me one last kick, placed to the right side of my back.

After I was carried off to the hole, they went back for Jack. He too gave them a fight, and also ended up with such a severe beating that he still had stitches in his head when we went to court for our arraignment.

While in the hole, my animosity grew out of proportion, as I plotted and planned various ways to cause the death of George.

Back in my jail cell I found the opportunity to steal a spoon. I broke off the scoop portion and kept the handle. I rubbed the broken end on the floor for days and days, until I had the handle pointed and sharp as a needle. I then placed the point into a clove of garlic until it turned green. My intention was to stab George in his fat abdomen on my way to court. I had heard that if the garlic-tarnished point penetrated into one's insides, it would create a horrible infection, ending in death. I was not concerned for myself anymore. I just wanted to get my revenge on this man.

As all hatred must, mine caused numerous sleepless nights and eventually a great deal of physical pain, as I accidentally stuck the garlic-treated point of my weapon into the palm of my own hand. The pain was excruciating. I washed the wound over and over again, in the hope it would not become infected. I tried cleansing the wound further by cutting it open and forcing it to bleed several times. My precautions were to no avail. After the third day my hand began to swell and became red and inflamed. I soaked it again and again in cold water, again to no avail, and the pain and swelling continued. By the end of the fifth or sixth day I could no longer stand the pain. I asked to see the jail doctor, who did not arrive until late the following day. When he saw my hand, he told me it would have to be incised and drained. By this time the pain was so intense that if he had said he would have to amputate, I would have consented with no hesitation.

As the doctor and I stood in the jail corridor, he used a sterile knife that had been washed off with iodine to incise my hand. No anesthetic or any other niceties accompanied the procedure. The amount of drainage that poured from the incision was unbelievable, as was the great amount of relief I experienced, as the pressure and infection were released from within the wound.

After all my efforts and needless suffering, the opportunity to stab George never materialized. My skillfully planned revenge had been turned on me. We were always taken to and from court by the U.S. Marshals, who, I might add, treated us extremely well.

Our crime had been committed in Ogden, Utah, and therefore whenever we had a court appearance we were transported to Ogden by car. On our first trip to Ogden from the Salt Lake City jail, we were told by the U.S. Marshal in charge that if we attempted to escape, he would kill us both. I believe he would have. He was a very kind person but had never lost a prisoner in all his years of service. He was not about to lose us just before his retirement. Escape was not too much on my mind, however, as I had developed a dull ache in my right side and had not felt at all well physically for quite a few weeks. I did not know the reason at that time, but was to find out in the months ahead.

Jack and I had decided not to plead guilty to anything and to demand a jury trial, even though we knew we did not have a chance to beat the charges. Our reasoning was to prolong our return to prison, thus giving us more time in the jail facilities, where it would be easier to find a way to escape. It was not any surprise to us when we were charged with violations of sections 408 and 408A. We went to trial on May 26, 1942, with a court-appointed attorney, in the U.S. District Court for the District of Utah, case number 14131.

The plans for prolongation had also proven to be just one more of my many stupid ideas, because the entire proceeding, including picking the jury, the trial, returning of the verdict, and sentencing, all took place in less than two hours. It was, at that time, the shortest trial time for a capital case in the United States.

Our lawyer never said a single word from start to finish, and as soon as we were sentenced he disappeared. Although he was appointed our attorney at an earlier hearing, we never consulted with him prior to our trial. We saw him for only five minutes on the day he was appointed to defend us; the next time we laid eyes on him was the day of the court trial. He did not want anything to do with defending us.

When we objected in court to the fact that we were never given an opportunity to discuss our case with our lawyer, Judge Tillman Johnson overruled our objection and ordered the case to continue. By then, it was quite obvious to everyone that our demanding a jury trial was as much a farce as was the trial itself. Even Jack and I knew that what we were doing was only antagonizing everyone.

It certainly antagonized Judge Johnson, because he sentenced us each to forty-five years in a federal penitentiary without so much as batting an eye.

When I heard that sentence I knew that, at age twenty-two, I had messed up my life. Little did I realize that in just three months, I would be in Alcatraz.

After being sentenced, we were returned to the Salt Lake City jail. Security was even greater than when we were first captured. Our remaining stay in that jail was uneventful, as was the trip to McNeil Island only a few days later. We were back in prison, only this time for much longer, and with very little hope that things would change in the future.

McNeil Island is a federal penitentiary located several miles off the coast of Washington state, in Puget Sound, a few miles south of Tacoma. It was a very modern prison, located on a fairly large island. Although it was a maximum-security institution, it did not, as a rule, house the hardened or incorrigible prisoner. All federal prisoners from California, Arizona, Nevada, Washington, and Utah are sent there. The Bureau of Prisons apparently never intended for Jack and I to stay.

I am sure that if such hadn't been the original plan, our attitudes would have brought it about in short order. We were sent through orientation just as is every other federal prisoner. After thirty days of orientation, which consisted of numerous interviews and tests, we were released into the general prison population. We were again put into another special cell unit and assigned single cells, but under much tighter security than the rest of the institution. It was obvious that we were really under the gun and could end up in trouble very easily if we were not careful.

We both tried to be casual about everything, but we were both looking to see if there was a way out. I was assigned to work in the laundry and Jack was put to work in another part of the institution. We looked at every possibility, but before we could even get started trying to put something together, the Bureau of Prisons decided to send us to Alcatraz at the earliest convenience. The reason, or at least pretense, being our long-term sentences and the fact we were great potential escape risks. In addition to Jack and me, two others were also selected to go, probably because of their friendship and association with Jack and me.

After coming back from dinner one night, we were taken to Administration and informed that we were being shipped out that night to Alcatraz. After just over two months at McNeil, we were being transferred without ever having a disciplinary action against us at this institution, which we felt was unjust. The other two were then brought in and told they were also going. It shook them up, as neither had very long sentences. Later that night we were asked to pack our few belongings and have them ready to go. Sometime during the night we were awakened, told to dress, taken to the basement, and all chained together. We were then taken to the mainland for the long train trip to Alcatraz.

10 Introduction to Alcatraz

During the Depression of the early 1930s, crime ran
rampant in the United States, and offenses of major pro-
portions went unpunished because of jurisdictional conflicts
between various states and the federal government.
Congress finally enacted legislation that gave the federal
government jurisdiction over certain criminal offenses
previously held by the states. Attorney General Homer
Cummings and Congress then decreed that a special prison
be built to house the long-term and incorrigible prisoners
who were responsible for these crimes. On October 13,
1933, Alcatraz was transferred from the Army to the
Department of Justice.

Alcatraz was designed and built to be a maximum-
security and minimum-privilege facility. In reality it went far
beyond this and became a prison where the sole purpose
was to degrade, deprive, humiliate, and break the inmates
physically, mentally, and spiritually, if possible. In many,
many cases, it was remarkably successful.

Alcatraz Island is 22 acres of solid rock and cliffs,

surrounded by the turbulent, fast-moving, cold water of San Francisco Bay. It lies in a beautiful setting inside the Golden Gate and is located approximately one and one-half miles from the nearest land. From the famous Fisherman's Wharf in San Francisco, it had often been called a brilliant jewel sitting in a field of green. This is easy to believe when seen at night from San Francisco. The lights from the island reflect off the waters of the bay and the lighthouse sends out flashes of light each minute, not unlike a diamond flashing its brilliance when exposed to the sun.

Above the steep cliffs of the island are a multitude of brilliantly colored flowers and plants that seem to flourish in the damp, cold, windy, foggy atmosphere that often shrouds the island in a blanket of white.

The entire history of Alcatraz has been associated with violence. In the mid-1800s, it was determined that the island would be an excellent choice for part of an inner defense line. The U.S. Army Corps of Engineers developed a plan of defense that would include Alcatraz, Angel Island, and Fort Mason (or Black Point, as it was then called). These installations would protect the entire harbor and mainland against any unwanted intrusion. A lighthouse was erected on Alcatraz and by 1859 the island housed Company H of the Third Army Artillery Regiment to man the new fortifications installed there. It did not take long for the fortress to become a prison also. Because of its location and the treacherous waters surrounding the island, it was soon being used to house military prisoners. In 1909, a new Army prison building was erected on the foundation of the old citadel, a defensive barracks at the top of the island. It housed many World War I prisoners, but as the years passed, these prisoners were transferred or released to other institutions.

My introduction to Alcatraz occurred the day following my arrival. At 7 a.m. a loud, ear-shattering bell indicated that we were to rise and prepare to be counted. The count was a simple procedure. Each inmate stood at his door, hands on the bars, as a guard walked down each tier counting every individual. As the count of each tier was completed, the count was called to the count center. If all were correct, a whistle blew and we were allowed to prepare for breakfast. It continued, hourly, even though prisoners were locked in their cells and asleep.

The night counts were very irritating, even though prisoners were not required to stand. The flash of light shining on our faces would wake us and drive home the realization that, even in sleep, we were being continuously watched.

We were not free, no matter what we dreamed. Our lives were being lived as others determined. We had no right to decide what we could do or say. It was of no consequence what we thought because we had violated the law; being incarcerated at Alcatraz made us outcasts, at the mercy of the whims of those in authority. It was a very unpleasant experience.

When it was time to go to the dining hall, tiers from B Block and C Block were opened simultaneously by guards at the end of each tier, using manually operated control levers. The entire tier population stepped out of their cells and proceeded single file into the dining hall. When the lines from B and C Blocks met at the dining hall door, they each maintained a single file down the center to the large steam table, where prisoners picked up trays and silverware. The lines split at this point and B Block turned right at the steam table and C Block turned left. (This might seem to be an insignificant point, but because the C Block side was in such close proximity to the guard standing outside the window with a machine gun, it often tended to dampen one's appetite, especially in times of stress and tension between guards and inmates. Which was quite often.)

As we passed along the steam table, we extended our trays to the inmate serving the line. He would give a measured portion of the food he was serving. If we did not want any particular dish, we were not obligated to take it; however, we were required to eat what we took or face disciplinary action.

Leaving the steam table, we took a seat at the first table we came to. Ten men were seated at each large table and were always eating with the inmates from their tier. This had the advantage of making it simple to get the inmates in and out of the dining hall and back to their cells, but it posed a problem at times for inmates, if there was bad blood between them.

The men never escaped the aggravation of eating with someone who irritated them, and this often caused great tension at the table. If a fight erupted in the dining hall and any kind of weapon was involved, it put everyone's life in jeopardy, for some guards, in my opinion, would not hesitate to shoot if the situation gave them the opportunity. I don't feel that was true of all the guards, but some lived for the day they could shoot a con. That might be considered a harsh statement to make, but I believe it to be true.

The dining hall in any institution is a very volatile and dangerous area. Plenty of murders and riots have occurred in this particular section of many prisons. Alcatraz was no exception to the rule, and guards and inmates alike were always relieved when the whistle blew for the return of the men to their own individual cells. I can remember several incidents that started in the other dining areas with no warning, and I am sure there could have been such incidents at Alcatraz, had the population not been older, wiser, and more institution-wise. Old cons knew the consequences for trouble erupting in this area. I also believe that the very close proximity of the machine-gun guard and a ceiling lined with ten tear gas canisters (which could be released instantaneously) had a quieting effect on the population.

The following is a daily routine for the long days at Alcatraz, Monday through Friday, year in and year out:

After breakfast, the inmates returned to their cells, single file, tier by tier, just as they had entered the dining hall. Each inmate entered his cell, the doors were closed, and a count was taken. After a correct count, one could relax until the doors were "racked" open and it was time for work. Tiers were opened one at a time and each inmate would proceed from his cell to the door leading to the recreation area. Outside the door leading to the yard, the inmate walked down a flight of stairs and passed through the metal detector (snitch box), which was magnetically and electrically operated. This was to detect any metal that was being taken from the cellhouse to the yard or work area.

The snitch box was hated and feared because it could be triggered by the guard to go off even if one were free of contraband. Not surprisingly, the snitch boxes were loved and appreciated by the guards because they were a means to punish, embarrass, and humiliate inmates they disliked. I know for the younger inmates (myself included, perhaps for having given a guard a bad time) this harassment in front of our peers was devastating and resented.

If the alarm was triggered, the inmate was pulled out of line and given a shakedown (patted over his entire body to determine if he was carrying contraband). He was then again sent through the snitch box, and if he was unfortunate enough to trigger the alarm again, he was subjected to a "skin search." This entailed stripping to the bare skin, while the guards searched every seam and inch of clothing. The inmate was personally examined from top to bottom, including the soles of his feet, while his peers observed as they passed by. Not only was this a disturbing incident mentally, in the winter it was also physically painful. The chill, wet wind that blew from the ocean would leave one so cold that it often took hours to feel warm again.

The inmates continued down another flight of stairs to the recreation area. Here they lined up along the painted lines on the pavement that designated the various shop details. The men in each shop area were then counted and checked against a roster for each shop. If all was correct, the captain of the guards gave the signal for the wall guard to lower the key to open the yard wall gate. Shop by shop, each crew moved through the gate and outside the yard walls. As each man stepped through the wall gate, he was again counted.

As one stepped through the gate, the view was beautiful. Directly in front was the Golden Gate Bridge and to the left was San Francisco. Each day this was a reminder of the freedom, love, and good things in life we had lost by our crimes. It is a reminder that has never left me. Passing through this gate, the crews, in single file, descended a long, steep flight of stairs. On a small, flat area was located a second snitch box. Each inmate passed through and descended another flight of stairs, similar to those above. At the bottom of these stairs, some crews turned off and went into shops located in that area. Others went down another short set of stairs and to their respective shops.

After arrival at their assigned work area, the inmates were again counted and after the count was verified as correct, the men went to their assigned workstations. All doors in the work area were locked and counts were taken every hour on the hour until the inmates were returned to the cellhouse at 11:30 a.m., after a final count in their shop. Although the return walk back to the cellhouse was repetitious, snitch box checks and all, it was also a more difficult trip in that the men were tired and irritable as they made the difficult uphill climb, only to return to a cold, gloomy cell.

The afternoon routine would be the same as the morning, except the men would be twice as exhausted and irritable as they made what seemed an even longer walk back to their cells. Those that were living on the "flats" were at least a bit more thankful perhaps, in that they did not have still two more flights of stairs to climb to reach their cells. The climbing was extremely difficult for the older inmates, yet in all the years I climbed these stairs, I never saw an older inmate falter or give up.

On my first day, I had the opportunity to observe the physical layout of the cellhouse. Inside a large, poorly lit building were four large cellblocks. Each cellblock was separated from the other by a corridor that ran the entire length of the building. A Block, the cellblock on the northeastern side of the cellhouse, was old and obsolete and had not been remodeled when the new construction of the institution had been done. It was far less secure than any of the other blocks and was used only to store supplies. Only one time after the new construction was it used to house prisoners. That was during the 1946 uprising.

B and C Blocks were the inside blocks. B and C were separated by a wide, highly polished corridor called "Broadway" by the inmates. It started at the entrance from the administration offices and armory and terminated at the entrance to the dining hall. Directly at its termination was located the west gun gallery, which gave the gun guard complete coverage of the three corridors and all tiers of the cellhouse. This gun gallery also had a clear view of the entire dining hall. It was to play an important part in the 1946 break.

Each of the cellblocks consisted of three tiers, the "flats," as the bottom cells were called, and the two tiers above. Each of the inner cellblocks (B and C) were approximately 150 feet long and divided at midpoint by a barred, empty area called the "cutoff," which was also to play an important part in the action that occurred on May 2, 1946. The cells on the A and D sides offered more privacy but were colder. The cells facing each other on Broadway offered no privacy but were warmer. The upper tiers on Broadway offered more light if one wished to read after the lights were out in the cells. Above the third tier was a large empty area, surrounded and enclosed on all sides by bars. It was divided in the center by the service corridor that contained all the plumbing for the block. It was possible to enter the service corridor on the flats and, by use of the plumbing, climb into this large barred area. (Barney Coy gained access to this locked area during the break of 1946 with keys taken from a cellhouse guard.)

The cutoff, as its name implies, separated the two sections of each block. It was a large, barred area that extended from the floor to the ceiling of the building. What its purpose was I have never understood.

Walled off from the main cellhouse on the southwest side was D Block, the disciplinary unit of the institution. It contained forty-two security cells, of which six were double-doored solitary confinement cells. They were called the "black holes." All the cells on D Block had steel walls, ceilings, and floors, as well as special tool-resistant barred fronts. Most of the cells in D Block were larger and better lighted than those in the main cellhouse, and faced the outer wall of the building. This had advantages as well as disadvantages. From some of the cells on the upper tier, the view was beautiful, but in the wet, windy, foggy weather, the windows were a curse because of the cold they allowed in, making it miserable for everyone.

All the cells in D Block had sliding-type doors like those in the main cellhouse. The "flats" or ground-floor cells were electrically operated from an extension of the west gun gallery into the block from the main cellhouse. Tiers two and three could be manually operated from the lock-box at the end of each tier. The solitary confinement cells (black holes) were both electrically and key-operated. The inner door had to be unlocked from the gun gallery and the outer by a key lowered by the gun gallery guard.

Confinement in D Block could be for a matter of one month to years. The only privilege allowed in this block was reading. You were locked in your cell twenty-four hours each day. Meals and all activity, except for a weekly bath, were in your cell. Talking was permitted to those who were housed in cells next to yours, but in a moderate tone only. Inmates were, by law, allowed a period of recreation in the prison yard, but this was never enforced for the D Block population. The hole was any of the six double-doored security cells on the lower floor. They were cold and dark. Confinement in the hole could be for any reason: intoxication, fighting, assaulting an officer, stealing food, destruction of government property, escape attempts, or possession of contraband of any nature.

Alcatraz was a prison where one was always aware that he was under the direct observation of well-armed guards, some willing to shoot with no hesitation. The only real security an inmate had was when locked in his cell, in certain portions of the hospital, or locked in his work area. Alcatraz had a complex system of gun towers, catwalks, and armed wall guards that gave protection to each other while keeping inmates under constant supervision and control. There was no outside area that was not under direct control of one or more gun towers, either in the recreation area or to and from the industrial buildings. It was this system of interlocking observation points that made any escape a futile venture from its very inception.

At Alcatraz, inmates were permitted one visitor a month. Actually, this could hardly be called a visit because it took place via a monitored phone, with a wall separating you from your visitor. You could see your visitor only by peering through a small slot in the glass. At times, this visit was more unbearable than gratifying, because if it was a loved one, a prisoner could not touch, hold, or kiss her, regardless of who it was or how long you had been separated. This in itself was a terrible price to pay and perhaps one of the most frustrating.

The only other means of communication with the outside world was somewhat unrewarding in that all mail was censored and often portions were deleted. In the early years, inmates were not given the opportunity to see the original letter that was sent; this policy changed in later years. Only two sheets of paper, twice a week, were issued to send mail outside of Alcatraz.

Reading material was limited to a few special magazines and the books contained in the library. There were hundreds of books listed but very few were of current issue. Of the books donated to the prison library, any that centered on or depicted crime were deleted.

It was mandatory that each inmate shave twice a week. A new razor blade was issued each month. The blades were retained by the institution and were passed out and retrieved after each use. To lose your blade was an automatic "solitary confinement" offense. Showers were permitted twice a week and haircuts were given once a month.

For several years, conversation was prohibited between inmates except on weekends, or in the yard. Cells were constantly searched for no particular reason—perhaps on the word of a snitch, or maybe to simply antagonize and annoy the prisoners. Cells had to be kept in perfect order at all times, with nothing draped or hung in such a matter that hindered the guard's view of the small vent in back of the cells, which opened into the service corridor.

Upon arrival at Alcatraz, all new inmates learned a fact of life that would not soon be forgotten. An escape attempt from this institution was often a death sentence. This was true even if the resultant death was not justified or even necessary to prevent an escape. This was particularly true of inmates actually discovered in the water. There was a feeling among the inmates that if one attempted to escape, he must be prepared to die. I believe some of the hand-picked keepers of the Alcatraz incorrigibles felt that death under these circumstances served as a deterrent to others who might be contemplating a similar move.

Retrospectively, it seemed the prison administration took an escape attempt as a personal affront to their capabilities. They were going to keep America's escape-proof prison escape-proof, regardless of method or cost to others, justifiable or otherwise. There would be no escapes.

The very methods under which the prison operated were conducive to several needless and unjustified deaths. What occurred at Alcatraz was never seriously questioned by the news media, as the authorities were very clever with half-truths, exploitation of occurrences, and one-sided versions of the uncontrollable, vicious criminals incarcerated within their prison walls. Misleading information or half-truths were released to prevent or eliminate any intrusion into the private hell of Alcatraz. Had the public been aware of the true facts, this prison would have surely been disbanded years earlier and perhaps many men would have been saved from the murder, suicide, execution, or insanity induced by

Alcatraz, with its deliberately calculated program to destroy its victims.

While it is true this prison housed violent men, many of whom had killed during the commission of their crimes, they were still human beings—a fact that seemed to be forgotten once incarcerated at Alcatraz. Also a fact: not all of the violent and vicious men found at Alcatraz wore numbers. Some wore uniforms and were protected by laws, society, and the wall of secrecy that surrounded that grim prison.

11 Alcatraz Early Years

Interview

All inmates, upon arrival, were interviewed by Warden Johnston and the associate warden. The purpose of the initial interview was twofold. It informed the inmate of all the rules and regulations that would govern his every activity and life, and it gave the warden and administrative staff a chance to know and personally judge him. This interview was a determining factor in how the inmate was going to get along and how he would be treated by administration and staff during his stay at this prison.

If the inmate was unresponsive, sullen, belligerent, or despondent, it was this attitude that was used as a criterion to judge him for years to come. It was often an unfair evaluation because many inmates would present a false facade of belligerence to hide their fears, anxieties, and despondency; they masked the inner turmoil they felt at having been placed in Alcatraz. It very often did not honestly reflect the inmate's true feelings and attitude, show what type of person he actually was, or how he truly intended to serve his sentence.

I was granted my initial interview with Warden Johnston on August 29, 1942. I can still recall the guard racking open my door and shouting, "Number 586, you have an interview with the warden." It seemed like a long walk from the top tier of C Block, where we had been assigned cells the previous night, to the interview area under the west gun gallery by the dining-hall door. At this point, I was very nervous and concerned as to how well this meeting would go. I was determined to keep my mouth shut and not make the same stupid mistakes I had made at McNeil Island, when I had refused to speak to, or shake hands with, the director of the Bureau of Prisons when he was introduced to me during an inspection of the island.

As I approached the desk, I was very conscious of the number of administrative personnel who were present. In addition to the warden, there were also the associate warden, the captain of the guards, and the day lieutenant. I was not aware of it as yet, but I was already considered a problem to them. They were concerned about my young age in a prison where the average inmate was about fifteen years older than me. The young are more apt to do things on impulse or create violence where an older and wiser inmate would ignore it and go about his business.

The interview started off with the warden explaining that I had been transferred to Alcatraz because I was an incorrigible and an escape risk, and was serving a long sentence with an escape detainer for the state of California. I was informed that my sentence of forty-five years could be served in thirty years if I did not forfeit any of the fifteen hundred days of good time I could earn during that period. It was also made very clear that there could be no transfer from Alcatraz to another prison unless any forfeited good time had been restored.

Escape was another topic that was discussed in great detail. I was informed, by tone and words, that my young age would not be a consideration in my punishment for any infractions or violation of the rules. I was also given the routine speech about "work is a privilege" and that to obtain this benefit, one had to apply to the warden in writing, asking for a work assignment.

I was given a list of rules for correspondence and visitors, along with an application form for the privileges I wanted to apply for. When I told Warden Johnston I would not be having correspondence or visitors, he was somewhat upset. Through these privileges, the administration had more insight into how well a prisoner was adjusting to his situation. It also gave them another means to make inmates comply with the rules. Visitors and correspondence were probably the most cherished privileges, because they were the inmate's only contact with family and the free world. An inmate with no contact with the outside had nothing to lose, having lost it already.

The interview was concluded with the warden giving me some good advice. He stated he had read my prison file and

The above photo was taken around 1925, and shows my mother and father at a carnival. They look so happy together. It is my only photo of my mother. Although I have some warm memories of her, my strongest recollection is of the unhappiness she caused my father, sister, and me.

An early photo of Dad holding my baby sister Kay with me standing near. We were still a family at this time.

With my father and Kay on the day of my first communion. As things with my mother became more difficult, my sister and I were often put in the care of relatives or neighbors, or left alone entirely.

Each day life was becoming harder for my sister and me.

USP-AC Form 175

Name QUILLEN, James J.   **No.** 586-AZ **Color** White **Rec'd** 8-28-42

Offense __KIDNAPPING & DYER ACT__

Date of Sentence __5-26-42__

Sentence __45 YEARS (1 5Yr.Concur)__

Sentence began __MAY 26, 1942__ 6-5-72

Minimum exp. date ~~AUGUST 11, 1972~~ 12-17-78

Maximum exp. date __MAY 25, 1987__

Parole date __MAY 25, 1957__

Good conduct credits __STAT.GT__ 5400

Credits forfeited 5-21-46: ~~2700 days~~** //3 day

Credits restored 365 days, 365, 383

District sentenced __Utah - Salt Lake City__

DETAINERS __7-18-42 Escape from Rd.Camp__ Calif. State Prison, San Quentin,Calif.

**Minimum date includes 16 days IGT, earned to 5-30-46.

Partners or co-defendants PEPPER,Jack 589-AZ

Received at Alcatraz Aug. 28, 1942, same day as subject.

Reason For Transfer

Subject, one of five men recently suspected of planning escape from Mc Neil. Other four men: Pepper,Wilson,Russ,Johnson. 1st. 3 above received at Alcatraz same time as subject.On 8-6-42 at McNeil five table knives were found concealed in his mattress, with note telling unknown accomplice how the knives were to be sharpened. To more secure Inst.

Former Institutional Rule Violatio[n]

SUBJECT ORIGINALLY SENTENCED TO MCNEIL ISLA[ND] TO ALCATRAZ BECAUSE OF SUSPECTED PLANNED ES[CAPE] 8-6-42: A leather sheath containing five s[t] found concealed in this inmate's bunk. A n[ote] ed to the sheath with instructions to grin[d] a sharp point. Sentenced to indefinite iso[lation] reg[?]tion unit; regular diet, by Assoc. Ward[en]

Criminal History

10-25-36 Juvenile Delinquency. Police p[?] 1-22-36 Burglary, robbery,G.T.(auto) en[?] Preston School of Indust. At Pr[eston] two escapes.

10-17-39 Viol. Sec.647-7 Pen.Code(sleepi[ng] 12-15-39 Robb. 1st. deg. Ventura,Calif. San Quentin Pr.5yrs to life. Gr[?] effective 1-9-43. Transf. Rd.Ca[mp] Co, on 1-5-42.

3-12-42 Info. received escaped from Rd 3-18-42 Kidnapping & Dyer Act. Sentenc[ed] OUTLINE OF INSTANT OFFENSE (U.[S.] Report)

Subject and co-defendant,#589-AZ P[?] 1941 Buick Seda in Ogden, Utah and kidn[apped] ported Ira Gourley and James Giles from Wyoming for the purpose of robbing then assist subjects in making their escape ing after escape from San Quentin Road [Camp]

FPI Inc—LK—6-26-40—200—1707-22

Escape record or attempt to escape

3-8-42 Escaped from Rd. Camp at San Quentin, Calif. with above co-defendant Suspected of planning escape at McNeil Is.8-6-42 discovered 5 table knives hidden in mattress with note.etc.

Medical, Neuro-Psychiatrical, Educational, Religious, Social and Employments.

MEDICAL EXAM: Physical condition good.

NEURO-PSYCH: M.A.16:10 I.Q. 105 St.Bn. [Ma]rital Status: Single; Catholic Religion; [8]th.Grd.education;Claims temperate drink[in]g;No drugs; Never knew real parents;Live[d wi]th step-parents in San Francisco & Oakland [re]al mother's name: J.A.Bittick (15 yrs ago [wa]s living in San Francisco.Disowned by [ple]asant step-parents: 1043 57thSt.Oakland.Calif

Prisoner AZ586.

Alcatraz – a life of sadness and pain led me to crime. Learning another way pulled me out of it.

The 'Rock Islanders' inmate band. Music helped fill a void in my life but did nothing to alleviate my loneliness and desire for freedom.

This photo shows the assault on D Block, which went on for roughly 36 hours. It could have been stopped in the first 8 hours.

Attack through the west wall.

WARNING
KEEP OFF
PERSONS ATTEMPTING
TO COME INSIDE BUOYS
WITHOUT PERMISSION
DO SO AT THEIR PERIL

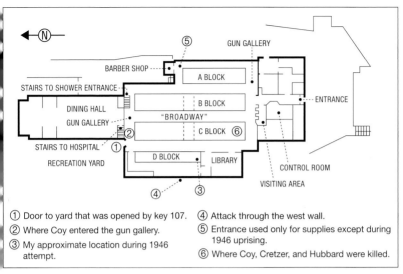

Cellhouse Diagram, 1946 Uprising.

An armed gun gallery guard controlled access to keys that opened various cellhouse doors. To get his hands on both keys and weapons, Coy had to get into the west gun gallery, which can be seen here above the entrance to the dining hall.

During cellhouse riots, inmates often trashed their own cells in protest.

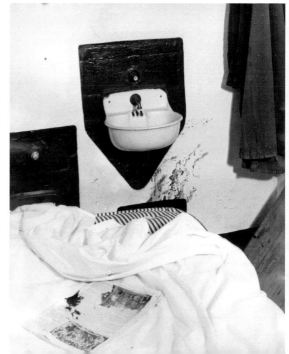

A close-up view. Cretzer carried out his mad revenge when he realized that the break-out attempt had been foiled.

the advice he was going to give me could be accepted or rejected as I so chose. I would do well, he informed me, to learn to control my temper and stop trying to solve my problems with my fists. He said that Alcatraz inmates would not find that solution to be acceptable and if I continued, as I had in other institutions, I would in all likelihood not survive to serve my time. He went on to state that if a fight did occur, I had better be aware that most inmates would not let the matter rest there; I would in all probability face a situation far more dangerous at some future date.

It was indeed good advice. His statements came true many times during my ten years on the island. Although I had not planned on trying to be an institution tough guy, it did give me something to seriously consider. I resolved that I would never be the aggressor in any situation unless there was no other alternative. I maintained this resolution, with the exception of two occasions.

Work Assignment

The day following the interview with Warden Johnston, I requested a work assignment, and was placed in the laundry. A fish (new inmate) could not ask for a specific work area, but a job change could be requested after a year. It was usually granted, unless it endangered security.

The following day I reported to the yard, where I was given directions to line up for my detail. I can still recall the beauty that met my eyes as I stepped through the wall gate for the first time. The Golden Gate Bridge was directly in front of me and there were wisps of fog behind it. The bay was smooth and calm. To my left was San Francisco and to my right, Sausalito and Marin, all reminders of the normal life I had thrown away. The detail continued down the stairs, through the snitch box, down a second long flight of stairs, and then turned off to enter the laundry.

The laundry was a huge new facility with all the modern equipment found in similar businesses in the free world. There were huge washers, dryers, extractors, presses, and mangles. I was assigned to work on a mangle with an old-time long-termer named Limpy.

Limpy was not at all pleased to have me paired with him. He was as unfriendly and uncommunicative as possible, without actually telling me out and out to get lost. I was offended and concerned. I had always been accepted as a good convict in every institution I had been in. I decided that, rather than have a confrontation so soon after arriving, I would ignore him and hope I would find out why he had taken a dislike to me. I soon learned the answer from another inmate.

At Alcatraz, fish had to earn their acceptance by minding their own business, doing their own time, and not causing trouble for other inmates. The old-timers at Alcatraz were skeptical of new and younger inmates because they had seen this breed try to build "tough guy" reputations at the expense of older inmates, who were in actuality trying to get along and do their time as easily as possible.

In a couple of weeks I finally gained some acceptance,

not only with Limpy but also from other old-timers who had been cold and distant at first.

I had only been working in the laundry approximately a month when I began to develop a severe pain in my right kidney region. I stayed in my cell that weekend, and on Monday morning reported to work as usual. By noon, I was having tremendous pain in my right side. I fell out for sick call after lunch and went to the hospital to have myself checked. Their assumption was "you're too young and healthy to be seriously ill." Thus, I was given two aspirin, a cell "lay-in" for the afternoon, then sent on my way. I went to my cell and fell asleep.

The following morning I reported for work, but by noon the pain was so severe I again went to sick call. I was given the same treatment. I reported to work the next two days, figuring it was a lost cause to return to the hospital. Each day I became more ill until, on Friday, I just could not take it any longer and almost passed out.

My co-inmates suggested returning to the hospital. If something wasn't done, I was told I should wreck the place so the warden would be notified and then I might get some results. I knew full well that threatening to wreck the hospital was not a wise idea, but I also felt if I didn't do something drastic soon, I would surely die. In desperation, I decided to take their advice. At that point I felt I had nothing to lose.

Once again I asked the laundry guard to send me to the hospital and he obliged. Again I was met with the same attitude as before. By then the pain was extremely intense. I was frightened, and knew I was in desperate need of medical attention. I intended to take the advice of the inmates, but did not get very far. I vaguely remember beginning to shout about how I would wreck the place, when everything went black. When I awoke, I was in a hospital bed, with many MTAs (medical technical assistants) and others attending me. I was examined, then blood and urine specimens were taken. I was actually being treated as though I was a paying patient in a private hospital.

I was aware of people around me, talking about appendicitis, ruptured appendix, and other things I did not understand. The only thing I was certain of at that point was that I was seriously ill and relieved to know I was going to get the medical attention I needed.

I was taken to surgery a few hours later where an abdominal exploratory and appendectomy were performed. Everything was found to be normal, thus after surgery and the normal findings, the attitude of the hospital personnel again changed. They felt they had been conned and my real purpose in the hospital was to attempt to escape. I was removed from the ward and locked in a security room just across the hallway from the guard station.

It was here I met Ludwig (Dutch) Schmidt, AZ-71, who I am sure is responsible for my being alive today. Dutch was a crime partner of the well-known bank robber and member of the Touey Gang, Basil (the Owl) Banghart, AZ-595. Dutch, a hospital orderly, was the only individual in the hospital who really believed I was still seriously ill. He would try to get me to eat and when I couldn't, he brought this to the attention of the doctors and MTAs. He was convinced I would die if something more wasn't done, and he expressed these feelings often to the hospital staff.

I still cannot understand why it was so difficult for the hospital staff to realize that something was seriously wrong with me. My weight dropped from 160 to 128 and I constantly ran abnormal blood counts and fever ranging from 102 to 104 degrees Fahrenheit. These certainly were not symptoms I could have faked.

Although I do not know what actually made the doctors finally relent, I would certainly tend to believe the persistence of Dutch played an important role. They agreed to bring in a surgeon from the Marine Hospital of San Francisco. A special boat was dispatched from the island, and he was picked up and returned to Alcatraz. Within one hour after his arrival, the diagnosis had been made and the operating room was readied. I was prepared for a second surgery. The Marine physician had discovered I had a perinephric abscess as a result of the beating and kicking I had received at the hands of George in the jail in Salt Lake City.

My recovery was a long, slow process; it was four months before I was discharged from the hospital. I asked for and was given a reassignment to the laundry. After the first day back to work, I discovered I was unable to continue. I could barely make the climb up and down the many stairs, let alone tolerate the workload. My side was still draining and I was extremely weak. Yet, in determination, I managed to report for work the following morning. However, I was pulled from the line by Captain Weinhold before our detail left the yard and was told to return to my cell. I had intended to ask for another assignment at noon, but the guards had observed my difficulties the previous day and had reported this to the captain. He removed me from my assignment on his own.

At noon, I asked the cellhouse officer to be called for an interview with the associate warden, Edward Miller. I intended to ask for another work assignment. When I got to the desk, Captain Weinhold told Jughead (a derogatory name given Mr. Miller by the inmates, as his head appeared to swell when he became angry) that he had removed me from the laundry crew because he heard reports from the guards that I was having trouble making it up and down the stairs. He said he felt that, since my surgery, this assignment was too strenuous for my condition. He also stated I was a good, willing worker, minded my own business, and was doing my own time. This was high praise coming from the captain. It created a good impression with Jughead and put me in his good graces through no effort of my own.

Captain Weinhold suggested I be classified as unassigned, but with full privileges. This was a tremendous break, because it allowed me yard privileges all day, every day. It also allowed me to see the monthly movie. These were privileges not granted to the inmate who refused to work, even though Warden Johnston said that working was a privilege.

Inmates working was important both to Warden Johnston and Associate Warden Miller, but not for the same reason. Warden Johnston thrived on the praise and publicity of the productivity of his forces. Jughead, on the other hand, was a sincere patriot and believed our work aided the war effort and the country's military forces.

Yardbird

This was the term given to the men who were assigned to work in the recreation area, a cement site enclosed by four walls. It was cold and unusually windy, and everyone tried to play his favorite sport in an enclosure far too small. Sports permitted were softball, handball, volleyball, and (although not a sport, but certainly great recreation) the card game of bridge.

Horseshoes had been allowed at one time, but had proven hazardous, after having been used numerous times by inmates to club one another over the head. Thus all horse-shoes were confiscated. Due to the very limited space, during the game of softball, if one hit a ball over the wall, it was considered an "out," rather than a home run. There were only two handball courts, which were always in use (as long as the balls lasted before accidentally being knocked over the wall!). Volleyball was seldom played, because it left too little room for those who wanted to walk without interfering with the game.

Finally, there were the bridge games. It was hardly the game the free world expected the country's most notorious inmates to be playing. Yet *Blackwood convention, finesse, grand slam, no trump*, and *bid* were terms that almost every inmate was familiar with. It was played with special dominoes, marked with blue, white, yellow, and green spots to denote the suits—they were the same as regular dominoes, except the double six (if blue) would represent the King of Spades, the double five became a Jack, etc. The dominoes were held by special boards that allowed a player to see his own cards but not his opponent's. Small tables and cotton-stuffed cushions were available to any four men who had a bag of rocks (dominoes) and wanted to play.

Bridge players congregated in the far end of the yard, away from the handball courts and where the wind deflected off the high buildings. Bridge was always played with great enthusiasm, vigor, and usually good humor. Seldom, if ever, was there an altercation over this game. It was played on the coldest, windiest days of the year if the men were permitted on the yard. It was a game well talked about and constantly played. I am sure it was even dreamed about by some of the men. Almost every inmate in the institution was familiar with the game to some extent, but to some it became another world—a way to escape from the reality of their lives within those walls.

Administration encouraged the game, and with good reason. It was quite evident that the men deeply involved with this game generally were not troublemakers, nor were they among those looking for attempts at escape. In retrospect, the bridge players had more or less found a form of escape in this card game. Thinking back, I can only name three inmates from this league who did attempt to escape.

Culbertson's Bridge for Beginners was beyond a doubt the most desired and read book in the prison's twenty-nine years of existence. When the warden permitted Auto Bridge (a device where an inmate could play the game by himself) to be ordered, it was to some inmates like Christmas had happened twice in one year.

Generally, the yardbirds working in this area had requested the job because, as soon as their limited amount of work was accomplished, they were free to spend the rest of the day playing bridge. And the inmates were not the only ones bitten by this bug. The yard wall guards also would become involved. Standing on the wall, they could usually see three of the four players' hands, and often became as involved as the participants.

The yard was now my assignment. My duties were to sweep the stairs to the yard and keep the small shed under the stairs (where the tables and cushions were stored) in order. It was a simple and easy job that took possibly thirty minutes to finish, leaving lots of free time. It was not long before I was introduced to bridge and soon learned to play, but not with the enthusiasm of my fellow inmates. With them it was a special world, but to me it was just a means to pass the time. Possibly because, being only a few months off the streets, I could not concentrate—my mind was always on freedom, and I kept looking for the possible escape.

I knew there was no possibility of escaping from the yard, but like, Ted Walters,* I kept watching in the hope I would see something others had missed. It never appeared to me, as it had Ted.

As my health and strength improved, I began to play handball. It was good for me physically as well as mentally, because it gave me something to do besides think of the free world outside. When I was not needed to make up a game of bridge, and it was too windy to play handball, I would return to my cell to read or sleep. It was an easy assignment, but one that, after a few months, bored me. I came to the decision it was time to ask for a new industrial area assignment.

The Federal Prison Industries

In 1934, through an act of Congress, the Federal Prison Industries was established. Its purpose was to manufacture several different products that could lower the cost of maintaining prisoners, create employment for inmates, and supply the military (and other prisons and government agencies) with services at a lower cost than could be obtained on the open market.

The industries were introduced at Alcatraz in mid-1936, but were not considered a great success until several years later, during the war.

_____

* See Appendix, p. 366

An inducement for working in the industries was the opportunity to earn additional good time. Industrial good time was computed on the basis of two additional days each month for the first year, four days each month for the next three years, and five days each month for the fifth and following years. For the inmate serving a short sentence, it was a great incentive. For the long-term inmate (fifty to one hundred years) with a detainer for another state, it meant little or nothing. Prior to my arrival at Alcatraz, a new industrial building had been built and opened in 1941. It was a clean, warm area in which to work.

During my months of recovery, while working as a yard-bird, still another incentive was given the inmates to work in the industries: a pay scale. Jobs were graded into four groups. Men on grade one earned twelve cents per hour; grade two, ten cents; grade three, seven and one-half cents; and grade four paid five cents. It was not much, but it made the men feel they were being rewarded for their labor.

One of the prime complaints at Alcatraz, however, was that the inmates were not afforded the privilege of a commissary. In other prisons, money had more significance because an inmate could buy some of the minor luxuries such as a candy bar, soap, shaving cream, cookies, and ready-made cigarettes. At Alcatraz, the earned money could only be spent to buy a limited number of subscriptions to magazines (from an approved list), a musical instrument, dominoes or bridge dominoes, *Culbertson's Bridge for Beginners*, or Auto Bridge. The pay scale was later upgraded to seventeen and one-half cents for maximum and six cents for minimum.

The minor amount of money it was possible to earn, at a later date, played an important part in the change in my life.

Job Change

After working as a yardbird for several months, I felt well enough to want to get another job. I had been playing handball at every opportunity, felt great, and felt certain administration would give me a change with a position in the industries. I decided to ask for an assignment in the brush shop. I put in a job change application and in a few days was given the assignment. I was soon to discover, however, that I had made a horrible choice. To a highly-strung, young and energetic individual such as myself, it was pure undiluted boredom and monotony.

To make a hair brush, the type used to sweep long corridors, an inmate was supplied with a board with a hundred or more tapered holes drilled in it, a crochet hook, a spool of very fine copper wire, a vise, and two pounds of horse hair. You clamped the board in a vise, pushed the hook through the hole, pulled the wire through the hole so it was double, opened the loop in the wire, then pulled the wire taut until the hair doubled over and seated itself in the tapered hole, without breaking the fine copper wire. This procedure was repeated over and over again, until all the holes were filled and the wire was tied off so all the hair could not fall out of the brush. A cap was screwed over the face of the wire, the brush was trimmed so that all the hair was even, and the brush was complete. Picture doing that over and over again for seven hours a day, five days a week.

This job proved to be the most frustrating and boring, not to mention aggravating, work I have ever done—before, during, or after my release from prison. After about six months, I could no longer stand it. I honestly thought I was going to go insane. I decided to once again ask for a new job assignment. I was certain it would be denied, but decided to try anyway. What did I have to lose at that point? Certainly not my sanity, because I was already slowly but surely losing that in the brush shop. I decided to put in for a work change to the kitchen. It offered more free time to do things I thought I would enjoy doing until my still-sought-after opportunity for escape would be found. I was convinced there was very little chance in the industrial area.

I had become interested in learning to play the guitar to pass the time, and working in the kitchen offered more time to pursue music without giving up searching for a way out. I thought it might be better also, as it would give me more areas to check out. The kitchen offered other benefits as well. Its small crew was housed together in a special section on Broadway, and not only worked together, but also played together, as the majority were interested in music, bridge, or handball.

Best of all, the kitchen area provided time away from the stress, strain, and tension that was always present on the mainline. Once assigned, I soon found it even offered companionship and camaraderie that existed in no other place on Alcatraz. Among other benefits, when food was appropriated or stolen, it was always shared. Sharing was expected of everyone.

For a short time I tried to learn to play the guitar but, due to an old fight injury, I found my fingers were too stiff, and thus I took up the saxophone, which did not require the finger dexterity of the guitar. Eventually the kitchen crew formed a small orchestra, in which I participated.

All this helped pass the time, but inside I felt something was lacking, and could not help but feel that somehow life was passing me by. Although music helped fill that void in my life, it did nothing to alleviate the loneliness or desire for freedom that was constantly present, especially during those long, cold nights when I could not sleep.

I had been continually searching for anything that would give me a small chance to again be in the free world. I could never resign myself to serving thirty years in prison. I was young, full of life and energy, and did not want to spend my life in prison. I knew my chances were slight to nonexistent, but I felt inside that somehow, some way, I had to escape. I did not want to commit suicide with some stupid escape attempt as others had done, but was willing to take my chances, whatever they might be, with the feared water surrounding the island. I knew my young age, good health, and athletic ability would all be to my advantage. I was doubly motivated by the conviction that, even after I had done my long sentence at Alcatraz, I would be returned to another state prison for still more years of imprisonment.

In my never-ending search to find a way out, whether mentally or physically, I noticed that of all departments in the kitchen, the bakery seemed to be the least observed, had more free time, and (because it had only three workers) was not constantly searched for things such as home brew. Thus I became a great contributor to the making of this "escape-for-a-few-magic-hours" brew.

In one instance, I had decided to experiment with a substitute alcoholic beverage called kumis, a Russian drink made from mare's milk. I obtained a quart I.V. bottle from the hospital, some milk, sugar, and yeast and followed the directions for making the drink. It required the ingredients to be mixed together, placed in a special, very heavily walled flask, sealed tightly, then buried several feet deep in the ground for ten days. I mixed the ingredients, filled the bottle, then sealed and wired it closed. My hiding place was the mixing compartment of a small ice cream mixer in a special room off the kitchen. This room was reserved for supplies and the barred doors were only unlocked when the cooks were being issued their supplies for the day. I waited my chance, then slipped it into its hiding place (a difficult fit, as the bottle and the mixing cylinder were almost exactly the same size).

I had decided I would wait the ten days, even though it might be discovered if ice cream were put on the officers' menu during that time. The mainline was not scheduled for ice cream for another month, so I felt it was relatively safe. Each morning I would slip in with the cooks and check to see if it had been discovered. All went well until the third night.

Lights were out in the cellhouse and all was quiet, when suddenly there was a large resounding crash in the kitchen. Shortly thereafter, we saw the goon squad hurry down Broadway and into the kitchen. Upon hearing someone comment about an explosion, I became aware of what I had done. The bottle had exploded from the constant, increasing pressure created by the fermentation of the sugar, milk, and yeast.

Shortly after the goon squad had entered the area, Warden Johnston also arrived. He too disappeared into the kitchen. It was not until we were released for work the next morning that we realized the officials of the prison were sincerely convinced that someone had created a bomb. When I had the opportunity to look into the supply room, I understood their consternation. The stainless-steel door to the mixer had been blown almost completely off the ice cream maker. The floor was littered with thousands of slivers and fragments of glass. Glass had even been driven into the inside of the mixing chamber. There was no smell, as normally associated with home brew, possibly because the mixture contained no malt and because the window adjoining the machine was open. Bits and pieces of wire and tape in the debris added to their suspicion that a bomb had exploded.

The "heat was on." The entire kitchen crew was under suspicion and an additional guard was assigned to the kitchen area. Individually, every worker in the kitchen was called out and questioned about the incident, including two known snitches. No one knew anything and in a month the incident was given less significance but not forgotten by the guards. I'm sure, until his death, the warden was convinced it was a bomb. It was also my last attempt to make any exotic or unusual happy juice.

A vacancy finally came open in the bakery and, because I had previous experience (San Quentin), I was given the assignment. It was not a sought-after position because it meant working with Alvin Karpis (AZ-325), who at times tried to impress others with his reputation as Public Enemy No. 1. His reputation outside did not as a rule impress those inside, and he in time became known as "Creepy Karpis" for his sometimes strange behavior in trying to impress his peers. He was not hard to work with, but at times he took himself and his reputation too seriously. Karpis was not a man given to physical activities and the only altercation I had with him during the two years we worked together came as a result of making happy juice.

It began when we had made some beer and, in order to have a daily supply, had hidden it in stale loaves of bread. (We had cut the bottoms off, hollowed out the centers, and then hid small I.V. bottles inside. When the bottoms were pushed back into place, the beer could not be detected.) We kept this supply in a special section of our bread rack where it was safe because no one had any use for stale bread and it could not be detected by smell (the entire bakery smelled of malt and yeast). We had a constant supply of beer, anytime we wanted it. To prevent detection, it was always kept within the bakery and, as a result, we got by with it for several months.

Unfortunately, due to an inadvertent mistake by Karpis or me, our personal brewery eventually came to an abrupt end. We had not brought out enough bread one evening and Officer Long (the kitchen guard), not seeing us close by, had gone into the bakery and pulled a couple of loaves of bread off the rack, only to have their bottoms fall off and our beer smash to the concrete floor. He then found some fresh bread, took it out to be sliced, and returned to the bakery, where he examined each loaf on the rack. Every time he found a bottle, he broke it on the floor, then threw the stale bread into the mess. After breaking our entire supply and creating a tremendous mess, he simply turned and walked away. When I returned to the bakery and found the mess, at first I thought Karpis had done it, but common sense told me that was unreasonable.

I immediately got a garbage can, and had just started cleaning up when Karpis returned. His first reaction was the same as mine, but he also realized this was a senseless thought. He was helping clean up the mess when the door of the bakery opened and in walked a stoolie. He announced he had a message from Officer Long. We were to clean up the mess and stop making beer, or we were going to the hole.

It was a break for us in the bakery, as the offense warranted nineteen days in the hole. The second part of the message was far more devastating: he informed us that if brew was made and found outside the bakery, where blame could not be placed on us, he would urinate in the container then put it back exactly where he had found it.

Needless to say, during the next few months, while Officer Long was assigned to the kitchen, no beer was made. Even after his assignment elsewhere, inmates set elaborate traps in order to make certain that Long had not passed on his threat to Officer Burdette, who replaced him.

I now entered a period of time when nothing seemed to interest me except the thought of escape. I had lost all interest in music and the things that had diverted my attention in the past. I again began to look for a way out, with an increased and intense obsession.

12 Attempted Escape

The kitchen had a large open area, and inmates (who were not at work) were permitted to walk its length until lockup, or until time to return to work. One day, while walking this area, I noticed two large steel plates embedded in the concrete floor. They were hinged and locked shut with a large steel bar and a heavy-duty institutional padlock. I had seen these plates hundreds of times and yet never thought of them in regard to escape. They were out in the open area, had been there for years, and had not attracted any attention from any old-timer or escape-minded convict. I wondered why, and decided to check them out.

I soon learned that they entered a three-by-three-foot tunnel that housed all the steam pipes for heating and much of the institution's cooking. I checked with a friend, who worked in the powerhouse located elsewhere on the island, and he confirmed that there was a direct connection between the tunnel in the kitchen and the power plant—but years before the institution had sealed it off by pouring a five-foot-thick concrete block at the powerhouse end. It was impossible to penetrate and gain passage to the powerhouse. At the other end, the tunnel terminated in the shower room and a large steam tank. I was also informed that the heat was so intense (because of radiation from the pipes) that it was impossible to tolerate and therefore an impossible way out. Although it did seem impossible, I was not ready to give up so soon. After all, there was nothing else in sight, so why not go as far as I could to determine if it had any other possibilities?

I spoke to my partner Jack and he said he was willing if I was. I decided to work out a plan where I could check out each step at a time, without getting so involved that I could not retreat and walk away.

The first step was to get into the tunnel to see if it was at all feasible. One of the inmates in the kitchen was an expert with locks, and was willing to pick the lock so we could check out the tunnel. It took Charlie about two minutes and we had free access into the narrow passageway. We slipped the lock back in place and decided to wait until the mainline was eating before we investigated any further.

When the mainline ate any meal, the kitchen guard and the steward stationed themselves at the bars that separated the kitchen from the dining room. This area was always locked so the inmates from the mainline could never have access to the kitchen area. When the mainline came in to eat dinner, we posted a lookout at the top of the stairs where he could watch the guard and steward, yet was in a position to give us a signal if anyone was to start down the stairs to the basement.

Jack, two other inmates, and I went to the basement and lifted the heavy iron plate. The tunnel was as described: narrow, shallow, and hot. Looking into the hole we could see a huge asbestos-covered pipe on the far side and bottom of the tunnel. On the bottom were two more pipes smaller in size. One was disconnected and the other was still in use. A large cut-off valve and another pipe were on our side. We could see the entire area was made of brick. Looking to the left we could only see for about three feet because it was so dark. Our hopes rose, as we felt the bricks would be easier to penetrate than concrete. We were also aware of the heat that arose from the hole, but there was no way we could determine if we could tolerate it without getting inside. We decided, as time was short, that we would close and lock the opening until the next day, when we could explore further.

We decided that if it proved to be a feasible option, we would work only during the evening meal, as there was little or no traffic to the basement. The evening meal always took longer and the kitchen guard and steward's attention were concentrated on the dining area, for if there was trouble, it usually occurred at this meal, when the men were tired and irritable after a long day's work.

The next day we again had Charlie pick the lock shortly before the mainline was to enter the dining room. When we were sure that Officer Long and Steward Bristow were at the barred doors, we again went to the basement and opened the trap door to the tunnel. This time I crawled down inside. The iron plate was closed and I moved a few feet to my left, away from the trap door. This was to be the crucial test as to how well and/or how long a person could stay enclosed in that hot, stifling environment without either passing out or panicking. As I crawled away from the door, I must admit, my heart was pounding not only from heat and anxiety, but also from a sincere case of claustrophobia. I was also in fear that I would push too hard on an old and ready-to-break pipe, causing it to rupture, at which time I would be scalded to death without the slightest chance of escape.

After moving possibly ten feet down the tunnel, I realized I had made several mistakes. First, I had crawled into the tunnel wearing only a T-shirt to protect my upper body, thinking the less clothing I wore, the better, because of the heat. The mistake became evident, however, the first time I touched the large pipe where the asbestos covering had fallen off. I received a burn that became a blister before I could move my arm. I was also sweating so profusely that the water dripped from my body and struck the hot pipe with a sizzling sound that did nothing to eliminate my anxieties.

My second mistake was in not checking before I moved away from the door, to determine if it was possible to turn around in this small, confining area. As I found out later, after several severe burns on my arms, this was indeed an impossibility. To get back to the door where Jack and the others were anxiously waiting, I had to crawl backwards.

Many thoughts passed through my mind as I waited. Most prevalent, the thought of being scalded to death, or passing out and dying of heat prostration. I kept telling myself not to panic or give up, because this was an important test, which would determine whether we should attempt this escape route. If I gave up too soon, it would discourage everyone and possibly cause us to lose an opportunity for freedom. I calmed down, stayed in one place, and made movements as though I was working. I knew Jack and the others were watching my time in the tunnel and felt reassured that, should I pass out, Jack would surely come to my rescue.

I stayed as long as I could and, when I began to feel slightly faint, started my slow, cautious, backward retreat to the door. When I reached a point where I could see light filtering in around the door, I felt a great sense of elation. I honestly thought we had a chance and this was to be our way out of the prison. As I got directly under the door, the intensity of the heat even seemed to dissipate to a degree, possibly because of the cool, fresh air from the basement.

When I believed I had reached the total limit of my endurance, I gently tapped the trap door. It was opened immediately and six hands reached in to pull me from the tunnel. When the cool air of the basement hit me, it was as though a giant cooling fan had been turned on. It felt like heaven, except that it seemed more difficult to breathe than in the tunnel. For a few minutes I experienced severe pains in my chest on each inhalation. This soon passed. I was soaked with perspiration, as though I had stepped into a shower with my clothing on. My face and body were red and flushed, and looked as if I had a tremendous sunburn.

Jack, having anticipated that I would look like this, had turned on the shower to lukewarm and laid out a change of clothing for me. With the help of the others, he took me to the shower, stripped my clothing off, and pushed me in. After a couple of minutes my normal color had returned and I was able to come out of the shower.

Time was running out, as Bart and George had to report to clean up the dining room, while Jack had to be at his station on the dishwashing machine. I had no reason to hurry, as my day's work had been completed before going to the basement. My only need was to appear normal and not show the elation I was feeling at this time.

I was convinced that if we were able to secure some tools and a flashlight, we had found a way out that had been overlooked or dismissed for years. I realized my feeling of confidence was based only on the fact that I had stayed fifteen minutes in the heat, but felt that if we were lucky, and willing to take the chance, we could cut our way through the bricks on the side, then crawl into the old discarded Spanish citadel that was the foundation for the newer military prison. If we could get under the building, then we could find our way through to the outside. Much of my daydreaming was based on speculation, which proved to be wrong, but I was certain the old fortified barracks existed beneath the newer prison. If this was the case, we had a good chance to make the water, away from the gun towers. John, George, Bart, and I held a meeting to determine the best way to use our newly acquired knowledge. We decided tools were our top priority, but they would be difficult, if not impossible, to obtain without the help of other inmates. It was apparent we needed a large, heavy hammer, a cold chisel, and a flashlight. The flashlight and extra batteries could be and were secured from the hospital, but the tools were a different matter. They would have to come from the industrial area.

Getting the tools up the hill from the industrial area posed a significant but not insurmountable barrier. I knew a system was in existence because a way had been found to bypass the snitch boxes. It was a very secretive operation and very few people knew exactly how it worked. I knew it had to do with and utilized the garbage cans. I did know an inmate on the mainline named Ray, who was "in the know" of the entire set-up, and, if he was willing, the whole chain could be put into operation to help us.

I arranged to talk to Ray the following weekend. He was somewhat skeptical, as he had been aware of the tunnel for years but also of the problem that must be encountered to put it to any practical use. Hearing that I had spent fifteen minutes alone in the enclosed area, and still felt it was possible, seemed to convince him to some degree. Ray was not willing to give me an answer just then. After all, he would be asking other inmates to jeopardize their good time and possibility of transfer if we were to goof up and involve others. He told me that he would contact others who would have to help and then get back to me with an answer. I was asked to make certain that we had a safe place to hide the tools, if we were given help, a place where they would have to stay a month or more to cool off. I agreed.

The whole process was now in the hands of others. All we could do was hope. A whole week passed before I received word Ray wanted to see me on the yard. I was concerned, because for the entire week I had walked around with an overwhelming sense of elation. The meeting, in some ways, was frightening, as I had gotten my hopes so high. All my dreams, at least at this time, could be smashed if no one was willing to help. The news was good, however, as we would get help, provided we hid the tools well and did not use them for six weeks. This was to provide protection for others involved and to give them a way and time to work out a means to replace or account for the loss of tools without concentrating or creating heat on a single inmate or shop.

We decided our safest hiding area for the tools would be the tunnel. Each time Charlie had to pick the lock, however, he faced the possibility of getting caught and losing his good time even though he had no plans to join our escape attempt. What was needed was a quick way to open the tunnel lock without the lock being picked.

We located a lock on an unused cabinet that was a

duplicate of the tunnel lock. Charlie picked this lock, as well as the lock on the tunnel. We switched the locks, hoping the unlocked cabinet would not be discovered, then sent the legitimate lock for the tunnel out to be modified. Under Ray's direction, it was wrapped and put in a full garbage can, then sent on its way. Somewhere in its route the lock was retrieved and sent to a shop, where it was modified by removing all but one tumbler; thus the lock would be opened by the officer's key, but also by us just by depressing the single remaining tumbler. The lock was reassembled and the next day was returned to the kitchen in a marked garbage can with a false bottom. The lock on the tunnel was picked and returned to the proper place without having been missed. The modified lock was snapped onto the tunnel opening.

We were in business and ready to hide the tools when they arrived. Our only concern now was the possibility of receiving the tools without too much concern on the administration's part. It was just a matter of waiting until the tools arrived. After two weeks I received word from Ray that the tools would arrive the following morning. We were told to watch out for a particular can, unload it, and return the can to its regular service.

The next day the tools arrived as planned, and were hidden as we had agreed. This time, it was much easier for me to enter and crawl down the passageway, as I had a light and seemed to have lost most of my fear and anxieties about being scalded to death. I even seemed to have less problem breathing. As I hid the tools, I believed this was surely the beginning of realizing my dream—freedom.

We had six weeks to wait to determine if the tools would be missed and, if they were, how severe the repercussions would be. We never knew who secured the tools, but each of us was constantly on the alert to see if anyone in the industries was removed from his job. Everything was quiet and never a word was heard about the missing tools. Ray never at any time gave us the smallest hint as to who was responsible for the help we had received. When three weeks had passed, we decided to watch, clock, and record in our minds all the actions of Officer Long, Steward Bristow, and the stoolie working in the officers' dining room.

It was easy to determine that neither the guard nor the steward would venture into the basement during this time frame. The stoolie in the officers' mess was always busy during this period, so we usually had thirty to forty minutes to do all the things needed. We estimated that each night we could have a maximum of twenty minutes from the time we entered the tunnel until we had to be out. This was fine because that allowed about fifteen minutes to work and five minutes to make the trip to and from the work area. We decided to work directly under the sallyport so there was no possibility of our activities being observed by opening the metal cover and shining a light down the tunnel. It did mean we had to crawl approximately twenty-five feet upon entering and leaving, but twenty minutes in that heat was all we could handle anyway.

Our plan was to attempt to knock the mortar out from around a brick and once we had one removed, start working on another. As each brick was removed, that would be less support for the others, as they tend to loosen, making their removal easier. It was also decided that Bart and I would make the first attempt. I was chosen because I was the youngest and Bart because he was the strongest. After starting to work, we planned to rotate so everyone took a turn in the heat.

After waiting an additional three weeks, I arranged to meet Ray, to make certain it was okay to start. He felt everything was normal and we were on our own.

Our first attempt in the tunnel was a learning experience. I backed down the tunnel, as Bart crawled forward. The further we advanced in the tunnel, the hotter it became. I could see that Bart was very nervous and seemed to be having considerable trouble breathing. It was then I realized I had made another mistake, in that if he fainted, I was not sure I could get past him to go to the door for help. I suggested to Bart that on this trip, we pick the area we were going to work in, then work our way back to the door. We located a place we thought was under the sallyport, then started back.

It was a slow trip, as Bart was really pooped out and his anxiety was growing by the minute. When we reached the door, Bart rapped and the door was unlocked and opened. Bart crawled out and, once in the air of the basement, was soon himself. He, like me, was soaked with sweat, but he did not have the red flush that always appeared on me. He walked around a couple of minutes and seemed to recover completely. I had to shower in cold water to get my color back to normal. Although I could recall how I felt the first time in the tunnel, I was still somewhat disappointed in Bart's being so anxious and nervous. I hoped that the next time he would be calmer.

The next night, George elected to try his luck. It was a lost cause. Bart had not even gotten the lid closed when George seemed to lose his senses. He scrambled and pushed over the top of me and was out before the lid was shut. He claimed the heat was too intense and he could not be confined in such a small place. We assured him it was all right and he could do his share outside the tunnel. We again quit for the night.

The next trip into the tunnel was to be Jack's turn. It too turned into an exercise in futility. Jack and I slipped into the passageway and at first everything seemed fine. As we started crawling to the area where we were to work, Jack, who had remained calm and showed no special signs of anxiety, suddenly asked me to stop. When I inquired why, he said the heat was too severe and he was certain that there was no possible way he could continue without passing out. He complained of severe chest pain and said he felt as though he would die if we didn't get out in short order. I realized that his was not a case of nerves but a real case of intolerance to the heat.

We slowly worked our way back to the door and, during

the short wait to have the door opened, Jack collapsed. He was not completely unconscious, but had reached a stage of exhaustion where he was incapable of doing much to help himself. George and Bart pulled him out, and he revived to a small degree. His color, unlike my own, was rather pale and he looked to me to be in poor condition. After a few minutes he seemed to regain some of his strength, but continued to complain about chest and head pain. In an hour he seemed to regain much of his normal function except that his movements were far more lethargic than usual.

At this point, it seemed the old-timers were correct. The heat was proving to be our downfall and there was nothing we could do to eliminate the problem. We were greatly depressed with the turn of events, but were not as yet ready or willing to give up.

I was still determined and decided, if necessary, I would attempt to do the job myself. The next night I again descended into the tunnel, crawled to the work area, and tried to work. It was impossible, as I could not hold the light, chisel, and still use the hammer. I tried shifting my body, turning, and getting into various positions, to no avail. All this movement did was exhaust me more rapidly. I crawled back to the door to be released. To my amazement, my co-conspirators were greatly concerned because I had been confined for over twenty minutes. I explained to them that it had to be a team effort, as it was an impossibility for a single individual.

There was a mutual feeling that we were beaten and in the process had jeopardized those who had helped us. It was a feeling that left each of us severely despondent. We decided to stay away from the tunnel for a few days while we tried to determine if there was any possible or feasible way to ventilate it with cool air from the basement. We could not come up with a solution of any kind, however.

Another option we investigated was the possibility of moving our work site closer to the trap door. This too was ruled out because after moving only three to five feet into the tunnel, the difference in heat was not perceptible. We considered moving closer to the door and working with the door open. This would prove exceptionally risky, though, as it would increase our chances of being caught in the act, or of having our work discovered when there was a routine inspection of the valves at the tunnel entrance. After many ideas and much deep concentration, it was determined we had to do it as originally planned, or give it up.

Bart and I decided that as a team we would again make another try and if we failed to make twenty minutes, we would quit. We decided to increase our salt intake, in the hope that retaining body fluids would increase our endurance. For two days, each of us radically increased our salt in a rather uninformed manner. We did not know what we were doing, but were desperately attempting to salvage a possibility that we had high hopes for.

With great apprehension, the night that was possibly to be our last attempt was selected. Bart seemed nervous, but more determined than on our previous attempt. I, on the other hand, was more relaxed and at ease than on previous trips. I believed Bart's previous failure was not from heat alone, but a combination of heat, fear, and anxiety. I now hoped that the realization that I had been in the tunnel on six occasions would give Bart more confidence that he could also stand it if he set his mind to it. I felt if I could just keep Bart from worrying, he would be able to tolerate the task.

Our plan was to take our time, move slowly, and give this our best effort. Bart was far calmer as we entered the tunnel, and less anxious. With no difficulty whatsoever we reached our designated work area. We were both doing just fine. We had to spend considerable time finding the best way to work, as we were severely hampered by the large hot pipe that took up much of the tunnel. We had to take extreme care using our hammer, as this pipe was cast iron and we were uncertain as to how hard a blow it could withstand without breaking. We knew that if we broke it we were dead, so we proceeded with extreme caution. After we had gotten into a reasonable, workable position, we began trying to chip out the mortar from between two bricks.

Immediately, we found we were in trouble, as the chisel would allow us to insert it only a short distance, and we could deliver only short blows with the hammer. The mortar was like stone, possibly because of the heat and the years it had been allowed to remain undisturbed under constant pressure. Just as we both began to feel very fatigued and decided it was time to leave, we heard a bang on the steel entrance plate, indicating our time was up.

Even considering the newfound obstacle, we still felt good about our prospects, but also realized that it was going to be a far more difficult and time-consuming task than we had anticipated. We were determined to give it our best shot regardless of how long it took or how hard it became. We believed we had beaten our major obstacles: fear and the heat.

Each night for the next three weeks, we worked on our project. We made an exception on Saturdays and Sundays because we found the substitute guard for Officer Long too unpredictable. We had, by increasing our salt intake, overcome our fears and anxieties about the heat and managed to work our fully allotted time each night. After considerable hard work, we were able to crack the surface and broke out actual small fragments of brick, rather than just dust. Our confidence and expectations (that we had found the way out) were rapidly increasing. Unfortunately, however, this was not the way it was to be.

Several times during the course of our work, other inmates became aware of what was occurring, since the only toilet facilities were in the basement and we were seen entering and leaving the tunnel. It was not what we had wanted, but it was inevitable. We were not overly concerned about this, as we felt our fellow inmates were friends and would not personally do anything to hurt our chances. Unfortunately, inmates often talk to other friends and tell things better kept silent. It is possible that someone from other than the kitchen, or associated with us, decided to give us up to increase his chances for a transfer. We were not actually caught, but our names were given to the authorities by someone.

13 Busted

The fatal blow to our dream came at midweek. I had gone to the yard in the afternoon to play handball, while Bart and George were playing bridge. Jack had remained in the kitchen. As I returned to the cellhouse, I was not permitted to return to the kitchen area and was instead escorted to my cell and placed in deadlock. As I passed Jack's cell, I saw it was empty. This relieved my mind because I felt if it was about the tunnel, Jack would have already been in deadlock. This was not long in coming, however, and then the full disciplinary board was convened. Suddenly my cell was racked open and I was ordered to proceed to the desk, where the board was assembled.

We saw the associate warden, captain, lieutenant, and Officer Long, and realized we were in serious trouble. For some reason, George and Bart were not there.

I was informed this was to be a disciplinary court for a serious breach of institutional rules and policies and that I was charged with attempted escape. The associate warden then informed me that I had been digging my way out of the tunnel and had been in possession of tools and a flashlight. I was also informed that I had been aided in this attempt by Jack.

Neither Jack nor I were questioned as to how we came into possession of the tools, who modified the lock, or anything that could or would involve others. This was very strange. If these items were in their possession, it would not have been too difficult to trace them to the area from which they had been taken. To this day, I do not believe they had actually retrieved the tools, but once the officials heard our attempt was in progress, led us to believe they had them. At any rate, we were removed from any possible further participation. Jack and I were each sentenced to nineteen days in the black hole, to be followed by indefinite segregation in D Block.

George and Bart were never questioned or removed from the kitchen. Also, oddly enough, George was soon placed on a transfer to Leavenworth. Whether this was coincidental or not, we would never know. Jack and I were lucky in one respect, in that neither of us forfeited any of our possible 5,400 days of good time. On the other hand, this ended our dream of escape and began a nightmare that almost cost me my life and did cause me to lose seven and a half years of my good time.

The Hole

A day in the hole was like an eternity. The day would start at 6:30 a.m. when the lights were turned on and a nerve-jangling bell was rung. This was soon followed by a guard unlocking the solid outer soundproof door and shouting for you to stand up. After you were accounted for, the guard would leave, closing the outer door again. The lights remained on and you were to prepare for breakfast. A short time later, your door would again open and a tray was passed through the narrow slot in the inside barred door. This was your morning meal.

Although one received the same food as the mainline, it was all dumped together in an unappetizing lump. Bread was buried in the oatmeal, prunes dumped on top, and no milk or sugar was allotted. A cup of warm coffee completed the meal. This was typical of how food was served in the hole. True, nutritional value was adequate, but the unappetizing manner in which it was served soon made one lose his desire to eat.

After approximately twenty minutes your tray was collected. If you could not stomach the meal, you had best dump it down the toilet, in order to prevent missing what might be a better noon meal. Shortly after your tray was collected, your door would open again and you would be instructed to roll up your blanket, pillow, and mattress and set them in the three-foot space separating the inner and outer doors. The guard would step out, relock the outer door, and open a metal peep slot and watch until you complied. After you were back inside the inner door, it was again relocked and the lights were turned off, leaving you in total darkness for the remainder of the day, except for meals.

There was nothing in the cell except a cold metal bed frame, a toilet, a sink, and you. There was total silence. The outer door was soundproof. It was also very cold, because of the limited clothing you were allowed. Inmates were given a pair of shorts, socks, and coveralls. These were inadequate to keep one warm, because the steel walls and floor of the cell retained the cold.

Worse than being cold, though, was the total feeling of isolation from the world. Being unable to see or hear is an awful experience for someone who has no physical impairment. Since total silence and darkness were to be my constant companions for twenty-four hours of each day of solitary confinement, it was imperative to find a way to keep my mind occupied, somehow. I invented a game simply to retain my sanity. I would tear a button from my coveralls, then fling it into the air, turn around in circles several times, and, with my eyes closed, get on the floor on my hands and knees and search for the button. When it was found, I would repeat the entire routine, over and over until I was exhausted, or my knees were so sore I could not continue.

When I could no longer hunt the button, I would pace back and forth between the toilet and the door. I would continue these routines until evening, since it was too cold to just sit and pacing helped pass the time. If not for the interruption of meals, it would have been easy to confuse night and day.

After the evening meal, our bedding was returned and I would get into bed and hope to fall asleep quickly. Nineteen consecutive days was the maximum time an inmate could be confined in solitary. If he behaved, he was not usually returned. If he still persisted in creating a problem, however, he was taken out, fed a full meal, allowed to brush his teeth, and then returned to solitary for another nineteen days.

Usually, nineteen days were sufficient.

If the inmate was released from solitary, he was usually confined to D Block for a period of time, depending on the circumstances leading up to his disciplinary action. When his offense had been minor, he was often released back to his old job, cell, and the general population.

I served my nineteen days in the hole and was moved into regular segregation. Before being assigned a cell, I was given a chance to shower, received a change of clothing, and was allowed to brush my teeth. Segregation was very boring and the days seemed endless. Even worse, there was far too much time to think. Because of the lack of activity, it was so easy to fall into a state of depression, brought about by our natural instinct to think back to better times of the past. It was also easy to think about how things could have been.

Once lost in this reverie, it was depressing to be brought back to our intolerable reality by the sound of a bell or the crash of a barred steel cell door. Nothing could blot out the knowledge of what and where you were, or the certainty that this was all that life held for you in the future. Man was never intended to live as a caged animal; I often speculated as to whether life was worth living under these conditions.

Being young, I had never understood or sympathized

with those who went insane or committed suicide, especially because of a situation they themselves had created. I had always lived by the philosophy that if one played the game, he must be willing to pay the price. Segregation and isolation were beginning to make me realize, however, that while these high-sounding macho ideals were easy to maintain when there was hope, it was far more difficult to cope with the undesirable and traumatic world of reality once hope was gone. This was what drove men to murder, insanity, and self-destruction.

This was brought home to me with great clarity when an inmate of D Block, shortly after my release from the hole, calmly and deliberately found a way to slash the major arteries in his wrists and elbows. He lay down on his bed, covered himself with a blanket, and silently bled to death. He had found his escape through a means that was often present in the minds of most hopelessly incarcerated inmates.

It is a release that is much easier to contemplate than to bring to actuality. Our natural instincts are to survive, and only after reaching the very bitter depths of despair can we bring it to this final conclusion. At Alcatraz, suicide was not an infrequent state of mind, and was often prevented only by tight security, the lack of privacy, and the lack of a means to accomplish it. One form of suicide was trying to escape, such as the attempts on May 23, 1938 and May 2, 1946.

I managed to make the best of D Block for the first six weeks after release from the hole. I had partially adjusted to the routine of boredom and depression. I would walk, read, and often sleep during the day to pass the time, but regardless of what I did, I could not relieve the terrible torment that seemed to rage within me. I would often awaken and feel that I just had to vent the anger or frustration that seemed to be destroying my sanity. I was very angry because I felt my opportunity for escape had been destroyed by someone who had used my chance at freedom to make his own life easier with a transfer, or to curry favor with administration. I was also angry at the prison administration because they had not caught me red-handed, yet locked me up on the word of another inmate. These were not facts I could prove, but it was something sincerely and wholeheartedly believed. I wanted somehow to relieve this rage by screaming, crying, and destroying something. Despite my often-expressed belief that "they couldn't break me," I felt I was slowly going insane.

An opportunity to relieve my inner tensions and rage was not long in coming. It was early March 1946. The weather was cold and gloomy and an air of depression and tension seemed to permeate the entire block. The inmates were irritable and restless. All that was needed was a spark to ignite a violent and very volatile confrontation. The spark was furnished by Bob Stroud (the infamous Birdman of Alcatraz).

14 Rebellion in D Block

The confrontation began about 8 p.m., when Bob Stroud complained that he was ill. The officer in charge of D Block called the hospital and requested that the prison doctor come to the block to examine him. He was informed the doctor was off the island, but that an MTA would examine Stroud when it was convenient. This seemed to pacify Stroud, but after an hour had passed and no medical personnel had appeared, he again commenced to complain. Another call to the hospital resulted in an angry response and an appearance by an MTA. Stroud was given a brief, perfunctory examination, then declared to be well.

After the passage of possibly another hour, Stroud again started complaining about severe abdominal pain and demanded to see the doctor who, by this time, had returned to the island. The doctor refused to come and again an angry MTA appeared. This time he examined Stroud more thoroughly, but again declared there were no acute or abnormal findings. The MTA then returned to his station in the hospital. All this commotion had aroused the anger of the tense and restless inmates of the unit. They were determined to take up Stroud's cause and force the doctor to come to the unit to give Stroud an examination.

This was the beginning of a night-long rebellion that seemed to involve all the inmates in the unit. We started by raking our tin drinking cups across the steel bars and shouting. After two hours of this racket, we received a response from administration. The associate warden and the goon squad paid us a visit. We were instructed to stop quieten down or we would individually receive a visit from the squad in our cells. This was greeted with jeers and catcalls from the now completely defiant inmates.

In response to this threat, the inmates issued administration an ultimatum of their own. It was to get the doctor into the block to examine and treat Stroud, or we would wreck our cells. At this point the squad left the block, knowing they could not "work over" every individual, and possibly hoping that their leaving would defuse the incident, and we would not carry out our threat. They also left with the knowledge they were not going to submit to our ultimatum. This was a miscalculation. The destruction began after another hour of waiting. Someone on the upper tier broke his toilet and washbasin—and then utter chaos followed.

I, like the rest, began a systematic destruction of my cell. I drained the water from the toilet, stuffed it with anything flammable, then set it afire. After waiting until the porcelain was hot, I pushed the flush button and the toilet was reduced to several large fragments. I used a fragment to smash the sink into pieces small enough to throw through the bars and break the outside windows.

Next, the mattress was destroyed by breaking the handle off the metal cup and using the jagged edge to rip open the cover so the stuffing could be pulled out and thrown to the flats below. Blankets and pillows were given the same treatment.

All around me, the same insane devastation was occurring. When our cells had been completely destroyed, we began throwing lighted toilet paper into the mass of cotton stuffing from mattresses. Several fires were started and the ensuing smoke began choking us. Each of us then made a concentrated effort to break out more windows to vent and dissipate the smoke. This had its advantages and disadvantages. With the windows out, we could breathe, but were far colder because of the cold wind blowing. The water flowing from the broken plumbing was a further cause for misery.

I believe the cold had a sobering effect on the block. Toward morning, the commotion and rebellion had ceased and all we could do was feel miserably cold and wonder about the consequences of our actions. We were aware there were going to be severe and continued repercussions. Speaking for myself, I didn't care. I felt relieved of much of the anger and hostility that had been consuming me. I felt free, elated, and more at peace with myself and others than I had for weeks.

Late the next morning, a crew was dispatched to the unit to clean up the horrible and still-smoldering mass of destruction our rage had created. I honestly don't believe there was a repentant participant in the entire group. After the debris had been cleared—but before we were fed—a disciplinary court was held. The dark holes were emptied to accommodate the first ones called. Whitey Franklin was among them. One by one, we were taken from our cells to face the judgment that would be meted out, not by an associate warden, but by Warden Johnston himself.

When I was to appear before the disciplinary board, I had to pass by Bob Stroud's cell. To my amazement and anger, his cell was undisturbed and in perfect order. I believe that Bob, the man the unit had united to help, had created a ruse. He had not been ill, but wanted to instigate a disturbance that would harass and annoy the officials. He was successful, using the sympathy of his fellow inmates with little or no regard for the consequences we would face for our actions. He was not alone. Twelve others who had indicated that they were participating had done nothing destructive or against prison rules. We had been used.

Warden Johnston's justice was swift and direct. Each inmate involved lost one-half of his good time, was sentenced to nineteen days in isolation and increased detention in D Block, and was ineligible for transfer to another institution until the damages were paid for and all forfeited good time had been restored. After the block isolation cells had been filled, the rest of us were returned to our destroyed cells, where we were to serve the same punishment.

It was a miserable nineteen days, as the broken windows made the heat ineffective against the cold weather and administration was in no hurry to alleviate the condition. Our toilet facilities were also allowed to wait for repair. We were issued a bucket, which we were permitted to empty once each day. It was the officials' way of saying to us, "Live with the situation you created."

After nineteen days, the windows and plumbing were repaired and D Block settled back into its lonely routine, but with less closeness and unity than before the insurrection. It was a learning experience for me, as it exposed a side of my fellow man that I had never experienced before. In a short time, I had been used twice. First by whoever gave me up for my escape attempt, and now by Bob Stroud.

The routine of the block continued under normal conditions until early on May 2, when all hell broke loose—not only in D Block, but the entire prison. This was the day for the big breakout.

15 Prelude to Breakout

That day (and events of the next two days) had a profound effect on D Block, Alcatraz, and many individuals. Many of those caught up in this tragedy were victims of circumstances, not choice. It was a revolt that changed and ended many lives. This escape plot was possibly one of the most vicious, desperate, and bloody uprisings to ever occur in this country's penal system. It was motivated by the same pressures (anger and frustration) that had overtaken the inmates of D Block a few weeks earlier. Only this time, they were of even greater magnitude.

Even more awesome was the overwhelming determination of those involved to accomplish their purpose or die. These men, in desperation and anger, challenged all the power of this country—its military strength, law agencies, and prison system—and the world in general. All this, simply because they could not endure incarceration in a prison like Alcatraz.

This was desperation at its maximum. The actions of men resolved to die, rather than exist in the exile imposed by the federal prison system and those paid to enforce it. The purpose of Alcatraz and men like Warden Johnston was to degrade, deprive, humiliate, and break inmates: spiritually, mentally, and physically. It was done under the guise of keeping society safe and free from the lawless element that was incarcerated on this miserable island. Brutality is a word that was synonymous with Alcatraz. Not physical brutality, usually, but mental brutality, which is far more difficult to endure, because it can be prolonged for years without obvious signs until the victim erupts like an exploding volcano. It is a process that develops a death wish in the victim because he can no longer endure the mental agony. And it is insidious; it occurs without the victim being aware of it.

Alcatraz's location was also conducive to the mental deterioration of its inhabitants. Each day, we saw the outside world in all its splendor, and each day that view served as a reminder that we had wasted and ruined our lives. On some occasions, when the wind was blowing from San Francisco toward the Rock, we could hear with great clarity the music, shouting, and laughter of people from the Yacht Club or from aboard a passing ship while we were in our dismal, lonely cells. Sights and sounds such as these, combined with pressure, stress, tension, despondency, and loneliness, often convinced us our lives would end in this environment. Additionally, our long sentences, and the constant reminders and implications we were "no good" and would die in prison, were always present in our minds.

Alcatraz was the epitome of hate, violence, anger, and loneliness; with these conditions, it is small wonder that some men could not continue to hold their lives, or the lives of others, in high esteem. The longer the sentence and the more the degradation, the more the feeling *Why do I continue to exist?* became part of one's every thought.

The only solution to the dilemma was escape, and this always was accompanied by the thought of death. I believe this often turned into a subconscious death wish by those who felt their lives were no longer worth living. Death often seemed preferable to a continuous painful existence. No one escaped these thoughts. This we see reflected in the occurrences of May 2, 1946.

I realize, as I write, that there will be those who say or feel that I am partial, and only see the side of the inmates, having been an inmate at Alcatraz. This is not true, because realizing I had such mixed emotions years ago, I delayed writing this book until I could be fair and objective. As an inmate, I did of course see situations only through the eyes of an inmate. However, now, having been a free man for twenty-six years and having re-earned my place in society as a worthwhile citizen (and as one who has worked hard to earn presidential and gubernatorial pardons), I feel I can and will look at past occurrences with an objective mind. I do know that many wrongful acts were committed on both sides. I also learned that law and authority do not always work hand in hand with righteous justice.

I will admit and honestly believe that a hopelessly

incarcerated inmate (because of crimes he knowingly committed) with no hope for the future does not have the right to take the life of another. I feel strongly that the forces of justice (i.e. the federal prison system) do not have the right to take a life when necessity and the preservation of security can be accomplished without so doing. This was not always the case, and several lives were sacrificed to act as a deterrent to escape.

Even at this late date, I have difficulty in understanding how the government could willfully justify their actions in attempting to kill twenty-six unarmed, trapped men who were not a party to, nor involved in, the "action" that occurred in the main cellhouse on that ill-fated day in 1946. Their justification for what they did is understandable to a point, but after that point it simply becomes, in my opinion, a cover-up to justify their desire for revenge. Being one of the twenty-six inmates who survived this murderous and unwarranted attack, I have to admit to some bitterness, even though forty years have elapsed. It is also true that violence is often a part of imprisonment and part of the price one must pay if one knowingly violates the law.

May 2, 1946 was not different in any respect in the lives of most inmates of Alcatraz, especially those of D Block. For all inmates, the day began with the usual routine: the ringing of the "wake-up bell" and the first count of the day. It also began with the usual cursing and swearing of the inmates who, for a few short hours while asleep, had escaped the routine, boredom, loneliness, and regimentation of the prison through dreams and an imaginary rejoining of the free world, their loved ones, and a normal life. The bell signaled the end of this escape and brought them back to the world of reality—prison. It was another day to face in hope of completing their prison sentence.

However, to other inmates in the prison, it was "the day," the day they would hit the free world and, in the process, "beat the Rock."

In D Block, we could hear preparations being made to start our long day with the serving of breakfast: the unlocking of D Block, the sound of the food cart being wheeled in and the crash of the cell door being opened for our cell tender, Louie Fliesh (AZ-574). Breakfast was certainly not thought of with great anticipation, knowing it would be exactly as it had been days and weeks before, again unappetizingly served in a sloppy manner, and with the usual cold, indifferent atmosphere of "eat it or leave it."

After breakfast was served and the trays collected, each inmate settled down into the routine that best helped him pass the long hours. Some walked, some read, and others merely spoke in a low tone to their neighbors. Little did we know our monotonous routine would be abruptly interrupted, and that May 2, 3, and 4 were going to be days that would live with us for the remainder of our lives. Within very few hours, D Block would become a major battleground, a scene of destruction and devastation. Alcatraz was to become a place of death and injury for many, both inmates and guards. It was a last and final confrontation between some desperate, determined, and "willing to die" inmates and those who had humiliated, degraded, and literally driven them to this self-destructive action.

This eventful battle eventually involved guards from Alcatraz, McNeil Island, Leavenworth, Atlanta, San Quentin, and Folsom, not to mention the U.S. Marine Corps and U.S. Navy Center, all utilized to subdue and kill three Alcatraz inmates armed with only one .45-caliber pistol and one rifle.

The encounter almost became a widespread, disastrous massacre due to the lies and distorted facts presented to the press and public by clever, manipulative officials. A system was created at Alcatraz that allowed some officials to have too much power and political influence. It also allowed the privilege of too much secrecy in determining how the men lived, survived, or died. Alcatraz was a law unto itself and it should be with shame that our federal prison system looks at this prison, rather than holding it in high esteem and considering it a success.

I realize the above statements reflect a feeling of hostility and bitterness. But to my knowledge, this is the first time the truth, from an inmate's point of view, is being written. As one of the few inmates of that era still alive, I somehow feel pressure on behalf of my fellows to reveal the true story concerning the attempted break: why it happened, and the three-day nightmare of the federal prison system and its bureaucrats trying to murder twenty-six inmates, including me.

On this day, the early morning passed in a routine manner for the inmates of D Block, until the daily disturbance of Harmon Waley (AZ-248). As always, Waley, serving a forty-five-year sentence for the $200,000 ransom kidnapping of the nine-year-old Weyerhaeuser child, began his usual and predictable tirade because he wanted a piano keyboard given him in his cell. He would often scream and carry on until he drove not only the guard in D Block to distraction, but the inmates as well. This day, the disturbance was not of its usual duration, but accomplished its purpose in angering everyone. He was, in return, soundly cursed and threatened with dire consequences of every degree if he didn't shut up. Following this episode, D Block settled down to wait for the noon meal. After lunch had been served, the trays collected, and the count taken, the majority of the inmates were napping and the block was still and quiet.

Suddenly, at about 1:40 p.m., we were startled by what sounded like a terrific fight taking place. We could hear cursing and thought that either a new inmate had been brought into D Block or an inmate was being worked over by the goon squad. It was difficult to determine just where the sound was originating. All inmates of the block made their way to their cell fronts in an effort to determine what was happening. Shortly thereafter the whispered word was passed down the tier that Pappy Burch, the guard in the west gun gallery, had been attacked and probably killed by another guard. This rumor was quickly dispelled when one of the inmates in a cell close to the gun gallery realized Bernard (Barney) Coy (AZ-415) had taken over the gun gallery. The "breakout" was underway.

The inmates were armed with the weapons from the gallery: a single 30.06 rifle, a .45-caliber automatic pistol, and 71 rounds of ammunition. This turn of events immediately raised many questions. How could an inmate breach the security of a gun gallery of the country's most secure and escape-proof prison? How could he attack and disarm a veteran prison guard? Why did it take over thirty-six hours for guards from six federal and state prisons, backed by the U.S. Marines, U.S. Navy, and gun boats, and armed with rifles, shotguns, automatic pistols, machine guns, flame throwers, grenades, tear gas, and demolition charges (with experts to use them), to subdue five inmates, of whom only two were armed?

From the point of view of an inmate who was present, who was inside (not simply an outside spectator), who was personal friends with most of the principal participants, and who almost lost his own life in a venture that was in all probability doomed from its inception, I will attempt to honestly answer these questions.

In order to fully understand what took place in those hours, one would have to know the participants and be able to understand their feelings and motivations during this tragic event. Actually, there were only five inmates involved in this episode, despite the official claim of six. Common bonds existed between three of the five inmates involved. First, each was predestined to escape or die in the attempt. Second, bitterness and hostility contributed as driving factors. These, as well as a lack of desire to correct or change their lives in the future, caused this event to take place.

Participants
Participant 1: Bernard P. Coy (AZ-415)

Barney Coy was in his early forties, a tall slender man with bushy eyebrows and a very nervous disposition; he was constantly on the move. He was polite and friendly to everyone and yet he was not entirely trusted by either the inmates or the guards. His accommodating demeanor earned him the reputation of being a "brown-noser" in some quarters and a jink, or "stoolie," in others (some of the "big-timers," such as the gutless "Public Enemy" Alvin "Creepy" Karpis, were responsible for the latter label). Neither was true.

Coy was born and raised in the hills of Kentucky, hence his reputation as an illiterate hillbilly who was an expert shot with a rifle. He had little formal education but was far from stupid. He ventured into crime at an early age and was twice convicted of bank robbery. He could be mean and vicious, as he proved in Atlanta, where his assault on another inmate resulted in his transfer to Alcatraz. On the island, he tried the legal system to have his sentence reversed and, when this failed, he determined he would escape.

Coy was not at all what his appearance and demeanor indicated. He was a crafty, observant, and patient man—and he was determined to escape or die. He was a dreamer, but also a man who had courage far in excess of most of the so-called public enemies or big names of the prison. It was this man who—by personal starvation, observation, and the willingness to expose himself to an instant death—brought the ill-fated plot to maturity. It was this man who also died in his quest for an unfulfillable dream.

Participant 2: Marvin Franklin Hubbard (AZ-645)

Marvin Hubbard was an unusual man. He based his entire life on the conviction that a man was only as good as his word and to give his word committed a man beyond question.

Hubbard was a quiet, unobtrusive man of thirty-six. Although he was strong and powerful, he wore glasses and spoke in a soft, low voice. Though not a loner, he was not given to close association with large groups of inmates. He was liked, respected, and on the surface seemed resigned to serve his time with no thought of escape or causing problems for the authorities.

Underneath his calm, quiet exterior was a man who had, on more than one occasion, faced what seemed to be overwhelming odds and death, yet managed to keep his cool and escape. He had been shot one or more times, yet was still willing to fight and die, if necessary, for his freedom. He had a long and violent history of crime.

For Hubbard, 1:30 p.m. on that fateful day was the beginning of the end. For this young man, raised in the backwoods of Alabama, death (and/or freedom) came on May 4, 1946, in a dirty, dark, smoke-filled, and bullet-riddled utility corridor in C Block at Alcatraz, far from the woods and mountains he so loved.

Participant 3: Joseph Paul Cretzer (AZ-547)

Joe Cretzer was a man who was predestined to meet a violent death. His entire way of life, from age fifteen, had led him toward a violent rendezvous with the Grim Reaper, in the service corridor with his friends Barney Coy and Marvin Hubbard.

Joe was, in many respects, a product of his environment. From a very early age, he was in trouble with the law and yet, because he was the youngest of three sons of deaf-mute parents, had been given many breaks and considerations not afforded others. His crimes, from age fifteen until his imprisonment at Alcatraz, grew in magnitude—burglary, car theft, robbery, bank robbery, and finally the ultimate: murder. He was not a man who looked back to see where his way of life had led him, but a man who looked forward with great ambition to other crimes.

Joe liked the notoriety of having been Public Enemy No. 5 and aspired to being no. 1. It was a way of life that held a great fascination for him and, with this attitude, his death was in keeping with his lifestyle and aspirations.

Joe was in all respects what a convict was reputed to be.

He was young, but also recognized by all as a man of his word in the world of prisons. He was tough and violent, a leader for those who wished to be led, and, above all, unafraid to face the consequences of his actions. He was felt to be too impulsive and impatient by many of the older, escape-minded inmates; as a consequence, he died for his actions. Had he used a little better judgment in the early hours of the breakout, he might have had a choice other than to die in the dirty service corridor or the gas chamber.

Participant 4: Miran Edgar (Buddy) Thompson (AZ-729)
Buddy was an acquaintance. He was not a man who inspired in me any great confidence either as an escape artist or as a tough inmate, despite his reputation as a "cop killer." In the institution, he had the reputation of being a solid convict who did his own time and handled his own beefs, yet he never would have been the person I would have chosen to protect my back in the event of trouble.

Buddy arrived at Alcatraz on November 22, 1945, on a transfer from Leavenworth, where he had been incarcerated with a term of ninety-nine years for car theft and kidnapping. Early in his incarceration, he was extradited to Texas, where he was convicted for the murder of a Texas police officer. For this crime, he was given a term of life imprisonment in a Texas state prison, but the federal government claimed jurisdiction and he was returned to Leavenworth to serve his federal sentence. His transfer to Alcatraz was probably precipitated by his long sentence, his detainer for the state of Texas, and his reputation as an escape artist (Buddy had successfully escaped from jails in Texas, Mississippi, and Alabama).

Participant 5: Clarence V. Carnes (AZ-714)

Clarence, or Joe, as he was known at Alcatraz, was the youngest inmate to be incarcerated in this institution. At the time of his arrival from Leavenworth he was nineteen years of age and, despite his ventures into crime, was very gullible and naive in this world of institution-wise inmates. Joe had the reputation of being capable and willing to fight, and as a consequence, was avoided by many inmates, who felt he was trouble. Yet he was accepted by others as a good convict. Joe was not a joiner, but neither was he a loner. He made certain friends and was content to be just another member of the group.

Joe Carnes was serving a ninety-nine-year sentence for a violation of the Lindbergh Act (kidnapping), the result of an escape from the Oklahoma State Reformatory at Granite, where he was serving a life sentence. He had received this life sentence for murder during an attempted robbery of a service station. The murder was an accident, but because it was committed during the commission of an armed robbery, it became first-degree murder, resulting in his long sentence.

I honestly do not believe Carnes was aware of, or anticipated, Joe Cretzer's insane action: the senseless shooting of helpless and defenseless guards in cells 402 and 403.

If Carnes had understood the determined death wish of

his companions, I truly believe he would have avoided the entire situation. I believe the proof of this statement is self-evident by the fact that, when he was instructed to go into the cells and "cut the throat" of "any screw" (guard) alive, he did not harm or injure anyone.

I don't believe he was fully cognizant of the fact that for this plot to even have a remote chance of success, it was necessary for all the guards in the surrounding gun towers to die. This was not the Clarence (Joe) Carnes I knew. I feel that, although the institution described him as a killer, he was not, and could not have deliberately taken this kind of action to achieve the one thing he desired most in life: freedom.

Participant 6: Samuel Richard Shockley (AZ-462)

Although Sam was not included as a participant by the actual five involved, he was indeed credited by the officials as such. Sam, the son of a poor sharecropper family in Oklahoma, was in every sense of the word the victim of a grievous and willful miscarriage of justice by our government and judicial system.

I knew very little about Sam until my incarceration in D Block. Before the forty-eight-hour siege of the block, he was just another voice and person who often carried on in many bizarre and erratic ways. It was said by all the inmates that he was crazy and was often characterized as "Crazy Sam."

I did not know the extent of his mental illness until we shared a single cell during the endless hours of assault on D

Block; then it became very apparent his mental capacity was definitely deficient (the Stanford–Binet test showed him as scoring in the area of sixty-eight). In addition to not being intelligent, Sam suffered from hallucinations and heard voices. He was hardly the dependable, stable personality that Coy, Cretzer, and Hubbard would have chosen to play such a vital and intricate part in their plan.

Sam Shockley was executed, however, in San Quentin's gas chamber, as it was alleged that he created the disturbance that afforded Coy the opportunity to gain access to the gun gallery. His "alleged" disturbance did not occur, and therefore Sam was not a premeditated participant to a crime that led to murder.

Sam was, in reality, a victim of the break. His involvement was only slightly more than my own, which was merely the result of sheer circumstances and not foreknowledge. Yet these circumstances led Sam to his death by execution.

16 For Want of a Key

Marvin Hubbard deliberately delayed completing his kitchen work assignment until the stage was set in the cell-house. It was essential to the plan that all inmates had left the main cellhouse to go to their work assignments, the recreation yard, or clothing-issue—or that they were locked in their cells. His arrival at the dining-hall door also had to coincide with the time interval when just one guard would be on duty in the cellhouse and the gallery officer was in D Block, leaving only Coy out of his cell and moving about freely.

The main obstacle was getting the gun gallery officer into D Block without creating a disturbance that would bring the goon squad into action, or alarm guards in nearby work areas (such as the kitchen, hospital, D Block, or clothing-issue section). Step one of the plan—capturing the cellhouse and gaining entry into the gun gallery— had to be accomplished quietly and quickly. It was rumored and believed by inmates that Coy had worked out this part of the plan well. His main tool was finding a means to relieve the boredom of the guard caged in the gun gallery.

Coy's work assignment as the cellhouse orderly included the distribution of new subscription magazines. This duty gave him great freedom of movement; opportunity to observe the habits, patterns, and actions of individual guards; and time to gain the confidence and trust of the regularly assigned cellblock guard.

His humble demeanor and apparent willingness to please the guards caused Coy to be suspected by some of his fellow inmates. Coy was aware of this fact and, considering the reason behind his actions, I am sure at times was hurt and angered by the treatment he received from those inmates.

For a considerable time, Coy had been sending magazines to various guards in the gun gallery. This I know to be a fact from personal observation. I believe many officers were also aware that this took place but, to my knowledge, never objected. I believe the magazines played an important role in getting the guard into D Block. If my theory is correct, and I believe it is, it offers a far more plausible and believable explanation than that offered by the institution— that Sam Shockley created a disturbance in D Block as a diversion to give Coy the necessary time to gain entrance to the gun gallery.

Coy surveyed the scene in the cellhouse. Everything was as planned: Officer Burdette was situated in D Block and the cellhouse was free of everyone except inmates locked in their cells. Officer Lageson had just gone to lunch and the only ones free in the block were Coy and Officer Miller. Coy gave the signal to Hubbard. It was on.

Hubbard asked permission to go to his cell. When it was granted, Hubbard, who had armed himself with a carving knife from the kitchen, walked to the locked door that separated the dining hall from the cellblock and knocked to catch Officer Miller's attention. Miller unlocked the door, looked to Officer Burdette to confirm Hubbard's release, then allowed Hubbard to enter the cellhouse.

When Hubbard stepped into the cellhouse, he made certain that Officer Burdette returned to his routine supervision of the kitchen inmates. This was according to plan. Hubbard moved to the designated area, where every inmate emerging from the kitchen stopped to be searched for contraband. Hubbard waited patiently as Officer Miller closed the dining-hall door. Coy, who had been lingering in the background, moved in closer as though he wished to start a conversation with either Miller or Hubbard.

When Officer Miller turned his back on Coy to search Hubbard, Coy moved swiftly. He grabbed Miller in a bear hug, then Hubbard smashed his fist into the helpless officer's face, knocking him out. Coy and Hubbard dragged the limp and unconscious officer around the corner of C Block, where there was no possibility that Officer Burdette, in the kitchen, could observe their actions.

Officer Miller was stripped of his keys, coat, and cap. While Hubbard was tying up the officer, Coy, using the keys he had obtained, opened cell 403 so Hubbard could hide the bound and gagged guard. While Hubbard was donning the officer's coat and cap, Coy unlocked the C Block service corridor and retrieved, from its depths, a bag containing a bar spreader.

Meanwhile, Hubbard, in his haste to gag and tie Officer Miller and to move him into cell 403 out of sight, made a mistake that would collapse Coy's carefully laid plans and turn the dream into a disaster. He missed key 107, which was essential to the plan because it opened the door from the cellhouse to the yard. Hubbard failed to search Officer Miller's pants pocket for any keys not on his ring. He had assumed key 107 was either on Miller's key ring or in the gun gallery, where it belonged. It was in neither place because Officer Miller, after using it, had slipped it into his pants pocket. It was, in fact, a serious breach of security for any cellhouse guard to retain this key when the gun gallery guard was in D Block.

After rendering Officer Miller helpless, Hubbard rejoined Coy in front of C Block. Hubbard was wearing the guard's cap and coat as a disguise. Coy directed Hubbard to keep watch down Broadway while he released the other inmates in on the plot.

After making certain that Officer Burdette in the kitchen would not observe his actions, Coy carefully crossed Broadway, then went to the northwest corner of B Block where the controls for opening the cells were located. He unlocked the control box and released the rest of the conspirators: Joe Cretzer, Miran Thompson, and Clarence

Carnes. The participants were then sent in different directions to prevent surprise intrusions.

It was time for Coy to accomplish the task he had been starving himself for. He stripped off his clothing to reveal an emaciated body he had to squeeze through a nine-inch gap in the bars.

While Coy stood naked, trembling in fear, excitement, and anticipation, Cretzer helped him apply a thick layer of grease. Special care was given to coat his head, shoulders, and hips—the most difficult parts to work through such a small opening. When he was totally covered, Cretzer checked to make certain Officer Ed Stucker could not see Coy when he climbed up the barred and screened stairwell that led to the basement and Officer Stucker's clothing-issue section. When Cretzer gave the signal, Coy climbed up on the stairwell, reached up, and caught the bottom of the gun gallery, then began to climb up the bars to the gallery's top level. Here, he carefully placed the bar spreader between two bars.

He tightened it until it was secure, then took a wrench from his bag and began to turn the nut, forcing the bolt outward and creating tremendous pressure on the bars. Coy continued twisting until the bars were spread as far as they would go. He removed the spreader, placed it back in the bag, and dropped it down to Cretzer. This was the moment of truth.

Coy slipped his skinny legs into the opening he had created. Getting his hips through proved very difficult;

finally, with much effort, tearing of skin, and bruising of muscles, he succeeded. Next, he worked his shoulders inside by twisting and turning. He was able to squeeze his head through without much difficulty. He was in.

Imagine the emotions Coy must have been experiencing. He knew that when he left the upper tier of the gun gallery and descended to the next level he was a dead man if he had miscalculated, in any way, the gallery officer's actions. In order to remain alive, he must successfully negotiate the stairs, cross half the width of the cellhouse, and disarm that guard.

Coy did not hesitate. He crossed the distance to the stairs and rapidly descended to the first level of the gallery. At the bottom he hesitated for just a moment to glance at Cretzer and Hubbard, who were standing in tense anticipation. When given the all-clear signal by Cretzer, he crossed the distance to the door leading into D Block. Here, he could glance inside D Block, locate the officer and determine how best he could use the element of surprise.

Cretzer was to give a single knock on the D Block door with Officer Miller's key, a customary signal to indicate that the officer was needed in the cellhouse for some minor reason. Cretzer and Hubbard were to stand out of sight under the gun gallery until they heard Coy attack the officer. At that moment, they were to unlock the D Block door and subdue Officer Corwin before he could reach the phone to give an alarm.

Coy gave the signal to Cretzer to rap on the door.

Motionless, all waited. Officer Corwin and the gallery officer heard the signal and Corwin remarked to Officer Burch that he was probably needed to release someone to the yard. Taking his time, Burch casually walked toward the door leading into the cellhouse. Coy crouched low behind the door, listening intently for the sound of the officer's shoes. He was now armed with a nightstick he had found in a weapons rack near the D Block door.

Coy waited until Burch was directly in front of the door, so that its inward swing would knock him off balance and afford Coy the opportunity to club the officer before he could respond. It almost worked as planned, but Burch was tougher than expected. He gave Coy a real battle before being choked into submission.

After searching Burch for keys, Coy secured the fallen officer's weapons, and lowered these (along with gas masks and another nightstick he had located in the weapons rack) to Cretzer, who, in the meantime, had successfully subdued and captured Officer Corwin. Corwin was hustled out of D Block, stripped, and then locked in cell 403 with Miller.

Coy now turned his attention to the unconscious officer. He located the lanyard used to lower keys to the cellhouse and secured the helpless guard's hands and feet with the rope before retracing his steps to the spread bars. Working his way out proved to be more difficult than his entrance, as the struggle with the officer had rubbed much of the grease from his body. After a long and painful effort, Coy rejoined his comrades in the main cellhouse.

While Coy was busy getting back into the cellblock, Cretzer and Hubbard had dressed themselves in the guards' uniforms in the event someone should appear upon the scene. Everything was working just as they had planned. The cellhouse and gallery had been captured, the only weapons inside the institution were in their possession, and no alarm had been sounded. No one was aware of this tense drama being enacted within the prison's walls.

First Problems

After Coy rejoined the others, they decided the time had come to release Whitey (Rufus Franklin) from his solitary confinement cell. Cretzer gathered all the keys they had accumulated and, upon entering the unit, asked cell tender Louie Fleish to pick the proper key, he being more familiar with them. After unlocking the outer door to the solitary cell, Cretzer realized that he had no key to open the barred inner door.

Quickly evaluating the situation, Cretzer told Whitey they would make Officer Corwin unlock the lever box at the end of the tier. As Cretzer brought Corwin into the block, Fleish warned him that if Corwin did not use the correct sequence of levers it would trigger an alarm in the armory. This definitely was not a risk the inmates could afford to take.

Cretzer, in his determination to release their friend Whitey, then decided the only other alternative was for Coy to re-enter the gun gallery and release him by use of an electrical switch box. This also presented a risk, as it was pointed out there was an indicator board in the armory that showed when any of the six solitary confinement cells were opened.

(At no time, day or night, was a solitary cell opened before the gun gallery guard had called the armory to obtain permission from a higher authority, such as the associate warden captain, or lieutenant of the guard. When the cell was again closed, it was mandatory that the gun gallery guard call in and indicate all was secure. In many cases, if the inmate was belligerent or combative, additional guards were sent to the block until the situation was under control.)

Confronted with this new information, Cretzer returned to Whitey's cell and told him that he couldn't get him out because the risk of detection was too great, and time was running out. Actually, this turned out to be a break for Whitey.

While Cretzer was consulting with Coy about how to release Whitey from his cell, several of us, Sam Shockley included, asked him to release us. The overwhelming desire to escape had driven any reasonable thinking from our minds. Had we used a little common sense, we would have realized that capturing the armory was impossible, let alone getting off the island by way of violence.

By now, Shockley was raising such a clamor to be released that Cretzer was concerned his noise would surely alert those in other work areas. While Coy was returning Officer

Corwin to cell 403, Cretzer released Shockley. Even after his release, Sam would not quiet down, and badgered Joe to release the rest of us. Cretzer finally gave Shockley the key and told him to release anyone he wished. With that, Sam released every inmate on both tiers, including Robert Stroud, even though Stroud indicated he indeed declined to be released. As we headed down the stairs to get to the main cellhouse, we were warned to stop and be quiet, as someone had entered the cellhouse. We waited in silence as Coy and Cretzer rejoined the others in the cellhouse.

It was Officer Bristow, who had been in administration and was returning to his duties in the kitchen. When he reached the end of Broadway, he realized the dining-hall door was partially opened, and became suspicious. Before he could turn to flee, he was captured by Hubbard and Thompson, who were lying in wait after having been warned of his presence by Carnes, who was watching the front gate. Bristow was escorted to cell 403.

As Sam, my partner Jack, and I were about to enter the cellhouse, we were again given a signal to get out of sight and be quiet. Jack Maylan and Lefty Egan, two inmate trusties, were coming in for lunch. They were also captured, but were simply taken to their cells and locked in.

Coy and Cretzer were now trying to locate key 107. But again the warning of someone approaching was given. This time it was Officer Lageson. He, like the others before him, walked down Broadway into the guns of Coy and Cretzer. He too was locked in cell 403. Right after the capture of

Lageson, Sam, Jack, Louie Fleish, and I emerged from D Block into the main cellhouse.

As we entered, we observed Thompson, Hubbard, and Cretzer trying, unsuccessfully, to unlock the door to the yard. After some quick consultation, they determined that the missing key had to be in Miller's pocket.

At this point, things began to take a bad turn for the convicts. Officer Burdette, in charge of the kitchen, had come into the dining hall to conduct a general inspection and caught a glimpse of Coy rapidly passing in front of the main dining-hall door. The fact that the door was unlocked and partially open aroused Burdette's suspicions. He made the mistake, however, of going to the door to check with either Miller or Lageson to make certain everything was in control. As he stepped into the cellhouse, he found himself face to face with the guns of Coy and Cretzer. He offered no resistance and was placed in cell 403, which was fast becoming crowded.

The inmates were still fortunate, in that no one was aware of what was occurring. But this would soon change. Time was running out and the plan's organization was beginning to crumble. A decision was reached to pull Miller from cell 403, search him, and, if necessary, beat the whereabouts of the key out of him. Coy was certain he had not overlooked the key while he was in the gun gallery; therefore, it could only be in Officer Miller's possession, or hidden in cell 403. It was the key to freedom and had to be retrieved at any cost.

Before Miller could be pulled from the cell and searched, the inmates were again interrupted. Miller, meanwhile, regained consciousness and informed his fellow officers that he had key 107 in his pocket. Realizing that the success of the escape revolved around the possession of this key, the guards obtained the key and forced it out of sight in the toilet, aware that its weight would prevent it from being flushed away into the main sewer.

Shortly thereafter, Miller was pulled from the cell. When no key was found, he was given a severe beating in a desperate effort to make him divulge its whereabouts. Miller, in spite of his pain, continued to maintain that the key had been returned to Officer Burch in the gun gallery. Officers Corwin, Burdette, and Lageson were then each searched. When no key was found, the officers were moved to cell 402 so the inmates could search cell 403. When they came up empty again, Coy became convinced that the key was hidden in the toilet. Before he could make a search, however, he was again distracted.

Officer Stucker, in charge of clothing-issue (located in the basement below the cellhouse), had released several inmates to return to the cellhouse or to their work assignments. Several of these inmates, assigned to the yard area and anxious to join a bridge game, proceeded to the top of the stairs leading into the cellhouse and rattled on the door, as was customary to attract Officer Miller's attention. After waiting several minutes they peeked through the screen, but could not see an officer. They returned to the basement and asked Officer Stucker to phone the cellhouse.

Officer Stucker, being the type of guard he was, did not believe the inmates and proceeded up the stairs to investigate for himself. As he peeked through the screen, he saw Cretzer in an officer's uniform with a .45-caliber pistol in his hand. At this same instant, Cretzer also observed Officer Stucker.

Cretzer made a mad dash across the cellhouse in an effort to stop Stucker from making a call to the armory. But Cretzer was too late, and Stucker locked the gate to the basement with a padlock.

Stucker made a headlong dash down the stairs, out of sight and out of range of Cretzer's pistol. When he reached the bottom, he realized he must keep the inmates in the basement from becoming aware of what was taking place in the cellhouse. This was a means of self-preservation, for he was now trapped in the basement with several inmates who detested him.

Stucker was an officer who went strictly "by the book," leaving no room for understanding or compassion where the inmates and their problems were concerned. He was one of those who would, with his arrogance, pettiness, and unaccommodating attitude, go out of his way to instigate punishment against any inmate for the most insignificant infraction of rules. He knew full well that if the inmates in his immediate charge realized what was occurring, his life would be in grave jeopardy.

He resorted to using the ruse that there were racial problems occurring in the cellhouse and, in order to keep the inmates from being involved, he wanted them in his office so they could not be blamed for whatever was taking place. It worked. The inmates complied. In reality, Stucker's main objective was getting the inmates away from the only telephone.

Stucker could see Cretzer working with desperate determination to force the basement door open. By now, Stucker was completely panicked; his call and conversation with the armory was short, incomplete, and, for the most part, incorrect.

Armory Officer Fish was not one to panic, nor react to a situation without a certain amount of investigation. He was a fair and just officer who understood inmates, but did not want his fellow guards to take the brunt of a vicious ploy. With the information received from Officer Stucker, he felt it might be a ruse to draw the goon squad into the cellhouse for a nonexistent emergency. This would elate the general population and embarrass and make the squad feel foolish. Credit must be given to Officer Fish for realizing that an incident such as this could occur. Rather than creating a problem by overreacting, he preferred to check out his facts before taking action. Of course, this worked to the inmates' advantage, buying them extra time.

Officer Fish, rather than sounding the escape alarm, called each of the nonresponsive stations again—the west gun gallery, kitchen, and cellhouse. Still cautious, he called the hospital, which was away from the cellhouse but in constant touch with the areas in question.

Officer Pherson responded from the hospital, stating he was unaware of any problems in the kitchen, cellhouse, or gun gallery. Although this made Fish feel a bit better, it did not completely relieve his anxieties. He then decided to re-establish contact with Officer Stucker in the basement, hoping for clarification of the situation.

Stucker hesitantly answered the telephone, still observing Cretzer and the others desperately working to gain entrance to the basement. By then in mortal fear for his life, his answer was curt, short, uninformative, and practically incoherent. He hung up and barricaded himself and his inmates in the basement office.

Had Cretzer and the others involved stopped to reason, they would have realized they could have gained entrance to the basement area via a large barred door off the inmate dining hall, to which they had the key. This was only one of several ways the inmates, in their frenzy, failed to utilize important options that might have gained them some precious time. They could have, for instance, forced Officer Stucker to call the armory and falsely report that everything was under control.

Holding It Together

As an observer of the events taking place, I felt at that point each of the inmates was trying, individually, to solve the problems facing the group. As a consequence, their overall prearranged plan was being discarded, piece by piece. Coy became aware of the mounting confusion, tension, loss of direction, and finally the evident deterioration of their plans. He realized that unless they were united, their escape was doomed to certain failure. He felt the one thing that would bring unity back into the picture would be to locate key 107.

Coy and Hubbard returned to cell 403. After searching every conceivable hiding place, Coy forced his slender hand into the toilet and felt the key at his fingertips. Straining, Coy was able to trap the key between two fingers. When he very carefully withdrew his hand and held the key up for Hubbard to see, it must have been a feeling akin to being reprieved from a death sentence at the last minute. But before they could share their jubilation with the others, they were interrupted by a warning that someone was entering the cellhouse. Everyone moved out of sight and into the best position to capture the intruder.

It was with some apprehension that the inmates realized the intruder was Captain of the Guard Weinhold. After receiving a call from Officer Fish, the captain had decided to ignore his own order that "no guard would enter the cellhouse alone if the possibility of trouble existed." Since Officer Fish had been unable to contact anyone, Weinhold decided to take it upon himself to enter the cellhouse, displaying his typical Prussian attitude that there were few problems he could not handle. In this case, it was a mistake that almost cost him his life.

The inmates' apprehension was warranted; the captain was not only a man with complete confidence in his ability to handle any problem, but also a fearless fighter. Unless taken by total surprise, he would have to be killed or battered into submission. But like others of the administrative staff he too had become very comfortable in the security of the prison walls and failed to take into consideration the ingenuity, patience, and determination of some inmates. He believed there was no possible way for inmates to break the impenetrable security of the gun gallery. Thus, taken quite unaware, the captain was captured without a struggle.

To this day, I can still remember the look of utter amazement on this man's face when he was confronted with guns from the gun gallery. His shock was so complete that he was unable to react in any manner whatever, let alone his normal manner. This, of course, proved to be still another break for the inmates. For had he reacted, it might have led to his shooting, and then the alarm, which would have brought the escape to an abrupt halt.

Immediately after the captain had been captured, Sam Shockley, for some reason, seemed to lose what little control he had over his emotions. He suddenly broke away from where Jack and I were standing and attacked the captain, who was being restrained by Carnes. Sam threw a vicious punch at Weinhold's head. The captain saw it coming and ducked, which enraged Sam even more. He then kicked at the captain's scrotum, again missing. Had he succeeded, Sam would have certainly incapacitated Captain Weinhold for a very long time, if not for life. This angered the captain and he lashed out with a backhand that caught Sam across the mouth, nearly knocking him to the floor.

Now Sam changed from an aggressive, belligerent inmate into a rather pathetic, whimpering, immature, and incoherent individual. He raged at Cretzer to kill the captain for hitting him, but by then, Cretzer was losing patience with Sam and asked us to get him out of the way. This was an impossible task, as Sam was not in control of his senses. He did, at our insistence, eventually move, but continued to pace back and forth in front of the D Block door, talking and muttering to himself. He was beyond the point of reasoning and I am sure Hubard, Coy, or Cretzer, with little hesitation, would have locked him in a cell had they been certain he would not have created a louder commotion. Sam was indeed a good friend and a good inmate, but at this point he was becoming a real detriment to their efforts.

By this time, I had determined things were not going to work out. Common sense pointed out that administration's concern must have been growing stronger, considering the unanswered phones and the mysterious silence of the officers who had gone inside and not returned. Even if Coy found the key, anyone who attempted to scale the wall would surely die in the attempt. Still, we decided to wait just a little longer, I suppose in the hope there would be a miraculous change in our favor.

We didn't have to wait long for the signal of someone else approaching! This time there were three: Lieutenant

Simpson, Officer Baker, and Officer Sundstrom. More easy prey for the guns of Coy and Cretzer. They too were locked in the cell with the others.

Although Officer Fish was aware that the warden was not feeling well, he decided it was his obligation and duty to inform the warden and associate warden of his fears. His concern for his fellow workers outweighed the possibility of the warden's disapproval.

17 Bad Marksmanship

Coy assembled the four principal inmates together and showed them key 107. At first there was a rush for the yard door, but Coy stopped them—there were still other factors to take care of before they made their assault on the wall. He instructed Cretzer, Thompson, and Carnes to return to their observation posts while he eliminated any threat from the towers surrounding the yard. It was now almost 2:30 p.m. and the count was soon due. Both luck and time had been pressed to the maximum. When the guards who were being held hostage failed to call in their counts at the given time, the escape alarm would be sounded, thus creating a "do or die" situation for the inmates.

Coy announced that he and Hubbard were going to clear their final hurdle—the towers. He asked Thompson, Carnes, and Cretzer to wait until they had returned before unlocking the yard door. Cretzer then informed the inmates from D Block that he thought too much time had been wasted, and felt that there was only a very slight chance that anyone was going to make it.

He told me that, since no one had been killed and none of us from D Block were too involved, now would be the time for us to go back. Knowing that in Sam's disturbed mental state there was no possible way for him to make it over the wall, Cretzer asked me to get Sam to go with me. This confirmed my earlier conviction that the break had definitely gone sour. There would be no miracle. Jack and I decided Cretzer made good sense, and that from this point on the break bordered on suicide.

We told Cretzer we were all heading back inside the block. I shook hands with Cretzer, wished him luck, then went to persuade Sam to return with us. Sam was still babbling incoherently, like some deranged imbecile. The only response I could get from him was "In just a minute!" I turned and looked at Cretzer. He indicated I should go into the block and that he would get Sam to follow. That was the last time we saw Cretzer, Coy, or Hubbard alive.

From this point on, I can only relate what I was told from inmate friends who were in a position to see what occurred as Coy made his final effort to bring the escape to fruition.

Coy and Hubbard entered the kitchen and proceeded on through to the bakery, the area that would afford Coy the best shot at Officer Besk, the guard in the hill tower. Seeing Besk relaxing in the glass-enclosed tower, Coy went from one window to another to determine which location would give him the best shot at the exposed and totally unsuspecting officer. Picking the best angle, Coy punched the glass out of a window, settled the gun on the window frame, and lined Besk up in his sights. He rapidly fired off two shots, both of which came very close to hitting him in the head. Before he was able to move, Coy squeezed off a third shot that apparently glanced off some object in the tower and hit him in the leg. The force of the shot knocked him from his stool, and the manner in which he fell convinced Coy he was dead. Elated with his apparent success, Coy decided to eliminate the yard wall officer and the road tower officer.

The bridge players in the yard scattered when they heard the shots, unaware of what was happening yet not wishing to be caught in any crossfire. Besk, in the meantime, played dead until he felt it was safe to cautiously peek out to determine where the shots had come from. The bullet holes in the glass of the tower indicated they had come from the bakery.

Coy and Hubbard now retreated from the bakery to the kitchen area. From here, it was only a matter of 150 feet to the yard wall and slightly further to the road tower. From this position, Coy could quickly, in succession, pick off both guards. For some reason, he elected to first shoot the tower guard rather than the yard wall guard, which did not make a great deal of sense, considering the timing. The yard guard had immediate access to cover behind the yard wall, whereas the tower guard was unprotected and would have been exposed as he ran for the cover of the wall.

At any rate, Coy's first shot at Levinson in the tower alerted Barker on the wall. As Coy fired, Levinson either moved or Coy out and out missed, but Levinson dropped, as though hit. Coy, confident he had killed him, immediately turned his attention to Officer Barker. Having heard the first shot, Barker was already starting to drop when Coy's shot whizzed past him. Thinking he had killed them both, Coy boasted of his capabilities as an accurate marksman to Hubbard. Believing that only the dock tower guard remained, they headed (with great confidence) for the inmate dining hall, and what Coy believed was his last challenge.

In reality, whatever possibilities they had had of making it over the wall had just ended. It was imperative that Officer Barker on the yard wall be completely eliminated, because he could move freely and safely. He could raise up and fire at anyone who attempted to climb the wall with minimum exposure; he had complete and absolute control of the yard wall.

But Coy was still confident when he found a window that gave him an unobstructed view of the dock tower and Guard Jim Comerford. He broke the window and carefully steadied the rifle against the sill. Comerford was standing outside the tower and in perfect position. Coy fired a shot he was convinced killed the guard instantly.

At that particular time, Comerford was talking to Associate Warden Miller, who had just returned from an inspection of several locations on the island. As the sound of the shot reverberated, Miller, realizing that Officer Comerford was under attack from an unknown source, shouted instructions to the officer to play dead until he could locate where the shot had come from. Comerford imme-diately responded.

Having been out of Coy's sight, Associate Warden Miller then hurried to the administration wing, keeping himself out of any possible gunfire from the cellhouse and surrounding areas. This was a wise move on his part, since Coy waited a few additional moments to see if there was any reaction or response to his shot at the tower.

When he observed none, Coy felt triumphant. He was doing his job well, and everything was under control. Hubbard and Coy left the dining hall and headed for the main cellhouse with great expectation that they were on their way over the wall.

At this point, while we were all climbing the stairs to the second tier, we heard Cretzer exclaim that key 107 would not unlock the door to the yard. This could possibly have been the result of the lock having been jammed during their attempts to open the door with other keys. With a feeling of sadness and grief, we continued into our cells, knowing full well that anyone who continued in the break from this point on was committing certain suicide. We also realized, with apprehension, that unless Sam returned to D Block within a very short time, he was going to become involved in something much more violent and serious than his confused, disturbed mind could possibly comprehend.

As we stood on the tier, debating whether it was feasible to re-enter the cellhouse and try to convince Sam to come back into the block, our decision was made for us. Officer Burch, who had been left bound hand and foot by Coy, somehow managed to raise his head above the solid partition of the gun gallery. He observed Jack, the others, and me gathered in a group on the second tier (this chance observation may have saved us from being indicted for escape or murder, as was Sam, because it placed us back in D Block before Cretzer went wild). Everyone was united in the decision that no amount of persuasion would convince Sam to return. Now was the time to prepare to protect ourselves from what might become a prolonged battle between prison authorities and armed inmates.

It was apparent that the only possible way for the authorities to regain control of the cellhouse was to take over the west gun gallery. This greatly concerned us, as the only entrance was a side door, which opened into the gallery from the catwalk that surrounded D Block and the outside. We realized the authorities would use this approach, it being the only logical option. We also realized that, in expectation of inmate resistance, there would be a heavy, concentrated volley of gunfire as the officers came charging through the entrance.

Retaking the east end of the cellhouse presented no real problem, as officers could enter from the administration wing of the building. It was utterly impossible, however, to quell or end this escape until both the west and east gun galleries were under control of the officials. A disastrous situation, which would endanger our lives, now seemed quite inevitable.

Associate Warden Miller had by now made his way to the administration area, and was filled in by Officer Fish. Miller instructed Fish to call the warden. He then armed himself with a gas gun and informed the remaining people in administration that he was going into the cellhouse to investigate. Against all advice, Miller was determined he would get to the heart of the problem. He wanted to have a full and comprehensive report to relay to the warden. Before entering the cellhouse, Miller instructed Officer Phillips, who was on the main entrance gate, to stay alert and be ready to let him back into the administrative offices should he run into trouble.

As Miller stepped into the cellhouse and heard the large steel gates lock behind him, I am sure that he had more than minor concerns about his bravado. He stood, waited, and observed. Everything seemed to be in perfect order. He moved cautiously, and peered down the long corridor that separated the old, unused A Block from the remodeled B Block. All was quiet. Feeling more secure, he decided to go back and walk down Broadway.

He, like Captain Weinhold, felt confident and comfortable with the security of the prison and its control of the inmates. Miller didn't know that his every move was being observed and relayed to the inmates at the west end of C Block. Despite this relative confidence, Miller did not move with the greatest of ease. Perhaps his instincts warned him of an impending trap—if so, they probably saved his life.

As he reached the cutoff (the halfway point of the blocks) Miller hesitated and appeared as though he were about to return to the main entrance. Afraid he would get away, Coy, dressed in an officer's uniform, tried to get close enough to Miller to subdue him.

Hiding the rifle along his side, Coy strolled out from behind the end of C Block as though intent on going to the administration wing. It was a ploy that only worked for seconds. Associate Warden Miller recognized Coy, turned, and made a mad dash for the exit.

Coy stopped, drew a bead on Miller, and fired. Again Coy missed. In his haste to escape, frantically pumping his fat body and arms, Miller accidentally discharged his own gas gun. The charge from the weapon burned Miller severely on his face and head, but did not slow him down.

Before Miller rounded the corner, Coy fired a second shot at the fleeing, terrified hulk who had, just minutes earlier, walked with arrogant confidence. Now, Jughead found himself reduced to panic—running, screaming for Officer Phillips to open the gate so he would not die. When Phillips had made certain there was no one else in close proximity, he unlocked the gate and allowed Miller to dash inside to safety.

Associate Warden Miller's first breathless words to the warden, who had by now arrived in the office, were that "Coy is inside, dressed in an officer's uniform resembling Captain Weinhold's, and armed with a rifle." Warden Johnston realized that if Miller was correct, he was in an untenable position; his policies and reputation (as the warden of the United States' most secure and escape-proof prison) were in grave jeopardy. He therefore chose to distort and misconstrue Miller's observation of the rifle. He announced that the inmates were in possession of submachine guns. He may have been thinking that he could claim the gun came from the outside, and would therefore not have to admit that the institution's security had been breached.

Miller, knowing the alarm must be sounded, looked to Warden Johnston to take action. Johnston appeared to be in a state of semi-shock, unable to believe the seriousness of the situation at hand. He may have been trying to determine his best move, taking into consideration the protection of his personal status. Feeling that Warden Johnston was stalling for time, Miller himself ordered the escape siren to be sounded.

Once the shrill, wailing siren had sounded, the possibility of an escape was totally gone. It automatically brought any and all police and authorized vessels to surround the island so no one could slip away in the water by boat or by swimming. Even if the inmates had made it to the wall, or (miraculously) over it, there was still nowhere for them to go. The bloody siege that was to commence was an unnecessarily created folly.

The long, loud siren also frightened the citizens of San Francisco and nearby cities because of the myth created by the federal government and Warden Johnston about the inmates of this grim prison. Both hoped that this myth, and Alcatraz's reputation, would take them off the "hot spot," justify Warden Johnston's actions, and even elevate them in the eyes of the general public (as defenders of justice). But the myth was untrue.

Had those in authority been less concerned about their personal reputations and prestige, the entire episode could have been handled in a low-key manner, the same way hundreds of prison breaks had been handled in the past. Instead, the incident became so blown out of proportion that it was heard of and read about throughout the entire United States.

18 Bail Out

When the siren sounded, Cretzer seemed to lose all control, common sense, and reason. Coy, Cretzer, and Hubbard decided there was no alternative except to shoot it out as long as possible before death overtook them. Once this decision was reached, Cretzer decided to kill all the captive officers. Hearing the conversation, Captain Weinhold knew the captives' chances were minimal, especially taking into consideration the inmates' frustration and anger at failing to gain the freedom they so desperately desired. He tried to reason with Cretzer, but to no avail. Cretzer walked up to cell 402, rested the .45-caliber pistol on the bars, and, in rapid succession, shot Captain Weinhold in the chest, Officer Miller in the arm, Corwin in the head, and Lageson in the cheek. As they fell into a heap, the crazed Cretzer then fired at Burdette, Sundstrom, and Bristow until the clip in the pistol was empty.

He reloaded the gun, moved to the next cell and began again. Baker was hit several times in the legs and thigh, Simpson twice in the chest and abdomen. Suddenly, the insane shooting seemed to bring Cretzer back to reality. He stood calmly, staring at the mass of bloody and critically wounded officers. All were still.

The frenzied shooting drew Carnes away from his observation post at the east end of C Block. When he saw the bloody mound of humanity Cretzer had created with his maniacal shootings, Carnes realized he was involved in a situation with men that he really did not know. He had not been made aware of the injuries and deaths that would be involved before this break had even a remote chance of success. Carnes realized he had been used.

Before he could react, he was instructed by Cretzer to enter the cells and cut the throats of any guard who might have survived the deadly gunfire. Carnes was determined to end his participation in this lost cause as soon as possible, without endangering his own life with the suicidal trio. It was obvious they were determined to die, but would in the process kill as many of their keepers as possible.

Although Carnes had killed in the commission of a crime, he was not the type of individual who could commit atrocious, cold-blooded murders. He entered the cells as though in search of any officers who might have survived the massacre, but he had decided that, regardless of what he found, he would tell Cretzer they were all dead. He realized that in so doing he would be endangering his own life, for he knew Cretzer, in his enraged state of mind, would not hesitate to kill him. Pretending he was through checking, he assured Cretzer they were indeed all dead. This seemed to satisfy Cretzer and he walked to the end of the tier to relock the cell doors. Carnes' decision probably kept him from receiving a death sentence.

During this time, Carnes decided he would return to his cell before he became involved any further. He was not ready or willing to die in this futile and suicidal venture. He found Coy, Cretzer, Hubbard, and Thompson at the end of C Block and told them of his decision. Coy told him it was okay. His cell was open and once inside he could close it, locking himself in. Thompson, at this point, despite his boasts he would stick to the end, lost his nerve and followed Carnes' lead, locking himself in as well. I am not certain where Sam was during the shooting of the guards, but he returned to the tier either before or shortly after Carnes and Thompson locked themselves in their cells.

Meanwhile in D Block, Jack, Bill, and I decided it would be advisable to get as far away from the gun gallery, and the D Block door into the main cellhouse, as possible. The gun gallery in D Block did not extend the entire length of the block, and if we chose a cell near the end of the second tier, it would be almost impossible to shoot directly into the cell. We never anticipated that in their fury and desire for revenge, the misinformed guards and the U.S. Marines would rain tear gas, rifle grenades, hand grenades, flares, smoke bombs, and bullets through the windows. They used pistols, rifles, machine guns, and every kind of weapon available to the assault force—at one point, they even considered flame-throwers and the bow guns of a Navy cutter.

Having decided where our best chance to survive would be, we hurriedly proceeded to find ways to protect ourselves. We knew there would be a great deal of random shooting when the guards entered the gallery. We thought, or perhaps hoped, it would be of short duration and figured if we survived the initial assault, it would soon be apparent to everyone that the inmates of the block were not involved, nor were we armed or a threatening factor.

Had we fully realized the events that were to take place (such as the total and expected anger of the guards, aggravated by Warden Johnston's distorted and exaggerated version of what was occurring, and the senseless shooting of the guards by Joe Cretzer), I'm sure that we would have been far more concerned. We knew we would come under some gunfire from the assault team, but we believed it would be in the form of a stream of bullets shot down the length of the tier to keep us back in our cells and away from the open cell doors.

We were totally unprepared for their planned terrorizing, and their savage, all-out attempt to spill convict blood. It was of no importance whether the potential victims were innocent, trapped bystanders or participants in the break. This was their perfect opportunity to avenge old insults and injuries and, at the same time, rid the institution and world of the incorrigibles of D Block with little or no repercussion from the outside world. After all, who would really care?

Bill, Jack, and I decided to gather as many mattresses as possible from empty cells and place them against the cell

Associate Warden Miller. Burns sustained while he was escaping from Coy. A tear gas club he was carrying exploded in his face.

Hole in the ceiling of the C Block cut-off, through which Marines on the prison's roof dropped armor-piercing bombs. The hole was never repaired, giving inmates a constant reminder of the futility of trying to escape.

C Block utility corridor where Cretzer, Coy, and Hubbard made their final stand, and died. When they entered this narrow, dark space, their fate was sealed; after guards secured the gun galleries, they had no way out.

Side by side… as they attempted to escape, fought, and died. The bodies of Coy, Cretzer and Hubbard.

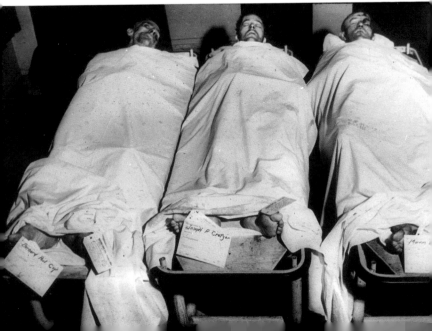

The prison launch transported the inmates' bodies to San Francisco; it was met at the dock by a van from the city morgue. (Reporters and news photographers also met the boat; their shadows can be seen in both photos.)

WARDEN JOHNSTON

Robert Stroud, the Birdman of Alcatraz (center), a divisive figure who caused a great deal of friction among fellow inmates, testified on behalf of Sam Shockley. Despite many favourable testimonies, including mine, Sam Schockley was convicted and executed.

On September 10, 1963, after a long year of waiting, Leone
became my wife. She has been the centre of my world since the
day I met her.

Our daughter Lori (above, with our beautiful granddaughters Mikki and little Shauni) taught me to appreciate life's precious moments.

My granddaughters make my days full.
It's a good life, a fine life, a free life!

Through twenty years of incarceration I learned that faith in God, family, and freedom are the most desirable objectives to be attained in this world.

front, providing ourselves with a barricade. We each found a mattress, and were in the process of erecting this soft wall, when Sam Shockley came and joined us. Where he came from or how long he had been back in D Block I do not know. Sam had ceased talking and muttering to himself. He seemed calm and relatively aware of all that was taking place. His conduct and calmness made it difficult to believe that he could have been on the scene (as claimed by administration officials) when Cretzer had unleashed his frustrated fury upon the helpless guards in cells 402 and 403.

We retreated into the cell and lay down on the floor behind our mattress barricade. Many frightening thoughts raced through our minds as we lay in wait. Just how safe were we? Would we survive or would we feel the cold steel messenger of death from one of the many weapons concentrated on our block? Would there be a tomorrow? I, for one, could feel cold, terrorizing chills creeping up and down my spine.

The expected assault was not long in coming.

The opening shot in the war to prevent administration from regaining control of Alcatraz was fired by Coy. He was positioned at the entrance to D Block when he heard movement, indicating that an assault on D Block by way of the entrance into the gun gallery on the D Block side was imminent. Coy waited until he was certain there was someone attempting to unlock the door, then fired. He missed his target, but certainly discouraged that particular assault.

The officials of Alcatraz seized this opportunity to introduce officers into the east gun gallery. Both Cretzer and

Hubbard, who were watching the east end of the block, heard the gallery door unlock and saw it open, but because of Cretzer's location, he was not able to get off a shot. The officers came in low and fast behind the gallery's thin but solid-metal lower portion. Had Cretzer fired, it would have been ineffective at best and would certainly have made him a sitting target for the officers. Realizing they were in an indefensible position, Cretzer and Hubbard beat a rapid retreat for the front of C Block.

When they reached the end of the block, Coy was there to greet them. He informed them he had gotten off a shot, but was certain he missed. Cretzer and Hubbard told him of the occupation of the east gallery. This worried Coy because he realized the inmates' movements would now be very limited. The east gallery now controlled all the aisles between A Block, Broadway, and D Block. Any movement from in front of C Block could expose them to tremendous gunfire from the east end.

Coy decided that if he could slip down Broadway under cover of the tier overhang, he might, by movement or sound, be able to pick off one or more officers, even though they were out of sight behind the metal portion of the gallery. He knew his rifle would penetrate it and would therefore give him an advantage that might turn the tide in the inmates' favor. But as Coy approached the cutoff, he was observed by Officer Virgil Cochenour in the gallery.

The officer waited patiently, undetected, until Coy was well within the range of his Winchester scattergun, loaded with double buckshot. He slipped the barrel of his gun between the bars, quickly raised up, and fired. Sheer instinct must have warned Coy he was in grave danger, for he suddenly turned and headed at a dead run for the protection at the end of C Block. Cochenour missed and was unable to get off another shot before Coy was safe and out of sight.

The officers now controlled half of the cellhouse and could limit the inmates' movements. It was an advantage the inmates knew they would not give up easily. When the officers captured the east end of the cellhouse, it should have put to rest the theory that inmates were freely entering D Block and shooting at the officers from within. Crossing the area between C Block and D Block was now very dangerous, or fatal. It was a short distance, but it was only crossed once, and then only in a desperate attempt to prevent the recapture of the west gun gallery.

Realizing that they had lost control of the cellhouse, the inmates were now forced to locate a position where they could kill as many guards as possible, and at the same time drive off any attempt on the west gun gallery. They chose the inside of the C Block service corridor.

Here they would be protected by a heavy metal door, but could still shoot at the officers as they entered the cellhouse. Leaving the door slightly ajar gave them a protected shooting port, and climbing up above the C Block cells gave them a clear, unobstructed shot at anyone entering the block. When lying flat, there was little chance of their being seen, and there was less chance of being hit by return fire because they could quickly retreat into the depths of the corridor.

From all appearances, it was an ideal location as long as they could keep the gallery unoccupied. In reality, the ingenuity of a combat-wise Marine turned this sanctuary into a tomb.

19 Running Out of Options

At sometime after 5 p.m., the institution officials decided the time had come to retake the west gun gallery. Warden Johnston had decided that as soon as the prison walls were manned with Marines, it would free enough officers to mount an assault via the entrance through D Block. It was as the inmates of D Block had anticipated.

Coy, Cretzer, and Hubbard were also anticipating this maneuver and were aware of the assault team as they converged on the catwalk outside D Block. They desperately sought a position that would give them an advantage when the catwalk door was opened. They decided to position themselves right inside the door to D Block, as this would leave them in the shadows while the officers assaulting the gallery would be silhouetted against the light from the door. Here the battle began. The assault team of Lieutenant Bergen, Officer Cochran, and Officer Stites were the first through the door. They were backed by another group of officers whose job it was to give cover fire and prevent the inmates from coming out of the entrance door if they were laying in wait inside the gun gallery.

As the guards entered the gallery, all was quiet. Nothing moved, no shots were fired, and the officers were convinced the inmates had abandoned this area. They were soon to learn it was a ruse.

Cretzer and Coy were there, waiting until the officers made a move toward the stairs that led to the middle level of the gallery, where they could enter the main cellhouse portion of the gallery.

As the officers moved toward the stairs, into their sights, Coy and Cretzer each fired a shot. Both missed. Their shots were answered with a barrage of firepower that must have amazed them. It seemed every kind of weapon imaginable was being fired in their direction, as well as into the whole of D Block.

The second attempt to retake the gun gallery produced a renewal of the bombardment. It was far more intense because we in D Block were now under fire from two directions: the gun gallery and the windows. The fire from the windows left us extremely vulnerable, as it was aimed directly into the cells. The protective construction of the building was the only thing that saved our lives.

As the outside catwalk was considerably lower than the windows, it forced the guards to extend their arms directly above their heads and fire blindly into the block if they did not want to expose themselves. This created an upward angle of fire that either struck the underside of the tier, its handrails, or the bars of the cell front; the bullets were deflected and ricocheted around, passing harmlessly over our heads or falling spent into the debris that was accumulating on the floor.

With each shot fired, it seemed our troubles increased. Bullets had started fires in several of the mattresses that other inmates were using as barricades. The smoke, tear gas, and constant hail of bullets were swiftly eroding any confidence that we had chosen a good position for our protection and survival.

Tracers illuminated the area, and shotguns, machine guns, pistols, and rifles filled D Block with smoke and bullets. Coy and Cretzer each fired a second shot at the officers before retreating to the C Block utility corridor where they were to make their last stand. In this exchange, the guards were not as fortunate as in the first encounter. Officer Cochran was hit in the shoulder and was seriously injured. Another officer was hit in the leg. The guards in the gallery drew back in order to remove Officer Cochran for treatment.

Once regrouped, though, the officers (including Lieutenant Bergen and Officers Stites, Mahan, and Oldham) decided to attempt to gain the middle level of the gun gallery. It was a risky, dangerous move, as this level was much lighter due to windows in the south and west walls. They would be well-illuminated targets for the inmates in D Block. On the other hand, it afforded them some additional protection not found on the flats, as a solid steel wall covered the lower portion of the gallery. They quietly and quickly moved across the flats and climbed the stairs as another unbelievable barrage of gunfire was unleashed into the cells of the inmates of D Block.

It was intended as cover fire, but was in reality totally indiscriminate, with no particular area or object in mind. The fact that twenty-six men were in those cells was of no consequence. If we all were killed, it did not matter. Sam, Jack, Bill, and I all lay on the floor behind our three mattresses. We could hear the bullets as they thudded into our lifesaving protection.

It was difficult to breathe because of the smoke. We could only lie flat on the floor behind our barricade and hope and pray we would not get hit. We lay for what seemed hours, with our arms covering our heads, waiting for this incredible volley of bullets to subside.

We thought of making a desperate dash for the main cellhouse, and possibly the protection of the kitchen. We all knew it would be futile and senseless, and would surely result in instant death the minute we were exposed on the tier, but at this point we were grabbing for any ideas that would keep us alive. We finally resigned ourselves to the fact that we had no choice but to stay down behind our barricade and pray. And believe me, I am sure each of us, in his own way, did pray.

We thought it was all over and were even beginning to feel confident enough to stand up. Fortunately we didn't, as what we thought was the end was just the beginning.

The assault team had now reached the middle level on D Block side. The difficult part was still before them, however. They had to pass through the swinging door into the main cellhouse, locate the inmates, and hope to stay alive as well. It is at this point that I can see and even understand the administration's belief that a gun was in D Block. When the officers reached the middle level, they split into two groups. Bergen and Mahan moved toward the door leading into the cellhouse, while Stites and Oldham turned in the opposite direction to allow Bergen and Mahan to position themselves to cover the gallery door into the main cellhouse. When the two were in position, Stites and Oldham were to join them. They would be forced to pass in front of a large window, which would make them excellent targets from either inside the block or outside the building.

At a prearranged signal, a tremendous volley of firepower was unleashed. The fire came from outside through the windows and from the back-up crew on the flats of the gun gallery. D Block was raked from top to bottom in this seemingly unending barrage.

Stites started his move to join Bergen and Mahan, but when he was centered in the window, he straightened up from his crouch, gave a cry, and fell, mortally wounded. Bergen and Mahan moved back to aid their stricken companion and Oldham moved forward. When he reached the window he too was shot, but not as seriously as Stites. With help from others from the back-up squad, the seriously wounded officers were removed from the gallery. Officer Stites died before reaching medical assistance.

Suddenly, although we felt our death was only a matter of minutes away, there came a lull in the attack.

We could hear sounds of movement in the gun gallery and it flashed though our minds that the guns had been located in the main cellhouse, or that the assault squad was going to concentrate its efforts elsewhere (because there had been no return fire from within the block). This was not to be. The lull was created by the death of Officer Stites and the wounding of Officer Oldham. It was a pause only to allow the guards to remove the injured from the gallery without being exposed to the possibility of being killed by their comrades.

With the killing of Stites and the severe wounding of Oldham, the block was about to become the focal point of a sustained attack that would continue to mount in intensity and destructive firepower for hours on end.

In my mind, I truly believe the actions taken against us were the result of Stites' death. It is true that he did die from a shot fired from a rifle. That was obvious from the wound he sustained. I can also understand the theory that he was killed from inside the block, except that he was hit in the back as he passed in front of a window (as was Oldham) and the fact that none of the guards giving support fire could recall seeing the flash of a gun in D Block returning fire. How could several men, looking directly at the area in question, fail to see or hear these indications of a weapon in the block? It was the very essence of what they were trying to locate.

Bergen and Mahan discussed where the shots could have come from. Neither could recall seeing a fire flash from anywhere in the D Block area. Again, Bergen and Mahan cautiously made their way back to the tier where the shooting had occurred. They were not fired at. While awaiting reinforcements, Bergen decided to check out the rest of the gallery in D Block. As he crawled along the floor toward the D Block gallery door, he discovered Officer Burch, still tied, cold, and battered. He was only semi-conscious, but soon recovered his composure. As they spoke, Bergen suggested he leave the area, but Burch wanted to stay and fight it out with the inmates. Bergen gave him a gun and arranged for some clothes. Burch was back in the fight.

Again a signal was given, and D Block came under another all-out bombardment to cover Bergen and Mahan's entrance into the cellhouse portion of the gallery. When the volley of fire subsided, the cellblock was quiet, semi-dark, and motionless. After exploring the entire length of the middle tier and finding nothing, the officers cautiously began checking out all the cells and corridors that they could see. Again, they observed nothing. No captured guards or armed inmates. The only unusual sight was the unlocked, partially open door leading into the C Block service corridor. Whenever the guards were in view of this door, their move-ments were slow, deliberate, and hidden from sight below the solid metal portion of the gallery. They had no intention of becoming a target for a hidden gun.

Bergen knew the upper level of the gallery had to be searched completely before they could feel secure that they controlled the gallery; he realized that the inmates could be lying in wait above. If they were, it would afford them the opportunity to fell another guard and possibly secure additional weapons. It was even conceivable that they could recapture the entire gallery, taking all the weapons, including a submachine gun that was now inside. Bergen, at this time, must have been experiencing many of the same fears and apprehensions that Coy had felt a few hours earlier. It could be a do-or-die situation for him now. He must climb the same stairs that Coy had descended. He also realized that he too faced the possibility of instant death in so doing.

Bergen began to climb the stairs. When he reached the top, he moved in rapidly, believing a moving target would be more difficult to hit. The gallery was empty as far as his eyes could see, but he knew he had to search the area behind the door leading into D Block. He worked his way rapidly but cautiously down the length of the gallery. When he reached the D Block door he hit it hard, forcing it open. He quickly scanned the area. It was empty. The guards now controlled both gun galleries, all the corridors, and the tiers of the cellhouse.

With the removal of Stites and Oldham from the gallery, the all-out attack again commenced. Its intensity and severity were increased, and several new destructive devices were pressed into use. Suddenly, series after series of rifle grenades were fired at our positions. Some say the grenades came from Marines, others say from the guards; it did not matter to us, as they were all under administration's command. They were fired at the windows located away from the gun gallery, making sure the officers in the gallery were not shelled.

The first indication we had of something new was a strange, muffled pop, after which we were literally lifted off the floor by the concussion, deafened by the explosion, and showered with thousands of shards from the remaining window glass. Red-hot fragments of metal lodged in several areas and started small fires. Acoustic tile was blasted from the walls and ceiling as the entire block shook from the explosion.

At first, we thought they were attempting to blast a hole in the side of the building with dynamite. It left us utterly stunned, not to mention overwhelmed with fear. But this blast was just the beginning. The strange sound and pop became very familiar to us. We knew that each time we heard it, another grenade was on its way, soon to be followed by an awesome explosion. The three last windows of D Block were the principal targets for the grenades, as the officials were aware that the majority of D Block inmates and those who had gone out into the cellhouse earlier had taken refuge in this particular area.

The cellhouse was now getting dark and still, no one was certain where the armed inmates were holed up. There were several possibilities. They could have retreated into the kitchen area, the basement, or the C Block service corridor. Bergen was now very concerned with locating the guards who had so mysteriously disappeared. He had expected to find their bodies scattered about the cellhouse when he peered down the corridors. The absence of this gave him hope they were alive.

After being certain the gallery was secure, he asked for additional men to cover all areas. After this was done, Bergen returned to D Block, where he opened direct communication with the front office and the warden via the gallery phone. He informed the warden that D Block and the entire west gun gallery were secure. The warden then instructed Bergen to stay in the gallery and make certain everything remained secure. This did not please Bergen, as he wanted to leave the gallery and lead an assault on the cellhouse to rescue his brother officers. The warden wasn't in agreement, however, and ordered Bergen to remain at his post and report regularly to the front office.

Bergen did as he was told and made several trips throughout the gallery to make certain all was secure. On one of his trips, he noticed three closely spaced holes in the lower steel portion of the gallery. The next time he returned, he noticed four holes instead of three. He became concerned, but because there were no sounds of shots from within the building, he dismissed it. A short time later he was again called to the phone. This time he saw five holes.

He suddenly realized what had happened to Officer Stites: he had been killed from outside, by his own men.

He called Mahan to inspect the holes, after cautioning him to avoid exposing himself to the window. The holes were smooth on the inside, indicating that the shot had exited into D Block. Curious, they took a coat and waved it in front of the same window. Instantly, they heard a shot from outside and there was a new hole in the wall, as well as in the coat. Bergen told the warden that they were being attacked by someone outside who fired whenever he saw action in the gallery near that window. A team was immediately sent to find, disarm, and remove whomever it might be.

If one can believe the officials' explanation, it was a drunk officer who had separated himself from the other guards. He had not heard the order not to shoot into those windows. The drunk officer was quickly removed from the island, but was never charged with any sort of crime. He was simply fired. This is a good example of the many men on the outside who wanted convict blood. Innocent or guilty, it was of no consequence, as long as they had a number and were incarcerated in D Block, the home of the incorrigibles.

We were fortunate (and are possibly alive today) because, upon reconstruction of the cellblock area used for housing federal incorrigibles, thousands of dollars were spent making the windows a very difficult, if not impossible, means of escape. These windows were extremely tough, with multiple bars, and this made it difficult to shoot a grenade directly into the block without it first hitting an offset bar, the interior frame, or some other obstacle, which would cause it to explode before penetrating. Had this not been the case, many of us would have died.

Because of the bars' toughness, their position, and the location from which the grenades were fired, it took several hours to establish obstruction-free access to the block.

During this time, dozens of grenades were fired, each of which covered the interior of the block with red-hot fragments, started fires, and stunned the inmates in close proximity to the explosions. Whitey Phillips was the first recipient of an unobstructed grenade.

Whitey was not a participant in the break, had never left his cell, and had had no knowledge of the impending break, yet his life was put into tremendous jeopardy simply because he was incarcerated in D Block. Whitey, lodged in the cell next to us, was in D Block for years—not for an escape, or its attempt, but because he had assaulted the warden with his fist for what he felt was unfair and selective tampering with his mail.

The grenade arched through a small opening in the window bars and exploded either on the cell front or inside, rupturing the water lines. Whitey, as the rest of us, in anticipation of the assault, had prepared his own area of protection. He had secured several mattresses and taken all his law books (acquired to overturn his conviction and sentence) and had piled them alongside his bed. This created a well-insulated cover, as his books were heavy and thick. When the grenade entered his cell and exploded, Whitey was hidden in his little cover. The explosion rocked the entire tier, fire belched from his cell, and the walls bowed from the tremendous concussion. Whitey was knocked unconscious and deafened, but was otherwise physically uninjured.

Jack, Bill, Sam, and I were stunned and totally disoriented, in addition to being unable to see or hear. We were, for a considerable time, convinced the grenade had exploded on the front bars of our own cell. When our reason returned, we were able to reconstruct what had actually occurred. We realized the grenade had exploded in Whitey's cell.

We repeatedly called to Whitey in the faint hope he was still alive. No response was forthcoming. We believed him dead and, in all probability, we would be next. The number of grenades entering the block without obstruction was increasing. There would have been more, but some were deflected without exploding, or fell short and detonated against the solid-faced isolation cells below.

With the explosion in Whitey's cell, we encountered a new problem. When the toilet and sink were destroyed, the water lines ruptured. This permitted a free and continuous flow of saltwater (water had to be hauled to the island by barge, so the toilets were plumbed for saltwater rather than fresh) down the tier. The tier soon became a river of water that was only slowed for a short period by the absorption of our mattress barricades. When the mattresses were saturated, each of the cells became inundated. Because we were unable to move or stand up, we were soon completely soaked. The wind also contributed to our misery; all the window glass had been blown out by the repeated bombings and rifle fire. We were now extremely cold, and our anxiety increased with each grenade, smoke bomb, and tear-gas exposure. To add to our discomfort, the saltwater irritated our skin.

Although detrimental in some respects, the broken plumbing and lack of glass in the windows did offer certain benefits. The mattresses, now waterlogged, were less subject to penetration by bullets or bomb fragments and no longer offered a source for fires. The tear gas and smoke quickly drifted out the broken windows, offering a welcome breath or two of fresh air.

The gun gallery was now secure, and the main cellhouse was enveloped in total darkness. All lights had been turned off and guards were dispatched by the warden to the catwalks outside the main building to offer the inmates a chance to surrender. This so infuriated Coy that he fired two shots at officers he could not see, but could hear. It was his defiant answer. After the shots were fired, the inmates realized it was a very serious mistake, in that they had given away their location. They also realized they were in a trap, boxed in and dead if an assault was initiated from the main gate. They had to get out.

They decided they must move from their corridor position and, if possible, make it into the kitchen area. Here, they could get a drink and food, and would have the opportunity to fight when the inevitable assault came. They cautiously moved toward the partially open corridor door, then hesitated, trying to determine if they could cross the few feet until they were under the gun gallery. Once under the gallery they would be safe from any fire and, if they were careful and lucky, could work their way back into the kitchen under the cover of darkness.

It was decided they had no choice except to try. They cautiously pushed the door open a few inches. Suddenly all hell broke loose. They were illuminated by a portable search-light and, as they desperately scrambled to get away from the door, all the guards in the gallery simultaneously opened fire. The volley was so intense that it slammed the corridor door shut.

After retreating from the door, the inmates decided to wait a couple of hours and try again, hoping to catch the guards unaware (thinking the inmates would not tempt fate again in the same way). Coy climbed up above the cells to see if he could get a shot at the searchlight. If they got the light, they might make it into the kitchen.

As Coy reached the top of the cells, Warden Johnston gave permission for the assault team to enter the cellhouse through the main gate. A team of twelve men, led by Lieutenant Faulk, was now inside the main cellhouse. They rapidly spread out and started a systematic search down each of the corridors. They were sure they had the armed inmates trapped in the service corridor and, by staying close to the cell fronts as they came down the corridors, were in no danger of being shot. The overhang from each of the tiers gave them protection from above, and the gun galleries adequately covered the ends of the cellblocks. If there was no one hidden in any of the cells, they would be in charge of the entire building except the C Block service corridor.

Coy, on top of the block, heard them enter but before he could get to the other end where he might have gotten a clear shot, they had dispersed and were under the overhang. In anger and frustration, Coy opened fire, shooting toward the D Block wall, hoping a shot would glance off and hit one or more guards.

When Coy started shooting, the guards in the gallery raked the top of the block with gunfire. The assault team retreated to the east end of the block, away from where the shots originated, and Coy made a mad dash to drop them inside the protective shelter of the service corridor.

Any hope of survival had ceased for the three inmates. They were caught in the corridor and their only escape now was not to the "free world," but in death. They gave up any hope of making it out of the corridor. Their only chance, and it wasn't much, was to surrender. If the guards did not kill them immediately, they would die in the gas chamber at San Quentin. They decided to retreat as deep into the corridor as possible and wait until the guards attempted to dislodge them, at which time they would make their last stand, killing as many guards as they could.

The assault team that had retreated to the east end of the block under Coy's fire restarted their relentless drive to capture the block and locate their fellow officers. As they moved toward the west gun gallery, each cell was inspected to make certain there would be no ambush. As they slowly progressed, they could hear moans emanating from the front cells. Carefully, they made their way toward the sounds. Upon reaching cells 402 and 403, they found their severely wounded friends lying in a bloody mass. It was obvious many needed immediate medical aid. Guards were dispatched to obtain stretchers.

Before proceeding with the transport of the victims, however, it was imperative to first make certain that the building was secured. At approximately 10:15 p.m. Lieutenant Faulk closed and locked the D Block entrance. The C Block service corridor was also secured, thus eliminating the possibility that Coy, Cretzer, or Hubbard could escape into the cellhouse. There was still fight in the inmates, however. Coy, sometime during this period, managed to get back to the top of C Block and shoot Lieutenant Roberts in the shoulder and back. He escaped into the corridor's depths before the guns in the gallery could pick him off. All open cells in the block were closed and locked. The cellhouse was secured. Guards and spotlights were stationed so Coy could not again get above the block to shoot.

Cell 402 was now opened, and removal of the officers begun. In 402 they found Captain Weinhold shot in the chest, Officer Corwin, in the face (with much of his jaw shot away), Officer Miller in the arm, and Officer Lageson grazed by a shot to his head. Officers Burdette and Bristow were unharmed. In cell 403, Lieutenant Simpson was found to have a gunshot wound to the chest and abdomen, Officer Baker had been shot in both legs, and Sundstrom was uninjured. The fact that these officers had been shot at approximately 2:30 p.m. and left unattended for eight hours, plus the very nature of the way Cretzer had so mercilessly tried to slaughter them, seemed to drive the guards into a frenzy of bitter anger.

20 The Final Hours

Sometime during the night, a new dimension was added to the retribution being showered upon the inmates of D Block. There would be a lull in the storm of destruction, and when we were beginning to feel slightly less apprehensive, a voice would call out, asking for a certain individual. Those called for had either been seen earlier in the main cellhouse (at the start of the break) or had been, in the past, a source of particular aggravation or irritation to the staff. It didn't take us long to realize that answering these inquiries only served to bring down a full-scale assault on the speaker. When the names of Jack, Bill, Sam, and I were called, we did not respond.

We knew they were aware of our location directly behind the bombarded windows, and it was simply a probe to determine if we were still alive. When we failed to respond, the bombardment began again.

Another tactic employed during the night was to halt the assault and demand that we surrender "the rifle." It was a nonexistent weapon and our reply that there was no such weapon in the block was their justification to continue to attempt to kill us. Asking for the rifle was simply a cover-up. It was a ploy and farce to gain credibility for their actions.

In the service corridor, the inmates realized that the rescue of the injured guards from cells 402 and 403 ended any vestige of hope they had retained. It was now all-out war, and the only victory they could possibly salvage would be in the satisfaction achieved from killing more guards. Surrender at this point was out of the question, even if they remotely considered the possibility. Thus their decision was to retreat as deep into the interior of the dark, damp, cold corridor as possible, erect a fort of planks from the overhead walkways, and force the guards to literally dig them out. They were certain that, when the assault came, it would be through the corridor doors at either end, or both.

Surprisingly, the inevitable attack did not come as they had anticipated and prepared for. Shortly before 11 p.m., an assault team assembled on the cellhouse roof and began dropping canisters of tear gas down the ventilator shafts that opened directly into the depths of the service corridor. The inmates were able to handle this portion of the attack, however, having acquired several gas masks from the gun gallery. To the dismay of the institution officials, it soon became evident the tactic was unsuccessful, which prompted their next plan of action.

This time, fragmentation bombs were dropped down the same shafts. The inmates were now in grave danger of being killed by either the fragmentation or the tremendous concussion, and this necessitated that they find still better protection. Driven to abandon their hastily constructed barricade, they crawled through and over fallen planks and plumbing and electrical lines. The corridor was actually demolished by the force of the bombs. The inmates returned to the cutoff and crawled into the tunnel that served as a connection between the east and west portions of the block.

Here they were protected by the foot or more of concrete above their heads. They were sheltered from fragments because the tunnel dipped down below floor level and there were no ventilator shafts over their heads. This area also afforded them an opportunity to fire at the end doors leading into the corridor from the cellhouse. This was neither a way out nor a solution to their problems, but only a brief respite in their unchangeable date with destiny. The guards realized that, once again, their tactics had failed. They were angry, tired, and frustrated, and felt the only solution was a direct assault on the corridor.

Associate Warden Miller and Lieutenant Faulk approached Warden Johnston with this plan. The warden, however, did not agree. He felt it was exactly what the armed inmates wanted, and that this endeavor would be too risky and costly to the guards. He informed the assault squad that a team of combat Marines was soon to arrive and they were bringing a new type explosive device that might drive the inmates out without exposing anyone, except the inmates, to death or injury.

Associate Warden Miller and Faulk were not overjoyed with his answer. They felt he was stalling, and they wanted to get this trio themselves. It was, as future events showed, a wise decision and one I am sure saved the lives of many guards.

Throughout the night, the deadly attack continued. Tear gas and fragmentation bombs rained into the corridor until the entire cellhouse was filled with gas and the smell of burnt cordite. The inmates huddled in the tunnel were cold and stunned, but determined to die rather than surrender. Coy and Cretzer, in complete frustration at being unable to get a shot at anyone, would periodically crawl from the tunnel, despite the danger, to take a few quick shots at the ventilators, in the hope their blind shots might find one of their tormentors.

On Friday, in the early morning hours, under the direction of Marine Buckner, a hole was cut in the roof directly over the cutoff and the tunnel. Through this opening the assault squad unleashed an incredible rain of demolition bombs onto the concrete directly over the inmates' heads. Although the bombs failed to penetrate the thick layer of concrete, the tremendous, repeated concussions drove the dazed and stunned men from their shelter.

Dawn without Respite

Friday was a repetition of what had transpired during the night. The only factor in our favor was that the attacks seemed a little less frequent and intense. They were still sufficiently vicious, however, to make us doubt our chances for survival. We could at times hear bits of conversation from the catwalk outside, which often increased our anxieties. Once we heard mention of the use of flame-throwers to drive us out into the open. On another occasion, we were threatened with the destruction of the block by dropping it onto our heads. This was not quite understood at the time, but later was made very clear to us.

In mid-afternoon, we could hear Bergen calling Bob Stroud's name. Every inmate was hopeful Bob would not respond, as it had been quiet for a short period of time and we felt that if he responded, the attack would commence again. After some hesitation, Bob did answer. He was told by Bergen that the outside shooting was going to cease and the inmates could get up and move about if they remained away from the front of the cells. He stated that any inmate who was seen at the cell door, or who ventured out into the tier, would be shot without question or hesitation.

Bob, as spokesman for the block, relayed this information to those inmates who had not heard it. There were many opinions as to whether it was a trap or in reality the end of the ordeal. Many wanted to believe it was safe, primarily because Lieutenant Bergen had a reputation for honesty and fairness. On the other hand, in view of what had occurred during the night, many were very skeptical and believed it to be a trap. We were among those who did not believe in the offer and chose to remain in what had proven to be a relatively safe position.

After probably thirty minutes, Stroud again called out to the block that everything seemed safe and that he had been up and moving about since he had last talked to us. This convinced most of us it was safe, and we too stood up to relieve the cold and cramps that had settled in our backs and legs. The soft hum of conversation soon spread between cells, as inmates checked to see if their friends had survived. I moved to the back of the cell and stood up on the bed frame to get a view of what might be happening outside.

Suddenly, the conversation about destroying the building was made clear. Just below us, with its bow guns aimed and manned, was a U.S. Navy or Coast Guard cutter. We knew then for certain they were not bluffing.

The situation remained stable and quiet for possibly an hour, when suddenly we heard the now all-too-familiar pop, followed by the explosion of a rifle grenade in the window. The bombardment commenced once again, with tear gas, rifle grenades, and rifle fire. We were caught completely off guard. The absence of shooting and Lieutenant Bergen's assurance had given us a false sense of security.

Many inmates felt that Bergen had set us up for this assault. I honestly do not believe this, however, as it also caught the guards in the gallery just as unaware. Bergen's angry voice could be heard during the height of the attack, demanding to know who had given the order to open fire and insisting that it be stopped. After what seemed a tremendously long time, the attack was brought to a halt. We were reassured that it had been a mistake and would not occur again. As you can imagine, this was met with considerable doubt. The inmates of the block had hit the deck at the start and remained that way for many more hours.

Back in the Main Cellhouse

The wreckage to the west end of the utility corridor was so extensive that it was almost impassable, thus the inmates retreated to the east end. Here they gathered whatever planks or other materials they could to give themselves as much shelter as possible, as the fragmentation bombs were still being dropped into the corridor. The assault squad changed their tactics and began dropping highly explosive demolition bombs down the ventilators directly into the corridor. This caused the inmates to open fire at the ventilators. It was a lost cause and again, the inmates were forced to retreat to the tunnel. Again and again, this series of tactics was repeated.

By this time, no one believed the inmates could have possibly survived. A halt was called to the bombardment around noon to determine whether there was any sign of survivors in the corridor. During this lull, the inmates in the yard, C Block, and on Broadway were evacuated from their areas and lodged in A Block. Officer Stucker and the inmates from the basement and kitchen area were also freed, and these inmates were locked up with the others. The entire prison population, with the exception of D Block and those in the corridor, was identified and accounted for.

After relocating and securing the general population, a watch was instituted to determine if anyone had survived. The corridor remained quiet the entire afternoon, except for the occasional bomb dropped down the ventilators in an effort to elicit a response. When none came, a meeting was conducted with the warden to seek permission to invade the corridor. Before the warden could come to a decision, however, a report was sent to him that a shot had been fired at Officer Joe Steere. It was a rifle shot fired blindly through the heavy metal service corridor in the hope of killing another guard. This gave the officials their answer. At least one inmate was alive and still wanted to fight.

At the warden's suggestion, a last effort was made to entice the survivor or survivors to surrender. The answer: silence. When no response was forthcoming, several officers stepped up and flooded the inside with bullets, then the heavy metal door was closed and locked for the remainder of the night. Throughout the night the corridor was quiet apart from an occasional bomb dropped down the ventilators and the dripping of water from broken plumbing. Not a sound was heard from the trapped inmates.

Darkness was now approaching and portable lights had been set up to illuminate the windows. All was quiet in D Block. The silence that filled the night was broken only by an occasional shot, to inform us they were still waiting and watching, or by the explosion of a bomb in the C Block corridor, giving Coy, Cretzer, and Hubbard the same message.

It was a very long night. The inmates were physically and mentally exhausted. In some aspects, the quiet was very hard to cope with because we were not convinced that it was over. The sound of the occasional bomb exploding in the main cellhouse was a constant reminder that it was still possible for all hell to break loose once again. Instead of relaxing us, the quiet made us even more aware of what should have been minor problems.

We were very cold and extremely miserable from lying in the water, and the freezing wind blowing in through the broken windows multiplied our discomfort. Our skin was very irritated from the saltwater, and we were starving. At times, we would drop off to sleep, only to suddenly awaken, heart pounding, gripped with anxiety and fear. The only thing one could seem to think about was what was going to happen next. The fact that bombs were still being exploded on occasion in the main cellhouse gave us hope our friends were still alive, but we knew if they continued to fight, it was just going to prolong the confrontation. What we did not know were the facts about the shooting of the guards (in cells 402 and 403, and in the towers) and, therefore, could not know that the trio (Coy, Cretzer, and Hubbard) had no other alternative at this point.

At the first light of day on Saturday, an assault team led by Associate Warden Miller came to retake the corridor. The metal door was unlocked and still another final offer to surrender was issued. Again, only silence. The assault team once again filled the corridor with hundreds of bullets and buckshot before they started their invasion.

Three of the officers entered the damp, dark, muck-and-sewage-filled area. Using a portable searchlight, they slowly and cautiously moved forward, .45-caliber pistols and machine guns ready for any event. Reaching the first of the barricades, the officers found the body of Coy. He was still wearing the captain's uniform and was sitting with a rifle pointed at the door. He had been riddled by several bullets, which had ripped their way through his head and body. Death and the dream of escape had come earlier for Coy than it had for his friends and companions. His emaciated body was cold and stiff.

As the team advanced deeper into the corridor, Cretzer's body was found amid the wreckage. He too had suffered multiple gunshot wounds to his head and body. He was also cold. In the filth, beyond Coy and Cretzer, the body of Hubbard was located. In the sewage near his body was the knife he had carried out of the kitchen.

He was the last to die, as his body was still warm.

Sometime in the early morning we were startled by a sudden outburst of rifle and shotgun fire in the main cell-house. Hundreds of rounds were fired as rapidly as possible. Each of us instinctively knew that it was over and our friends were dead. The block was suddenly silent and quiet. I believe each of us gave thought at that time to these friends whose dreams of escape had now been fulfilled.

I believe the reader must give serious thought in an attempt to determine what drove these men to such extremes. Were they filled with fear and terror at the thought of dying under these circumstances? Was their hate due to the regimentation and monotony of daily routines that were designed to punish, humiliate, and break men physically, mentally, and morally? Did they think of home, family, and loved ones as they waited to die? Or did they feel that being dead was preferable to continuing the existence that was called "living" at Alcatraz?

To me, it is apparent they simply chose to die.

21 Survivors

For several hours, nothing was heard in the block until the silence was broken by the sound of the D Block door being unlocked. Suddenly, the loud, harsh, commanding voice of Assistant Warden Miller was heard giving instructions to the force that was now going to invade the block. We could hear him instructing the squad to be careful where they walked, as there were many unexploded rifle grenades scattered among the broken acoustic tiles, burnt or smoldering bedding, spent shell casings, and empty tear-gas canisters that littered the floor. Before letting the force enter the block, he had some instructions and advice for us inmates also.

We were to "get on the floor, away from the door, and remain there until instructed to do otherwise." He also stated, and I quote, "Do anything else and we will blow your ass off!" It was quite evident to every inmate that if Miller's instructions were not carried out as ordered, there would be no question about what would happen—we would be shot. After complying with his orders, we could hear the sound of many officers making their way through the litter to position themselves. After each guard had reached his assigned position, we were given more instructions.

As our names were called, we were to stand up, remove every article of clothing, and then wait until given orders to step slowly out on the tier, arms extended straight out so they were the first part of the body to emerge from the cell. We were then to proceed to the handrail. There, we were to bend over the rail with our arms on the outside and remain in that position until ordered otherwise.

The first name to be called was Bob Stroud. He did as instructed and everything went as planned. I can recall, as my name was called, being extremely nervous and concerned that I might trip as I stepped over our barricade and be shot as a result. Carefully following instructions, I stood up, stripped, and slowly moved out onto the tier. If I had known the sight that was going to be presented when I stepped out, I would have been far more nervous, if that was possible.

The entire flat was covered with armed, nervous, and tired guards. Each guard had been assigned an inmate to cover as he stepped from his cell. The guard assigned to me was a stranger, possibly from another institution. He was armed with a shotgun and was so nervous that I could see the gun trembling in his hands. His nervousness convinced me the best thing I could do would be to follow instructions to the letter, bend over as told, and not look at him again.

After each inmate had been called from his cell and had

draped himself over the handrail, we were instructed to side-step slowly to the far end of the tier. This permitted several unarmed guards to come up on the tier and strip the first cell of all its contents. As the cells were stripped, individuals were then moved down the tier, searched, and locked into cells with instructions to sit down and not move. Finally it was done. Every inmate and cell had been searched and every inmate was accounted for.

There were no deaths or serious injuries to any inmate of the block. Our mattress barricades had served us well, especially Whitey Phillips, who had escaped unscathed except for some loss of hearing. We had all survived what should have been a massacre.

Back in our cells, it was very difficult to believe we had survived. There had to be someone special who had protected us through this ordeal and we each knew who it was. As can be expected, we were all very anxious to learn what had happened to our friends. Many, who had not gone into the cellhouse, were totally unaware of what had taken place. But when we looked at the guards, we knew that now was the time for silence, a time to be seen but not heard, as it was obvious that many guards were still angry.

Shortly after we were resettled in our cells, a demolition team entered the block to remove the unexploded, but still deadly, rifle grenades. A string was attached to the fin of each grenade, a path was cleared, and each grenade was dragged to an area where it could be disposed of. While I was standing on the tier, I counted seventeen unexploded grenades in our cell area. I doubt that there were many more toward the gallery; the windows there had escaped heavy attack because of their close proximity to the guards in the gallery.

It took several hours for the guards to clean up the debris from the floor and tiers, and to stop the flow of water. While this work was being done, we were sitting naked and silent in our cells. No one dared to comment that we were freezing from the wind. Finally, Jughead issued an order to give each inmate a blanket, which warded off the cold somewhat. It was the first act of consideration that had been extended to us since the takeover of the block. It seemed to break the overt hostility the guards were showing to us, at least to a degree.

Later in the evening, after the block had been cleaned up, we were each brought a mattress, an additional blanket, and a change of clothing. It was wonderful to change into clean, dry clothing and have the prospect of sleeping a full, undisturbed night's sleep without fear of bombs or rifle fire. We were brought soup, sandwiches, and coffee—the first food since Thursday at noon.

Later, one at a time, we were permitted to take a quick shower to remove the accumulated saltwater residue from our skin. It was wonderful to be relieved from the tensions that had plagued the preceding thirty-plus hours. It was over. We knew we would have to face the consequences of whatever action we had taken during the break, but didn't mind, as we were still busy being thankful to be alive.

Shortly after we had cleaned up, we heard the door of a cell racked open and Sam Shockley was removed from the block to be incarcerated in a special cell prepared for him in A Block. It was the last time I saw Sam until I testified, on his behalf, concerning his sanity in court in San Francisco.

22 Taking Stock

I honestly feel there were many injustices committed during, and as a result of, this escape attempt (if it can truly be called that, and not simply a very elaborate and well-planned mutual suicide). The prosecution and execution of Sam Shockley was one of them.

I must admit that I cannot recall, at this late date, whether or not Sam was with us when we heard the shots in the main cellhouse, but there could not have been an interval of longer than ten minutes between the time of our re-entry into the block and the bloody revenge carried out by Cretzer. I do not believe that Sam was a party to that frenzied shooting, nor was there evidence to prove it.

Consider: if Sam had indeed witnessed the slaughter, and then came into our cell as calm and composed as he did, this calmness would then tend to indicate he was completely and undeniably insane. From the moment he came to help us, until the entire confrontation was ended, he was never more than three feet away from Jack, Bill, or me. During this time Sam did not indicate that he participated in or witnessed the event. In the remote chance that the administration was correct, however, it only verifies the theory that Sam was insane, as no rational individual in control of his emotions could have witnessed or participated in that scene—an attempted massacre of nine men—and, within a matter of minutes, attain and present such a calm composure.

Our federal penal system should have tried to help Sam during the earlier years, when it was obvious to officials as well as inmates that this man was, day by day and year by year, losing all control over his emotions and mental faculties. Instead, he was ignored, isolated, and left to deteriorate into a state where he was unaccountable for and unable to control his behavior.

I feel that the prison officials should have been held responsible for any part Sam played, although I do not believe that Sam was any more responsible for the shooting of the guards, or for the actions of Joe Cretzer, than I was. Executing Sam was equivalent to killing a mentally ill child who strikes a parent in the process of a temper tantrum. His death by execution was a travesty of justice and should be viewed as such.

I truly believe that Sam Shockley was a victim of the break, not a knowledgeable co-conspirator. I also believe that the U.S. government put to death, by execution, a man who was not only insane, but who was the victim of angered, frustrated, and revengeful people who wanted "convict blood" for the death and injuries sustained by their fellow workers during a tragic incident.

And then there was the vicious and indiscriminate bombardment of D Block.

There are many excuses and explanations offered for what took place during those many hours, but none will stand up under careful scrutiny. Not only do they vary in degree, some statements even contradict each other. Let us examine the facts.

The primary reasoning and/or excuse for the thirty hours of bombardment of D Block was based on the statement there was a gun inside. First, it is hard to conceive that guards who were observant enough to scrawl the names of the participants of the break on their cell wall, and who were in the best position to observe who entered or left D Block, failed to see the three inmates and their weapons retreat from the block after the confrontation when the D Block portion of the gun gallery was recaptured—the last time a weapon was fired in D Block by the inmates.

How did the uninjured officers in cells 402 and 403 fail to hear the three inmates conversing and moving in the corridor when they were waiting to ambush the guards as they entered the cellhouse portion of the gun gallery? Or when they were moving into position to attempt to leave the corridor in hopes of fleeing into the kitchen? There was a vent in the cell just above floor level that opened into where the inmates were waiting. Had there been enough light, the guards could have actually seen them, and the inmates were not concerned about being heard because they thought the guards were all dead, having been assured of this fact by Carnes.

And how did they account for the fact the first assault team was forced to retreat from Coy's rifle fire coming from the top of C Block? If the rifle was in D Block, then how was Lieutenant Roberts shot while crossing Broadway?

Of still further interest would be an accounting of how either the pistol or the rifle could have been in D Block, when these very weapons were fired on the roof attack team as they dropped bombs into the C Block service corridor.

And why were there no reports of gunfire for hours from D Block by any of the guards who controlled the gun gallery? It was said shots were fired out the window of D Block, yet those inside the block—as well as those in the gun gallery—neither heard these shots nor saw any muzzle flashes.

Knowing for a fact (and completely confident) that there was no gun in the block, Bob Stroud offered to strip naked and walk to the center of D Block as a willing hostage while officers entered the block to search for the supposed gun. Bob was not a man who would jeopardize his own life for others (as high officials of the prison system both recognized and admitted). Stroud would not have taken the risk, knowing full well that he would die under the guns of the armed officers, if there had been any chance of the "legendary" gun appearing. Yet his offer was flatly rejected.

Why, when the names selected to call were supposed to have been of those seen in the main cellhouse during the initial part of the break, did they call such individuals as Harmon Waley? This inmate never once left his cell during the entire encounter. Could it have been simply in the name of revenge for his past encounters and differences with the keepers of Alcatraz? What better opportunity to eliminate those particularly disliked incorrigibles?

I also believe that the escapees' failure to release Whitey Franklin was a good indication that no one in D Block had been aware of the break prior to its occurrence. Had Whitey or Sam Shockley known of the plans, they certainly would not have participated in the riot in March; Whitey was in solitary for his participation and Sam (along with the rest of us) could have been, had there been enough solitary cells available. If Sam was to have been a key figure in helping Coy enter the gun gallery, he would not have risked being placed in solitary by smashing and setting fire to his cell. Whitey, too, would have refrained from joining in.

I find it very difficult to dismiss all these occurrences and coincidences. I honestly believe they were attempting to kill every inmate who had in any degree been involved in the break, as well as those most disliked on general principles. I feel the attempt was made as retribution for previous insults or injuries incurred by guards and administration.

It is also my opinion that it was an attempt to magnify the number of inmates involved and thus divert attention away from the fact that, despite the hundreds of thousands of dollars spent, the so-called impregnable security of Alcatraz had been penetrated. Those who for years had enjoyed and basked in the reputation and prestige of being the "keepers of America's most dangerous convicts" had been tarnished and soiled by the audacity of the very inmates they had brutalized and degraded over the years.

I feel the sustained and unwarranted attack on D Block was motivated not only by the genuine anger of some guards following what they believed to be reliable information, but also by the many bruised and battered egos that had been deflated and deglamorized, as had the invincibility of the security of Alcatraz.

23 New Beginning

It took several months before any semblance of normality returned to the prison. There was much bitterness and anger on both sides. Guards and inmates alike were tense, mistrusting, and aware that any minor confrontation could flare into another bloody uprising. Everyone was very cognizant that each side must be careful not to upset the delicate balance that now prevailed, but there was far more antagonism on the part of the inmates than the guards.

This delicate and unstable situation was handled with great expertise by Associate Warden Miller. He made certain that the practice of harassing inmates over infractions of small rules was stopped. He improved the quality and quantity of food and made several other minor concessions. These concessions were not meant to be nor interpreted as signs of weakness on the part of the administration, but rather as a means to let the population know that many of the petty rules were not significant and to enforce them did nothing to alleviate the tension that had engulfed the prison.

After all, how important can the failure to button the top of your shirt be?

Inmates and guards alike realized that unless we were to continue to exist in a state of nervous tension, both sides would need to make concessions. As time passed, the sullenness and anger lessened, and the situation returned to relative normalcy. Both sides had learned lessons. The inmates realized there were no extremes the officials would not employ to ensure the inescapability of the prison. Administration learned that there was a time when pettiness, degradation, and humiliation must stop, or others (like Coy, Cretzer, and Hubbard) would reach the point where life was no longer important.

I remained in D Block for several more months, which gave me considerable time to think about my future. I realized that escaping was now an utter impossibility. I would not, for years, be allowed to work in any area that was not "under the gun." I also knew there would never be a chance for Jack and I to work in the same location, since we were both considered "hot" and officials would keep a very close watch on us. Although I realized that the dream of escape was certainly far from reality, I had not actually given up all hope just yet. I did realize I had been burned twice, and was not willing to trust anyone except Jack. There was no choice but to let time pass and hope that the future would reveal still another chance, somehow, some way.

Upon being released from D Block I was given the choice of going to work in the industries to earn the $150 I needed to pay for the damages I had created in my cell, or remaining in continuous lockup. I chose to go back to work in the laundry. I was again assigned to work on the mangle. Life went on day by day, and my only accomplishment was that, after approximately eighteen months, I had repaid the institution the money I owed.

It was an exceptionally depressing period for me. I was watched day and night. Old friends were often reluctant to associate with me for any length of time for fear the officials would assume there was an escape plot in the making. In retrospect, I can understand their position. Many had put in sufficient years without trouble or loss of good time and were hopeful of a transfer to a less restrictive prison. All had long ago given up any idea of escape. It hurt to know that because I wanted out, I had in turn become a threat to the future of my friends. I realized that some of them were ashamed of their actions, but an old axiom of prison life was "protect yourself because no one else will." It was a saying that I never believed in but, as years passed, I began to learn its truth.

I became somewhat of a loner, never talking to anyone except for short, open conversations because I did not want to be part of anything that would be detrimental to the future of others. I played a great deal of handball and saw little of Jack because he spent most of his weekends in his cell, away from our former companions. It was a very lonely period, but after a year, things began to improve.

After a period of time, Jack and I were allowed to share a short time together, walking and talking, on the weekends. Other inmates were becoming less apprehensive about being seen in our company, but security was not relaxed to any noticeable degree. It was a very desperate time in my life. I was again in a state of limbo, as my hopes for escape had obviously dwindled; security was so close, it was uncomfortable and the time I could associate with my friend and partner was very restricted. During this period, I began to associate with "Lifetime Murphy," an old-timer who had served twenty-six years and was soon to be transferred to Leavenworth, from where he expected to be paroled within five years.

Indirectly, through my friendship with Murphy, and his position as the Catholic altar boy, many dramatic changes were to occur in my life. I became better acquainted with Father Clark, the Catholic chaplain for Alcatraz. It was this trusted and respected man who influenced my life in many ways and was ultimately responsible for my changed outlook on life. Father Clark was always seeking ways to make the inmate's life better. His good advice could be depended upon, and inmates were certain of his confidentiality, with never a breach, regardless of pressure used by the administration. The inmates considered him to be one of us. After services, he spent Sundays walking the yard, unescorted, with the inmates. We were his "boys." During my period of severe depression, I had attended a couple of services. This was not because I had changed, but because I hoped to change my image in the view of administration. I was still very escape-minded.

After my having associated with Murphy for a short time, it became apparent that Father Clark was seeking me out to walk with more frequently. I am sure this can be partially attributed to Murphy's telling him what a tough time it was for me. Our conversations were very seldom of a religious nature, usually centering on such sports as baseball and boxing, which he knew I was interested in.

For several visits, our conversation remained in this area, until one day he asked me to tell him about my family. When he learned we had been estranged for years, he was very concerned and wanted to know why. He found it difficult to believe that my family, who could see the prison daily with little effort, had not written or seen me during my years in captivity. He wanted to immediately contact my family and effect a reconciliation, if possible. I refused to allow it, as I felt they had suffered more than their share of shame and humiliation for my unlawful acts. Additionally, I had not resolved to serve my sentence, and re-establishing a relationship with my family would leave me, I felt, accountable and obligated not to try to escape.

After my refusal, he again asked me to reconsider and, reluctantly, I consented, but in my heart I already knew my decision: I was no longer a part of their lives and it was best it remain that way.

All this talk about family had started me thinking about my mother. I began to wonder if she was still alive and destitute, and could use the twenty to thirty dollars I was now earning each month. I decided to ask Father Clark to attempt to locate her, but only on the condition that under no circumstances would my family be contacted. He was agreeable and enthusiastic because he felt if I had someone, even if only an alcoholic mother, my chances of rehabilitation would increase. I could give him no more information than I related earlier in this book. He was confident that it was sufficient because he had made many friends and contacts during his years in San Francisco.

Father Clark was somewhat over-optimistic. He utilized many of his contacts and friends, but to no avail. It was as though she had disappeared from the face of the earth. But he would not give up on his determined quest to bring someone into my life. During this period, the approval for Murphy's transfer was received. This meant that Father Clark would soon be without an altar boy.

I was asked by Murphy if I would consider replacing him, but I refused for several reasons. First, I had not been a churchgoer in previous years. Second, I felt it would be hypocritical of me to take the position when I was not at all certain about my feelings for the Church and its functions. And third, I was concerned about peer pressure. Many inmates felt if you had any religious beliefs or affiliations, you were weak and possibly a stoolie. It had taken Murphy several years to overcome this stigma in the minds of many inmates. I had not, at that time, reached a point of maturity where I could disregard the reputation and credibility I had as a solid inmate. I wanted to change my image in the view of administration, but not at the possible expense of my good reputation with the inmates.

I was also approached by Father Clark to take the position, if only on a temporary basis, until I could be replaced. Father Clark was very understanding when I refused, as he knew the code that prevailed among a large portion of the population. As time went on, Father Clark continued in his efforts to locate my mother and I began to have many second thoughts concerning my refusal of the altar boy position. Many nights I lay awake, thinking about my decision. One thought that repeatedly crossed my mind was, *Why do you have to prove yourself?* I had always been a good convict and had no intention of changing, so why was I concerned about what others thought? It was a question I could not find a logical answer for, and the more I considered it, the more I realized I had nothing to prove and possibly much to gain. I also considered the fact that I had been burned twice by my fellow inmates and no one seemed to care. After a great amount of thought, I decided to take the position. It was, in all probability, the first mature decision I had made in all my years of prison. Father Clark was delighted, even though he was aware of my mixed feelings about the Church.

The first Sunday that I served Mass was a very difficult day for me. After services were concluded, I went to the recreation yard to face whatever ridicule or antagonism I might receive from my fellow inmates. To my surprise, I was treated as cordially as always. This continued to be the case during my remaining years at Alcatraz.

After I had served with Father Clark for several months, he told me that he had been given a temporary assignment at another institution, but would return in a few months. He asked if I would continue to serve with his replacement until his return, and I consented. The following week, Father Clark brought his replacement to the island. He was a young and dedicated priest—a younger version of Father Clark.

Upon the word of his predecessor, Father Hastings was readily accepted by the inmates. Shortly before departing for his temporary assignment, Father Clark informed me that even though it seemed hopeless, Father Hastings was going to see if he could make any connections that would help locate my mother. I had by now given up hope, but felt there was nothing to lose if they wished to continue the search. After an absence of three months, Father Clark returned and resumed his Alcatraz duties in conjunction with Father Hastings. There had still been no word of my mother.

Approximately a month later, during Mass, it appeared to me that Father Clark had something on his mind that was disturbing him. He asked me to meet him on the yard in the early afternoon. I was concerned and nervous. My intuition told me it concerned my mother. I felt the news was not going to be good. I went to the yard after lunch and was surprised to see both Father Clark and Father Hastings walking alone and in deep conversation. When they saw me they waved for me to join them. From the look on their faces, I knew before I heard the words. Father Clark gently informed me that Father Hastings had discovered my mother had been dead for several years. Although I had felt this might be the news, I found myself stunned and over-whelmed with sorrow.

Father Hastings had found this information by going through untold numbers of death certificates. She had died at age forty-four in a county hospital in San Francisco and was buried in a pauper's grave. Her love and/or need for alcohol had killed her at an age when her life could and should have been at its best. What I did not learn until later was that Father Hastings had also gone to see my father in Oakland in an effort to attain a lead to my mother's where-abouts. I never was sure whether Father Hastings had not understood that he was not to contact my family, or whether he felt he could get the information needed without revealing my whereabouts.

Somehow, whatever his good intentions, my family soon learned he was doing the search on my behalf. This led to a quick request on the part of my father to leave and not return. The antagonism and anger were still present despite the passage of years. Father Hastings left, feeling sure that he had made a terrible mistake that opened old wounds. He did not know how to tell me about the reception he had received and had decided to wait for Father Clark's return.

About three weeks after his visit, Father Hastings received a call from my father, inviting him to dinner. The reception this time was far more cordial and much of the antagonism was gone. Father Hastings was asked not to inform me about the dinner or the fact they were concerned about me in any manner. It must have been a very emotional evening, as Father Hastings told them I was at Alcatraz, had been there for several years, and at this point was hopelessly incarcerated, with little incentive to go on. My asking Father Clark to search for my mother was a last, desperate effort to add some meaning to my life. Though I had never admitted it, even to myself, it was true.

I was saddened by the news, even though so many years had passed since the last time I had seen my mother when I was a small child. My life was so empty that I had let myself build up hope that I would have someone in the outside world to communicate and share with. It was a hard blow to handle, even though I had known at the start it would probably be hopeless. For several weeks, I struggled with my disappointment and anger. I was angry at myself for not having tried to locate her when I was free, and disappointed for the selfish reason that I was still alone.

Then, one Sunday afternoon on a cold and windy day, the door to my cell was suddenly opened. I stepped out on the tier and was told I had a visitor. I informed the guard it was a mistake, as I had no one on the approved visitor or correspondence list. I went back inside my cell and it was promptly relocked. Shortly thereafter, my cell was once again opened and I was again informed I had a visitor and was to report to the visiting area.

I protested, but was told to report as ordered; if it was a mistake, I would be sent back to my cell. Realizing that further argument was useless, I proceeded to the visiting area. Despite my better judgment, I began to hope it was not a mistake, but could not imagine who could possibly come to see me. I was certain it was not my family.

When I reached the visiting area, I saw that two of the visiting booths were occupied. I tried unsuccessfully to peer through the small slot of glass at the unoccupied booths as I passed. Because of their construction, it was impossible to see anyone. I reported to the officer in charge and was directed to a booth. When I hesitated, he asked me if I was #586 and I said I was. He then told me to get to my booth before I wasted any further visiting time.

It is still very vivid in my mind, the feeling that I experienced as I walked toward that booth. I was so nervous I was trembling, worried that it was a mistake, yet more afraid to face whoever sat behind that glass.

When I reached the booth, I immediately peered through the glass. There sat my father and stepmother, crying as though their hearts would break. From their location, they had been able to see me as I approached the visiting area along the tier. It was more than they could bear and they simply went to pieces. All the bitterness and antagonism of the past years were washed away with that flood of tears, to be replaced by love, kindness, and encouragement. I was nervous and overjoyed, yet trembling so violently, the visitor guard came over, helped me into my chair, and handed me the phone. My first words must have been indistinguishable, as my mouth was so dry and the tears so profuse that I could hardly speak. It took several minutes before we were able to begin a rational conversation and this was periodically interrupted by unexpected spells of crying on both sides.

Gone was the tough, independent, and self-sufficient convict and in his place was a joyful, emotional man who was determined never to inflict pain, hurt, or suffering on his family again, regardless of the circumstances. In that moment, when I saw their tears and anguish, a new man was born. A man who was determined to forget the ways of the past and use every fiber of his body to make amends for his mistakes. I knew that nothing I could do would remove the pain they were experiencing seeing me in this infamous place, but I was never going to complain again. Instead, I would make a wholehearted effort to do something that would give them hope and peace about the future.

In that short span of time, any thoughts of escape or suicide vanished. Nothing I would do in the future would hurt them. The visiting time passed so rapidly that it was impossible to ask or answer all the questions that were racing through all of our minds. As they were told their time was over, the tears again began to flow on both sides. They assured me they would be back in the near future and would, on their way out, fill out the necessary forms to be permitted to correspond with me by mail.

It is difficult to explain how I felt. I was filled with sorrow that I could not also go, yet when I returned to my cell, there was a feeling of warmth and peace, and a degree of content that I had not known for many long years. As I looked about the cellhouse, it did not seem as grim and dreary as it had just a short time earlier. I guess I was looking at my surroundings through rose-tinted glasses, as nothing had changed in the prison, but certainly had in my heart and mind. My entire attitude had changed. I now had someone who cared, existed, and who would share my future, regardless of what it held. I was not just a lonely number in prison anymore, but a man with a caring family.

The following Sunday I was again called for a visit. I felt it was a mistake, but this time did not argue. When I arrived at the visiting area, I was informed that the warden had given special permission for me to have a second visit in the same month. This was unheard of, as Warden Johnston was a firm enforcer of any and all regulations in the books. Why he broke his own rule for this occasion I have never understood. Possibly it was because he was aware of how desperate I had been prior to my previous visit, or perhaps he felt a little kindness on his part would have a beneficial effect on me, one of his most incorrigible and rebellious inmates. If either of these were his reasons, he was correct.

I hurried to the visiting booth with great expectations of seeing my parents again. I was unprepared for what I encountered, however. Sitting there was a beautiful young lady and a handsome, large man. I was shocked as the realization came: this was my baby sister and the young man was her husband, Tom. It was difficult for me to grasp that Kay was not the same little child I had last seen. Somehow in my mind, I had not realized that during all the years I had been imprisoned, she was growing up.

After the same type of tearful reunion, which I'm sure embarrassed her husband, we began talking. I could sense she was uncomfortable and when after a time the tension did not subside, I asked her what was troubling her. It was then she told me that Tom was a police officer for the City of Oakland. My sister had been somewhat reluctant to bring him because she was uncertain what my reaction would be. It did not surprise me, but also made me feel that he must be a special person to come with her to a place like Alcatraz. (I was indeed correct in feeling he was special, as over the years to come, he did many things to help me and there was never any criticism of what I had done in my life.)

Once Kay made the facts known she relaxed, and our visit was a wonderful experience. It was Tom who taught me a lesson that day, one that I have never forgotten. I learned that no one should be judged because of his occupation. I knew my incarceration on Alcatraz could be a source of tremendous embarrassment to my family, were it known. I decided to devote all my time and energy toward doing things that would get my good time restored and a transfer away from Alcatraz, but I never betrayed a trust or in any manner harmed my friends or fellow prisoners. I decided I would take as many correspondence courses from the University of California as possible to earn credits toward a high school diploma.

As rehabilitation was not a part of the policy at Alcatraz, funds were very limited. I selected three courses, and the cost of these alone used the total fund for the year. It was very slow going, as each lesson took two to three weeks to be returned before I could start on the next section. Fortunately, at this time, Mr. James V. Bennett, director of the Bureau of Prisons, made a trip to check on the institution. I requested, and was granted, an interview with him. I told him my plans to finish high school and earn the restoration of my forfeited good time. I also told him I felt the system was not encouraging this type of activity by limiting the funds allocated for courses and related materials, such as books.

He stated he was unaware that there were insufficient funds, but would investigate and, if it was true, he would personally see that whatever funds were needed were made available to me. He also assured me that if I would continue to work and study for two years, he would recommend that at least five years of my forfeited good time be restored. It was a challenge that I accepted.

For the next two years I worked hard in the net shop in the industries and studied six nights each week. I allowed myself Sunday off. At the end of this period I had completed all the correspondence courses I could use for credits toward my diploma. The remaining few credits I needed would have to wait until I was transferred to an institution with a school program like that at McNeil Island.

Mr. Bennett was true to his word about my good time. On Christmas Day 1950, I was called to an interview with Warden Johnston. He handed me a letter the director had written him, recommending that five years of my good time be restored. At the bottom of the letter was the warden's signature approving the restoration. I was then given a talk by Warden Johnston, who stated he had never at Alcatraz had anyone who tried harder. He encouraged me to continue, and said that possibly in the next year, the remainder of my good time could be restored. I was greatly pleased, as was my family, who had continued to visit me each month.

A Close Call

Everything had been going so well and then, suddenly, it almost fell completely apart. One day, without warning, I developed a tremor over my entire body.

It lasted only a few minutes, then quit. The next day the same thing occurred, except it was more intense and of longer duration. I again dismissed it as tension, or the fact that I had become somewhat worn down during the previous two years. It was not to be dismissed easily, however.

Each day, the frequency and duration of the attacks grew more severe. I checked in for sick call and was examined by the doctor and found to be in good health. I again dismissed it as nerves and tension. The attacks continued, and each day grew more acute. They were on several occasions witnessed by guards and inmates alike. I was sent one time to the hospital by a guard who thought I was having a seizure. When I reached the hospital the tremors stopped, yet just minutes before I had been trembling so hard my teeth were chattering. I was again given a thorough examination and found to be normal. It was in essence a repetition of my first few weeks on Alcatraz.

After the second trip to the hospital with no abnormal findings, I was scheduled for a visit with a San Francisco psychiatrist who came to the island each month. I had no objection, as I was frightened and believed I was going insane. This examination also revealed no abnormalities either mentally or physically; yet the attacks continued, but never in the presence of medical personnel. I was losing weight and was now unable to sleep nights. I again went to the hospital and this time the attack continued and was witnessed by the doctor. My story was finally believed and I was hospitalized. I was given several treatments, but nothing seemed to help.

As a last resort, the doctor decided to try a treatment used in some mental hospitals to calm belligerent and aggressive patients. The treatment consisted of being laid naked on a large table, arms along my sides and mummy-wrapped tightly in several layers of cold, wet sheets. The doors were closed and lights turned off for the next hour. The first time I was given this treatment I was first miserably cold, then panic-stricken because of my helplessness. I fought to release myself until I was exhausted, and then a strange thing began to occur. I started to feel warm, comfortable, and strangely at peace. In a short while, I fell into the most restful sleep I had ever experienced in my years in the prison. It was so peaceful that I had a feeling of disappointment when the hour was up and I was released.

I was admitted to the hospital for two weeks of these treatments. It was effective and the attacks gradually subsided in frequency and intensity. It was during this period I was exposed to the type of work that would become my life's occupation. Due to a shortage of help during a flu epidemic, in my spare time I was permitted to help care for my ill friends. It was a very rewarding experience to see the appreciation shown for some simple kindness.

I continued my treatment for the two-week period, then was discharged back to the mainline. The tremors were gone and I never experienced a recurrence. It was wonderful to know I was not losing my mind. I continued to work in the net shop until I heard there was to be an opening for an orderly in the hospital. I decided to apply, but thought my chances were very poor, in view of my past conduct. Surprisingly I was given the assignment. This allowed me to live in the hospital and allowed more freedom from under the gun.

Soon after my assignment, I was given responsibilities not normally associated with orderly work and soon became engrossed in all aspects of hospital care. Noting my obvious desire to learn, the resident doctor and several MTAs took it upon themselves to teach me various tests and procedures. As I learned and acquired more proficiency in these phases,

I was given other duties, such as giving hypodermic injections and preparing surgical packs. My desire to learn seemed to have no limit. Each day was a new adventure that I looked forward to with great anticipation. After several months, I was given the chance to take an X-ray. It so intrigued me that I determined, if and when I was transferred to another institution, I would ask to be trained in this phase of hospital work.

Christmas 1951 arrived and, again on the recommendation of Director Bennett and the warden, the remainder of my forfeited good time was restored. I was informed I was also eligible for transfer to another institution if and when approval was granted by the Washington Bureau of Prisons. I was pleased I was eligible to leave, but held no high hopes. My feeling was that I would stay a minimum of three more years, although I had not been involved in any major confrontations since 1946.

The first eight months of 1952 proceeded in much the same fashion as the previous year. I was continually learning and doing my job well. My life had settled down into a routine that, while not a happy life, was not the painful struggle that I had previously experienced. Each month, I received a visit from some member of my family, and the maximum mail permitted.

On August 28, 1952, a transfer was brought from USP McNeil Island. As a coincidence, it was on the tenth anniversary of my arrival at Alcatraz. Later in the evening, as I was doing my final duties for the night, I was summoned into the chief medical officer's office. This was not a good omen, as it usually indicated you were in trouble.

While I walked down the long corridor to the office, my brain was racing. I could not think of anything that I had done that would result in my being summoned there. As I opened the door and entered, I realized there was more than the usual complement of personnel. I then saw the associate warden and my heart sank. The only thought running through my mind was *what had I done, or been accused of doing*?

My feelings must have been apparent on my face, as suddenly everyone was laughing and congratulating me. I still did not understand until the associate warden told me I was leaving Alcatraz the next evening for McNeil Island. Ten years and one day of hell were coming to a close, and the relief and happiness I felt at that minute defy description. I had made it.

The next day I said goodbye to friends and lastly Jack, who was now working as the warden's cook. At this parting, we felt we were saying goodbye for the remainder of our lives. It was very hard, as we had been together for over twelve years and shared many experiences, both good and bad.

24 Major Changes

Early the next evening, I was taken to the administrative office, where I was joined by three others who were also being transferred. We were going to a new world. We were handcuffed, shackled, and then chained together as a group. We were transported to the dock, where the prison launch waited to take us to Oakland.

In Oakland, we boarded a train. The rear car had been sectioned off and only prisoners and guards were permitted in this area. Once inside the car, the chain that held us together as a group was removed. Each of us, however, remained handcuffed and shackled to a partner. This made any movement difficult, especially the use of the restroom. At meals our handcuffs were removed but, as added security, our shackles were chained to the base of the seat. This eliminated any sudden movement or possible attack on the guards. Much of this close security was taken because of my long sentence and history of escapes. The trip was uneventful, and after many hours we arrived in Steilacoom, Washington, where we disembarked for the van and boat trip to the island.

Upon arriving at the prison, we were given a shower, a skin search, and a new issue of clothing. Again the marking ink gave me a new identity. I was now #15874. This time, however, I was not required to participate in the thirty-day orientation program.

I was again housed in the maximum-security section. The remainder of the week consisted of a series of interviews with the warden, associate warden, and captain of the guards. Each interview repeated the same theme: escape or any major infraction of the rules would result in a return to Alcatraz. I was not particularly impressed, as I had no intention of trying to escape, but was concerned by their preoccupation with the subject. I realized I had better be careful or this stay might be as short as my previous one.

The first productive meeting I had was with Mr. Case, director of education. When he learned I wanted to complete my high school education, he was very enthusiastic in setting up a program to allow me to do so. I was not interviewed by the committee for a work assignment. I requested placement in the X-ray department, but because it was a position for only one man and required more experience than I had, I was assigned to the hospital as an orderly.

McNeil had a far larger hospital than Alcatraz, and the work was quite different from what I had previously done. Here surgery was done five days a week by many skilled and specialized surgeons who volunteered their time to make life better for the inmates. Acute and reconstructive surgery was done by those doctors, who came from Tacoma and Seattle. One particularly talented plastic surgeon, Dr. Banfield, did considerable facial reconstruction and his ability and willingness gave many disfigured inmates a very positive psychological boost.

The concepts and policies of this institution were the extreme opposite of Alcatraz's. McNeil operated on the principle that we were individuals who had broken the law and our punishment was incarceration. We were not in prison to be abused and degraded, but to be rehabilitated and returned to society, more responsible and skilled than when we had arrived. This concept was demonstrated by the many vocational and educational opportunities available to every inmate.

The most difficult change for me was adapting to the freedom allowed the inmates. Cells were open until 9 p.m. and inmates were allowed to visit, go to night school, attend educational movies in the auditorium, or go to the gymnasium. During the summer months, additional activities were available in the outside yard area. Each cell was equipped with two-station earphones that remained on until 11 p.m. A commissary was provided and inmates were allowed to spend $15 each month for such luxuries as cigarettes, candy, cookies, and toilet articles. Magazines and daily newspapers were available by monthly subscription.

I went to work in the hospital and soon fell into the routine of the surgical floor. After a short period on this floor

I was given a new assignment. I was placed in charge of the tuberculosis unit. Here I was responsible for all shots, medications, and necessary charting. This was a good assignment for me, as it provided study time for the classes I was taking at night school.

A vacancy was created in surgery and I requested, and was given, the new position. I learned to assemble various surgical packs and, as I became more proficient, earned more responsibilities. I learned to scrub in as instrument nurse and often worked as the surgeon's assistant on simple surgeries.

While I was working in the surgical department, a new psychiatrist joined the staff. I decided to ask for his counseling in an effort to determine why I had not conformed to the acceptable code of behavior, as had most people. To this day, I am not certain that I was ever given a clear, definite answer, but just being able to talk to him gave me a new perspective on many things. Dr. Garvey finally told me I had found my own answers and future sessions would not help me. He felt I could and would make it in the free world, if released.

During the period when I was working in surgery, Jack was transferred back to McNeil Island and assigned to work in the dental laboratory. He too was housed in the maximum-security unit. We agreed that for our own protection, we would limit our time together to meals. This, we hoped, would eliminate any possibility of administration thinking we were conspiring to escape.

The following year, the State of Washington approved a pilot Vocational Nursing Program for the inmates. Completion of the intense, year-long program and taking the state examination would allow for state licensure in this field. It was a program designed to attract men into nursing, especially into the state mental hospital system. The curricula and examination for licensure were closely monitored by the State Board of Professional Nursing. I applied for and was given the opportunity of taking the class. After completion, I took the examination and passed with the second highest grade in the state for that year.

The following year, I was selected by the hospital staff and prison administration to act as assistant to the registered nurse teaching the course. This I felt was quite an honor. These were all fine achievements, but I still had not been able to get into the field that most intrigued me: X-ray. The day finally came when the X-ray technician was discharged and, because I had been spending my free time learning all I could from my predecessor, I was given the assignment. As I became more knowledgeable in X-ray, I began to realize that I had acquired a well-rounded versatility in the medical profession.

I now began to think seriously about my future and the possibility of parole. I thought of the personal achievements I could present at my hearing, which was rapidly approaching. I felt I had met and surpassed the criteria usually applied to determine eligibility for parole. Among my accomplishments were completion of high school and receiving my high school diploma, and licensure as a practical nurse. I was also competent and qualified in most phases of hospital work, had received psychiatric counseling, and was active in the teaching programs. Additionally, I had been free of any major disciplinary action for many years. These accomplishments looked good on my record but I still had some major obstacles to overcome.

The first of these was the conflict between the State of California and the U.S. Parole Board. I was caught in the middle between these powerful bureaus and the policies each had adopted. The problem was that the U.S. Parole Board would not parole an inmate to another institution and the State of California would never drop a detainer on an escaped inmate. While both sides maintained their respective positions, my personal accomplishments toward rehabilitating myself meant nothing. I was destined, by virtue of these policies, to serve another fifteen years unless someone was willing to compromise. I felt certain California would not change its policy that an escapee must always return.

After much thought, I felt my best chance was to attempt to get the U.S. Parole Board to reconsider its position. I wrote to the director of the Bureau of Prisons to enlist his assistance. While sympathetic, he informed me it was not within his jurisdiction to help me. He did make a suggestion that later proved invaluable: to have a member of my family locate and contact the victims of my crime. If they were willing to appeal to the parole board for my release, it might have an impact on the members. My family immediately started working and, after much effort, located one of the victims. He stated he felt I had been punished sufficiently and had no objection to my release and would write the necessary letter. I was now beginning to have a glimmer of hope. I also realized that this was only one of the hurdles I had to get over. Mr. Jack Minihane, an MTA and a friend who had taught me surgical procedures, suggested writing to the judge who had sentenced me. The judge had died, but I decided to write the judge who had replaced him on the bench.

In my first letter, I informed him of my accomplishments, the feelings of the victim of my crime, and the dilemma in which I was caught. His response was less than enthusiastic and appeared to show little interest in another judge's case, especially one fifteen years old. I am certain he received many letters such as mine concerning cases he had sentenced. I was determined not to give up as I believed his recommendation would have a great influence on the members of the board. The importance of a letter from him justified my persistence and the possibility that I might antagonize him. What did I have to lose? I wrote again and received a prompt reply but no indication of a willingness to help. I resolved to write each month until I had an affirmative or absolute refusal to help. After many letters, each of which was very similar in content, the time came when I did not receive a reply. I felt I had lost and he had outright refused my request. I was very disheartened.

After several weeks, a ray of hope suddenly appeared. Judge Ritter had written Dr. Garvey for a copy of my psychiatric evaluation. I waited each day for a letter from the judge, but it never came. I did not know what to do. To write again might offend him, yet the suspense was almost unbearable. Knowing that he had at last shown an interest raised my hopes, and it was hard not to be optimistic. I decided to live with what I knew. I realized my criminal record was going to weigh heavily against me at my hearing, and even a letter from Judge Ritter did not assure me of any positive action by the board.

I was now in my fifteenth year, and my parole hearing was scheduled for May. I submitted all the necessary applications and copies of my achievements. From the outside, my family was writing and submitting everything they felt would be beneficial to my case. Once these things were done, there was nothing left to do but put it in the hands of the Lord and wait. During the waiting, I received a personal letter from Judge Ritter. He said that, after studying my past criminal record, my conduct during fifteen years of imprisonment at Alcatraz and McNeil, and my efforts to change my life and rehabilitate myself, he had recommended that I be granted parole.

Jack had also applied but had not made any special effort to enlist help from anyone. He had done well since 1946 and had become an excellent dental technician. It was now just a matter of waiting until we were notified by mail what our future held.

It was a trying four to six weeks, for an application's early return usually indicated a denial of parole. Each night for the next two weeks, I worried every time the mail was delivered. At the end of the third week my application was returned, as was Jack's. I was afraid to open it, but with pounding heart and trembling fingers I tore open the envelope. Before reading the enclosed letter, I said a prayer that I would be able to cope with the results. I quickly scanned the contents, looking for the word *denied*. It wasn't there. I had been granted parole to San Quentin, effective in four months. Suddenly I heard a yell from the other side of the cellhouse. It was Jack, and he had also been granted parole.

The next four months at McNeil saw many changes in the routine of the hospital and my life. The work hours of the MTAs were changed and the island had no free medical personnel on duty after 7 p.m. The institution physician lived on the island but was subject to call only in the event of major incidents such as stabbings or other life-threatening emergencies. I was offered the opportunity to live in the hospital with my own room, and access to the hospital diet kitchen, in exchange for attending to the medical problems that arose after the hospital was closed. It was a challenge, as I was given more authority related to the hospital than had been given any previous inmate.

My duties included giving all narcotics ordered, running specific lab tests, and determining if an inmate's illness necessitated being hospitalized. I also took care of minor abrasions, cuts, and lacerations. I had learned to suture while I was in surgery and was permitted to administer this type of treatment. If I had any doubts about my ability to handle a situation, I was allowed to call the doctor at any time.

One problem associated with the position was the possibility of inmates using my inexperience in diagnosis to gain admission to the hospital. A favorite method was to create a fever, and there were many very ingenious tricks in this area. It was often done by putting lye soap under the armpit, drinking a hot liquid just before having a temperature taken, or catching me off guard and rubbing the bulb of the thermometer rapidly on their clothing. These cases were usually easy to detect, as the visible signs of fever sufficient to necessitate admission would be absent. In these incidents, the inmates were given a repeat of the test while being more closely observed. Most were normal upon the second attempt. They were then given two aspirin and told to return in the morning for an examination by the doctor. Amazingly, very few ever returned.

A more difficult problem was the patient who complained of a kidney stone. The usual criterion for the presence of a stone was blood in the urine. During the first urine sample, the inmates were usually allowed to go to the restroom alone. This often resulted in the microscopic examination showing gross blood. This was accomplished by the faker pricking his finger with a pin and dripping the blood into the specimen. A repeat sample, taken while being observed, was usually negative. The most devious and hardest to detect was the smart, hospital-wise inmate who would take a pin or a straightened paper clip, slip it into the urethra, and create a small laceration that was undetectable. This inmate could then produce a specimen positive for blood either with or without my presence. On these cases, I called the doctor, who would then have a record check made to determine if the inmate was incarcerated for drugs or their use. If the patient was not involved in drugs, they were often given narcotics, thereby eliminating the necessity for surgery. I am sure that, on occasion, the narcotic offender was unjustly denied the medical attention he deserved, but it was always a decision made by others, not me.

Closing In on Freedom

The remaining four months of my sentence passed incredibly slowly, even with my new job. I found it difficult to sleep because I now had hope of being in the free world. I still had several problems to overcome before this could be a reality. There were endless possibilities in how the State of California Adult Authority would handle my case. Among them: let the original fifty-year sentence stand, rehear my case and reduce my sentence, or have me brought up for a hearing each year until they were willing to release me. This would leave me in a perpetual state of limbo, year after year, not knowing my future.

The other factor determining how soon or when I would get out was related to the untried charge of escape. It could be dropped or I could be tried. If I was tried, and the sentence run consecutively to my original sentence, it could add years of incarceration in San Quentin. My hope was that, after looking at my attempt to change, my accomplishments in learning a profession, and my clean record since 1946, the Adult Authority would drop the escape episode and give me a quick board hearing and a reasonably early release. These thoughts were always in my mind.

After what seemed an eternity, September arrived. It was our month, the month we would leave the care of the federal government. We were fitted with our civilian clothing, probably the one occasion thus far that made it seem more than just a dream. We were required to attend several interviews and classes designed to impress in our minds the conditions of our release and how to readjust to society. They were that we return to San Quentin and satisfy the sentence the Adult Authority imposed on us for our original sentence and the escape charge, after which we would again become federal parolees. It was rather complicated, but the one certainty was that the State of California had to be very cognizant of my efforts to rehabilitate myself or I was still doomed to many years of prison.

The day before our discharge, we were summoned to the associate warden's office and introduced to the two men who would be taking us back to San Quentin. An unusual aspect of the meeting was that one man, Louis Nelson, the associate warden of San Quentin, had been a lieutenant at Alcatraz during our imprisonment there. He was a well-liked and respected individual whom both Jack and I had gotten along with well. The other man was the captain of the guards. Both had a great deal of expertise in transporting prisoners.

All the paperwork was completed, as we were to leave early the following morning. Needless to say, it was a long and sleepless night. In the morning we were transported by the island launch to the dock at Steilacoom, where we were met by Louis Nelson and the captain. Here, Mr. Nelson gave Jack and me an alternative. Give our word not to run and he would use only handcuffs; if not, it would be shackles and cuffs all the way. He also informed us that the comfort of the trip would be determined by our actions. He assured us there would be no escape.

We were handcuffed and driven to the Tacoma airport. Here we were to catch a plane to San Francisco. It was very strange indeed to be in the midst of all the hustle and bustle of the busy airport. Each officer had brought a topcoat that they gave to us to drape over our cuffs so no one would be aware that we were under restraint. We had arrived early, and it was very exciting just to sit and observe the actions of the hurried people. Only two minor incidents occurred during the trip.

The first took place as we boarded the plane. The stewardess who greeted the oncoming passengers somehow observed the fact that Jack and I were handcuffed and refused us permission to board until the cuffs were removed. Louis refused. The stewardess then called for the captain of the plane. He agreed to let us be seated under the condition that once the plane was closed up and we were ready to take off, they would remove our cuffs and not reapply them until the plane was again safely on the ground. The two guards agreed and we were ready to go. The plane taxied away to our runway and the cuffs were removed as agreed. Soon we were airborne and everyone relaxed. Jack was even allowed to use the restroom unaccompanied.

The second incident occurred when another stewardess was making rounds, passing out complimentary champagne. Jack, the first of our group asked, accepted. This forced Louis to inform the confused young lady that we were prisoners and that the entire group, himself included, would have to decline. I never knew why Jack accepted, possibly as a joke, but for a few minutes it strained the congenial atmosphere we had achieved. It soon passed, however, and the stewardess made a concerted effort to make our trip memorable, bringing candy, soft drinks, and anything she felt we would enjoy.

Our trip was over too soon. We landed at San Francisco, and this time Louis did not recuff us. He said we were on our honor not to run. If ever temptation was placed in front of a man, it was as we worked our way through the crowded airport. I had a constant desire to run, to be a part of the life that was all about me. Escaping could have, and would have, been easy. I knew Jack experienced the same feelings. Many thoughts raced through my mind. I thought of freedom, and the right to do as I wanted, when I wanted to; fortunately, I also thought of my family,

Alcatraz, and the trust that had been placed in me. I just couldn't throw them all away, even though I did not know what the future held, except prison and bars, and both within a very short time.

The prison van was there to meet us and soon we were on our way to the grim walls of San Quentin. Just prior to our arrival at the prison, Louis and the captain thanked us for our cooperation in making it a pleasant trip. Louis then apologized, but said he was going to recuff us to eliminate any criticism that could be directed at him for not doing so when we disembarked.

When we arrived within sight of the prison, I was suddenly overwhelmed by a tremendous feeling of depression. I had the recurring thought I should have run at the airport. I knew I could have made it easily. The problem was, I would again have had to return to crime and its lifestyle. This would have soon led to my demise, as I would never have let them capture me alive. It was not what I wanted, or what I had worked so hard to achieve during the past several years, but being back inside San Quentin was not what I wanted either. Once inside those walls, my life and future were in the hands of the Adult Authority.

San Quentin Again

We returned to the prison with the usual routine for any new admission. We were wished well by Louis Nelson and the captain, and I became another minute particle of the large mass of humanity of San Quentin. I was #64452, an

Jim Quillen

old-timer among the thousands who inhabited this holding
pen for the dregs of California's society.

San Quentin's population was composed of doctors,
lawyers, and Indian chiefs, as well as psychopaths, sexual
deviants, killers, forgers, and some of the most vicious men
ever to inhabit the world of crime. Present also were the
affluent and influential, now far removed from their former
lives and companions. From the minute one stepped inside
those walls, feelings of the restlessness, turmoil, tension, and
suppressed violence were ever present.

After being dressed in and complying with all the requirements of a new admission, I was escorted across the "Big
Yard" to South Block, where I was to cell. South Block was
a huge, cold, five-tier cellhouse that contained 1,000 cells
and housed 2,000 men. Each and every cell was constantly
under the gun force from a guard walking the gun rails
surrounding the block. As I crossed the yard I was greeted
by several old friends, some of whom had been released and
returned, others who had been there since my escape.

I was housed on the fourth tier and, after placing my
newly issued clothing in the cell, was started on a round of
interviews and psychological and psychiatric testing. These
took most of the remainder of the day. I was then turned
out into the yard where I could visit for an hour with old
friends.

A special friend, whom I had known since I was in prison,
was waiting to see me. He warned me of the great changes
that had occurred during the fifteen years I was in federal

prison. San Quentin was no longer a place where an inmate could peacefully do his time, but a cauldron of boiling violence, precipitated by overcrowding, the formation of rival gangs, and the young age of the majority of the offenders. Among the young, violence was a way of creating excitement, and a status symbol. There need not be a rationale for the violence; it could occur for any reason. A look, an accidental bump, or even just knowing or being with someone could involve you in a major and often violent, deadly confrontation.

The old code of ethics that an inmate did his own time was gone. Gang rule was the way of life, and if an inmate did not or would not belong, he had to constantly be on guard and prepared to protect himself.

C.D., as my friend was known, told me he would get me a shiv (knife) and bring it in the morning. I refused his offer, but he said he would meet me after breakfast and we would discuss it. I had not located Jack, as he was housed in North Block; thus I went to dinner alone. It was a strange and somewhat frightening experience to be thrown in among 5,000 men, of whom I possibly knew ten to twenty. I now faced a new routine, and might have to confront a young punk looking to build a reputation (especially if he found out I had been at Alcatraz).

The next two nights at San Quentin were to be a real nightmare. I returned to my assigned cell and when the bar was lifted, I entered. Whoever was my cell partner was not there, so I left the door ajar so the bar could not drop, so my partner would not get a "lockup" (loss of weekend yard privileges for being late). I heard the gun gallery guard yell for me to close the door, and just as I started to do so my cell partner arrived and rushed in, closing the door. It was immediately apparent that he was not pleased to have me as a cellmate, even though I had just done him a favor.

I introduced myself after the count and was met with total silence. I decided to let the matter rest and go about my own business. I made my bed and then turned to store my personal belongings on one of the two shelves provided. I asked him which shelf he preferred and again received no response. As the bottom shelf was usually preferred, I removed his belongings and put them in this area. Although he was watching, nothing was said, and he made no effort to help. I completed the job and then lay down on the bed. Not one word was spoken the entire evening, until just prior to lights out, when he stood up and told me to get a cell change the next day or he would throw me and my belongings over the tier the next night. I did not respond, as my temper was starting to get out of hand, and I knew a serious problem would result if I let it. I did not sleep that night, as I did not know what to do or even what he might do. I didn't even know his name.

I had the option to go to the "porch" (the front office, where cell changes were made) but getting a cell change after one night in an overcrowded prison was not going to be easy without divulging the true situation. I could not go and snitch on him, so I decided to talk to C.D. in the morning. Upon leaving the cell, I was again warned by my as-yet-unknown cell partner not to be there on his return that night. I met C.D. in the yard and informed him of what had occurred. He asked what I intended to do and I told him I did not know, but I was not going to move. I was nervous and on edge and still had another interview to attend that day for job placement. C.D. said he had not gotten me a shiv as I had said I didn't want one. About that time, my cell partner passed and I pointed him out. C.D. said he would find out what he could about the guy and meet me for lunch. I agreed, and left to attend my job interview. I again asked for assignment to the X-ray department, but it was full. I was assigned instead to surgery, effective the following week.

I met C.D. for lunch, but the only information he could get on my cell partner was that he was a loner, in for murder, and was considered crazy by the few inmates C.D. could get information from. My friend had to leave, but told me to wait for him for supper. I started hunting through the yard for Jack, but because he ate in a different dining room I was unable to find him.

I was really uptight now. I couldn't run, I couldn't snitch, and yet returning to my cell that night might ruin everything I had been working all these years to accomplish. I gave some thought to attempting to be admitted to the hospital, but I just could not run. I knew it was crazy, but I just had to see this through—call his bluff (if that's what it was) or face the consequences, if he was serious. Once one starts to run in prison, he is finished and everyone will take advantage of this weakness. I had faced too many confrontations in my life to begin to run now.

I met C.D. for supper, and as we were filing into the dining room, he slipped me a shiv. I didn't want to take it, yet I was afraid not to. If I was caught with this in my possession, my future was gone; but if I didn't take it, I might lose my life. I quickly slipped the knife inside my shirt and continued on to dinner. After eating, C.D. wished me luck, said he would see me in the morning, and left. I was on my own with a major problem to face.

I returned to my cell and my cell partner was late again. I left the door ajar as I had the night before. The early part of the evening was a repetition of the previous night. No one spoke. About 8 p.m. my cell partner climbed down from his bunk, took off his shirt, and confronted me. I assumed he had been working himself up for this moment. He then started to tell me how he was going to take me apart and by the time the cell was opened, I would be dead. He was considerably younger than me and it was obvious he was strong.

I realized there was no way, in these close quarters, I stood a chance in a fight with him. The more he talked, the more enraged he seemed to become. I made the decision that if he attacked me, I was going to use the knife. I had slipped it up my sleeve while he was lying clown. As I stood by the sink in the back of the cell, he started toward me. I exposed the knife and told him to stop or I would kill him. He hesitated a few seconds as though debating in his mind if I was serious or not. It must have been apparent I was, as he turned, put on his shirt, and climbed back on his bed. Neither of us spoke or slept the remainder of the night. In order to be certain I would not fall asleep, I sat on the toilet all night. I am sure at times I must have dozed off, but the slightest sound caused my heart to pound and I was instantly ready for whatever might come. The night finally passed and we both went to breakfast without washing or even brushing our teeth.

As the day was warm, after seeing C.D. and giving him the details of what had occurred I found a spot on a bench against the cellhouse and fell asleep. I woke for lunch, ate, and then returned to my spot to sleep. Dinner time finally arrived, and after eating, it was time to return to the cell for another night of anxiety and torment. I entered the cell and left the door ajar. Again I was given a warning by the gun guard to pull the door shut. The count bell rang, but my cell partner had not appeared. Suddenly I realized his personal possessions were gone. He had moved and it was over. It was the last incident of trouble that happened during the remainder of my stay in San Quentin.

While awaiting my work assignment, I had time to think about the events of the recent past. Since my return I had been forced into a situation where I could have taken a man's life. I would have also destroyed the relationship with my family, for they would not have understood the code by which I had to live. I also had time to view the changes in the prison from past years.

Fifteen years earlier, the prison had been run and controlled entirely by the officials, but not so now. Gone was the creed that personal conflicts were settled one-on-one. Today the prison was controlled in many aspects by the young, vicious, and terroristic gangs who inhabited the prison. Individual problems of gang members were settled not by the individual, but by the gang. Disputes were not settled face to face, but often by a silent knife in the back wielded by someone unknown to the victim. Inmates not involved in gangs found it wise and prudent to be ever-watchful, careful with what they said, where they went, and with whom they associated. Gang members were easy to offend and responded with violence. This gave them added prestige and status with their faction peers.

Members of gangs were easy to identify. They were young and ran in packs like wolves. Each gang had its own symbol, such as tattoos or sweat bands or colored bandanas worn on their heads. They were loud, boisterous bullies. Each gang had a special area of the yard they had confiscated as their own turf. Intrusion into this area, even unintentionally, could generate a confrontation of verbal, if not physical, abuse. Old-timers avoided these areas as if they were plague-infested. Watching these young bullies in action made me realize why it had been difficult for the old-timers to accept me when I first arrived at Alcatraz.

Gang vengeance was often quick, quiet, and undetected until too late. The victim would be caught in the big yard when several thousand inmates were waiting at the entrance to the mess hall. He would suddenly be surrounded by gang members (who had removed their gang identity) and quickly struck with a knife in the back or abdomen. The perpetrators would then disperse among the large mass of the general population. Often the incident would be discovered only when everyone moved away from the area to eliminate any possibility of involvement. The victim could then be seen lying on the ground, severely injured or dead.

If the victim was a gang member, this would be the beginning of a vicious cycle. Every gang, as a matter of honor, felt compelled to seek revenge for its brother members. If the victim was not a gang member, the incident was soon forgotten by all except the officials. They were, however, limited in what they could do. No one would talk, so their only response was to create a "lock down" and increase the constant and ongoing search for weapons.

These situations were not the fault of the authorities, but rather attributable to overcrowding and the type of individuals being incarcerated. These inmates refused to work or utilize the educational and vocational opportunities available to them; violence, power, and brutality were their goals in life. San Quentin had always been a tough prison because of the indeterminate sentence law, the guards, and the system in general. But now it was a tough prison to do time in because of this new rebellious breed of inmates.

My choice to work in the hospital proved to be a good one. It gave me benefits I had not been aware of. I was moved from the noisy, crowded South Block to hospital row and ate all my meals in the hospital dining room. This was allowed because surgeries often ran over their allotted time, and it was easier to feed us there rather than in the main mess halls. I liked this, as it freed me from the possibility of becoming involved in an altercation with the vicious punks who dominated so much of the prison.

Approximately ten days after my return, I was informed that the Adult Authority had reviewed my case and given me a year postponement for a parole hearing. This was expected. I had been sentenced under California's now-changed indeterminate sentence law. This made it mandatory that I receive a minimum sentence of five years. At my original hearing I had received fifty years with parole after three calendar years served.

Because of my escapes, the best I could now hope for would be the minimum of five calendar years, which at this time left me with approximately two years, if I was lucky. I was informed no new detainers had been lodged against me since my return, and my escape detainer had been dropped several years before. I realized that I was now able to see light at the end of the tunnel of what had been a hopeless future.

The holiday season came and went and I was doing well in my assignment. I had progressed from suite 1, surgical unit, to suite 3, where major facial reconstructive surgery was performed. It was an easy transition for me, as I had considerable experience in this specialty at McNeil Island. Here, too, the volunteer surgeons from the surrounding areas were pleasant and easy to work with. The year until my appearance before the Adult Authority passed quickly.

My appearance was scheduled for late November, and my family and I immediately started working to secure as many favorable recommendations as possible. The most outstanding thing I can recall about that day was the mental anguish each inmate subjects himself to while waiting on the hot seat—because he is next in line to make a personal appearance before a group that has great influence on his future.

This is a time of indescribable tension and apprehension and, like the myth of the drowning man, the inmate's past flashes before his eyes. My personal fear was that I had not accomplished enough to overcome the experiences of the past. I could visualize the board members looking at my rap sheet and seeing my long list of crimes. I could, in my mind, even hear them discussing my record of three convictions of robbery with a gun, burglary, car theft, kidnapping, and—last but not least—my escape record. Especially my last escape, which had led to an extensive crime spree. I also worried about what effect Renaldo's confession all those years ago would have on my chances.

Finally, after what seemed an eternity, the buzzer sounded, indicating I was to enter the room. It was judgment day and the culmination of my efforts over the past ten years.

With pounding heart, dry mouth, and sweating palms, I entered the room. I saw a very long conference table with several individuals seated on one side and on the other, in the center, one lone chair facing them. This was in many ways the epitome of being alone, yet in the midst of others.

As I took my seat I quickly and nervously glanced at the entire group. To my amazement, none appeared to be hostile. As I entered the room, I was greeted by the chairman of the board. His voice was friendly as he told me to take the vacant seat. His first words were very comforting, as he informed me that each of the board members was aware of the tremendous anxiety the appearance of the board created. He suggested that we merely chat for a few minutes before proceeding. This did a great deal to allow me to regain my composure and to think more clearly.

After introducing each of the board members, the chairman inquired as to whether I was ready to proceed. For the next few minutes, each of the members discussed my past criminal record, my failure to reform, and the fact that I had continually involved myself in a way of life that was not only unacceptable to society, but each time more serious—not only to the public, but to me as well. I was asked if I had a statement to present to the board. My only response was that I had changed, had been reunited with my family, and was willing to let the record of my last ten years of incarceration speak on my behalf.

It was impossible to determine from their tone or questions if I had pleaded my case well. Finally I was told the interview was concluded and I was free to leave. As I thanked each individual for his time and courtesy in making me feel at ease, I was given a quick wink from one of the members. In my search for optimism, I interpreted this to be a favorable sign and left the boardroom in an elated mood, not because of what had or had not been said, but on the basis of a friendly gesture.

The time interval before one knew of the board's decision was determined by the number of inmates on each calendar. My date had been advanced because of the upcoming holidays. December was the month when the members tried to limit, or even eliminate, meetings; therefore, it was a long hearing session, with many cases pending. All results were to be released at the same time, thus another anxiety-filled wait. After a period of two weeks, a rumor was circulated around the institution that the results would be out that night.

I had a short surgery schedule that day, so I immediately returned to my cell. I wanted to wait there for the mail delivery that would, I hoped, include the long-awaited results of the hearing. After count, I could hear the guard passing out mail. There were several shouts of joy from those who had received their parole "ducket," as well as cries of disappointment from others who had been denied. Finally it was my turn. I tore open the envelope and, as at McNeil, I scanned its contents for the word *denied*. Again, it was not there. I had actually been granted release. It was almost unbelievable. I had slightly over a year to serve, as I had been given the minimum sentence allowed by law. My sentence was set at five calendar years, but I could earn additional days off.

The next morning, I met Jack in the yard. He too had been released, but had an additional year to serve after my release. During our year at San Quentin, we had seen little of each other, therefore the pain of knowing we were soon going to be separated for good was far easier to bear.

I reported to work at the hospital as usual and amid the congratulations of my fellow workers I saw Associate Warden Louis Nelson walking down the hall. I immediately hurried out into the hall to tell him my good news. As I approached him, he turned and saw me. I instantly knew that I need not say a word, as the look and smile on his face indicated he already knew. He congratulated me and expressed his satisfaction with the decision of the board. I was sure that in some way, he had used his position to help me.

He then surprised me by inquiring if I was interested in going to camp. It would give me the opportunity to earn extra days off my sentence and acquire some money for my release. It was the opportunity of a lifetime. I told him I was interested and he instructed me to send a personal request to him and he would see if it was possible. That night I wrote my request and submitted it to his office, but with little expectation, as I had already escaped from a similar camp. The remainder of November and month of December passed with no response to my request. I believed my request had been denied, yet as I had learned from the past, anything can happen. The holidays passed, and because I realized this was to be my last Christmas and New Years in prison, they were very easy to cope with. As for my real Christmas, it came early in January. I received a letter from the work committee indicating that the following week, I would be transferred to a Division of Forestry Camp in Humboldt County. Needless to say, I was overwhelmed.

Forestry Camp

On Wednesday of the following week, I was told to have my personal property packed and ready to turn in early the next morning, as I was being transferred to camp. In the morning, I was taken from my cell before the institution was awake. It was a different world crossing the dark, deserted big yard to reach the mess hall. It was quiet and calm, yet within an hour it would become a world of turmoil and stress. In the mess hall, I joined three other inmates who were also going to camp. I was not acquainted with any of them but, because of the elation each of us felt at leaving the walls, it was soon a congenial and friendly group.

After being fed, we were taken outside the walls to a waiting station wagon. Our possessions were already strapped onto the roof and we were on our way. We were not handcuffed or restrained in any manner. As we left the prison grounds, one of the two guards turned and spoke to us. His message was plain and simple. He said they were not armed, and were not there to keep us from escaping, but simply to transport us to another facility.

He stated that we would eat a box lunch provided by the institution at noon, and should arrive at camp in time for dinner. He informed us they would make several fifteen-minute rest stops and it would be our responsibility to remain in close contact with our group. This was difficult to comprehend. A few minutes earlier, we had been behind bars and walls, and now there was absolutely nothing to prevent us from just walking away. The entire trip was a world of pleasure, as everything was so enjoyable about this newfound freedom.

We arrived at camp just in time for an excellent dinner. The food was well prepared and we could eat as much as we wished. It was difficult to tell much about the camp, as when we arrived it had already turned dark. After dinner we were taken to a large, clean, and well-lighted barracks. There were sixty individual spring beds and lockers. The area also contained numerous toilet and bathing facilities.

Reading my parole ducket seemed unreal. Ten years ago, I was hopelessly incarcerated with a possible ninety-five-year sentence hanging heavily over my head, and now the outside world was just a year away. It seemed impossible, yet the paper in my hand told me it was true. I had now only to avoid any confrontation or situation that might make me lose my release date.

We were assigned our beds and lockers, then freed to meet our friends and view the recreation room. This was a warm, comfortable area with sections set aside to play cards or ping-pong, read, or watch television. After being behind walls at various prisons for so many years, the total freedom and lack of close and suspicious supervision was unbelievable. I walked through the recreation room, greeted several old friends, and then went outside to walk in the unfenced compound area.

The night was clear and the moon and stars were absolutely brilliant. For the first time in eighteen years, I was alone, outside under the stars and unrestrained by bars, fences, or uniformed guards with guns. It was such a wonderful feeling to be free of the tension and stress that I had an overwhelming desire to cry. I walked for several minutes before I was roused from dreams of the future by the sharp sound of a whistle indicating it was time for bed.

It was a restful and peaceful night. The next morning, we were awakened by the same whistle, indicating that breakfast was in fifteen minutes. Breakfast was as excellent as the previous meal. During the night, the rains had begun again. Our arrival day had been the first break in the weather for several weeks. When everyone had eaten, it was time for the crews to leave camp for their assignments. We new arrivals were held in camp so we could attend an orientation meeting about our jobs and the rules. We were issued clothing and rain gear. We were each assigned to a work crew and instructed how to determine our work truck.

Rules were far from rigid and were basically no stealing, fighting, missing work, or missing count. The most definite and serious infraction was to be caught outside camp limits. This was an automatic return back inside the walls of the institution. The rules were easy and not difficult to comply with. A congenial and friendly atmosphere prevailed over camp and there was no legitimate reason to breach the rules.

We were informed that although we were still inmates serving our convictions, our labors were contracted for and we were working with the California Department of Forestry and the Department of Parks and Recreation. We would be paid by the state at the rate of $1.50 per hour, and at the end of each month, our keep for the month (room and board) would be deducted from our wages before the remainder was deposited in our accounts. It was possible to earn and save $30 to $75 each month. In addition, we would be earning five additional days off our sentences each month. That meant I could earn almost two months off my year. The camp was run by the institution, but only had three guards for the sixty men housed there, two on days and one during the night. At work, we were under the supervision of the Department of Forestry. After we had been issued our clothing, briefed on the rules, and given our assignments, we were free for the remainder of the day.

Camp was a beautiful place. It was nestled high in the hills on a plateau and surrounded by massive redwood trees. The air was clean and fresh, and deer and other animals often freely wandered through the grounds, seemingly undisturbed by our presence. At times they were pests, as they would eat the flowers that had been planted by the inmates to add color to our beautiful surroundings. It took time to adjust to the serene, restful, and quiet beauty of our new home, and to free oneself from the tension and stress of years behind walls.

As we learned the next day, this serenity and peace came with a price of sorts. We were going to earn it all. The work was either wet, hot, or cold and much of the time dangerous. In winter, we were to make certain the fast-moving Eel River was free of obstructions during the high runoff periods, or to evacuate people and property when the river overflowed its banks and flooded the low-lying areas. In summer, we were firefighters, on twenty-four-hour call to respond to any fire where help was needed within the state. This was the most dangerous of our assignments, as we were the front-line crew.

During the fire season, we worked directly under well-trained Department of Forestry rangers who were experts in their field and very cognizant of the blunderous situations that we, the untrained, could manage to get ourselves into. They were constantly watching over us, as somehow a raging fire became a challenge to our ability to subdue it.

We would often work twelve to fourteen hours at a time, and I saw men protest at being relieved of their duties, even though they were exhausted. A fire was a challenge they wished to see to its conclusion. I am certain a competent psychiatrist could explain why such a challenge became an obsession for most inmates. Our duties, when not fighting the rampaging Eel River or hot forest fires, was to build state parks. It was a cold, wet winter, and at times we wished we were fighting a fire. On the fire lines, we had often wished for the winter.

The months passed rapidly and, as my time grew shorter, I began marking each completed day off the calendar. When I came down to the thirtieth day before my release, I was taken back to San Quentin, but this time I did not mind in the least, as it was not for a violation of camp rules, but instead for a selection and fitting of my release clothing. It was actually a treat, as I was taken by one lone guard and treated as though I was already a free man. After the fitting and signing of some release papers, I was returned to camp. I had also been informed I had calculated my release correctly. I was to be released from California's custody, free of any attachments and placed under the provision of parole granted me by the federal government. My release date, determined with extra days off earned, was to be November 26, 1958. At this time, I would begin my thirty-year parole for the federal government.

I immediately wrote my family and gave them the good news. My brother-in-law Tom elected to drive the six hours necessary to pick me up from camp. I was going home.

Tom and my sister had arranged a room for me in their home. I could stay with them free of charge until such time as I was able to find employment and support myself. During the month prior to my release, my sister had inquired into the possibility of my employment at the State Mental Hospital in Ukiah, their home town. Prospects were very good, and my sister was told to encourage me to apply upon my release. She was told I had more than enough qualifications for employment and my criminal past would not be a deterrent, except that I would be on a longer probationary period than most new employees.

The next month was somewhat a dream. I was going home, I had a place to live, and had exceptional prospects for a good paying job. The days passed quickly except for the final night. Not being able to sleep, I walked the camp compound. Captain McEmery was understanding and helped me pass the long night. Finally dawn broke, camp woke up, breakfast was served, and I was called to "dress out." While I was dressing, Tom arrived, and within a matter of minutes I said my goodbyes and left camp with Tom.

No one could possibly understand the emotions I felt as I waved goodbye to my friends and headed out to an entirely different world. I was exceedingly fearful that I would fail, and sad that Jack was still incarcerated, yet extremely happy to be free. One fact that became apparent as we left camp behind was that "I was free!" Honestly, truly free. It was a feeling and situation I never again wished to impair.

25 Life after Prison

As I rode home with Tom that day, I was in my own private
world of unreality. I was confident I could and would
conquer the world. I was to learn it was goodbye to the
world of fantasy, however, and hello to the world of reality.
There were still many days of worry and fear to be faced
despite the fact that I was again in the world of the free and
the brave. The realization came that one needed to indeed
be brave—brave enough to face society and those with
self-righteous attitudes toward individuals who have been
imprisoned. I am certain, had it not been for the support
and encouragement of Tom and Kay, I would have surely
failed.

I soon learned there were only two things of which I was
absolutely certain. First, I would never willingly commit
another criminal act; and second, under no circumstances
would I allow myself to be returned to prison.

There were times soon after my release when I was
uncertain that gaining my freedom was the best thing. These
were only fleeting moments of discouragement, however,

which quickly passed when I thought of prison and its environment. I felt that, having survived those many years of prison, I could cope with that segment of the world that had a condemning, unforgiving, and judgmental attitude. Actually, that attitude in others was not as difficult to cope with as my own fear.

It is very difficult to describe the fear that lies hidden in the minds of those who have been in prison. It is an insidious threat that can suddenly rise to the surface and explode like an overlooked time bomb. It can be triggered by a word, a glance, a gesture, or just the close proximity of a stranger. This sudden eruption can toss you into a sea of self-doubt and uncertainty, and leave you struggling against the feeling of being somehow obviously marked for the public to see as a criminal and an undesirable. I knew this fear was just a figment of my imagination, yet it was real to me. The unfortunate part is that one cannot communicate these feelings to another, regardless of how close the relationship might be.

Tom and I finally arrived home in Ukiah, where I was given a warm welcome by my sister and a niece and nephew whom I had never met. My discharge had occurred on the day before Thanksgiving and, as a result, I had a four-day reprieve before going to make application and taking the examinations for employment at the state mental hospital.

I was confident, after learning I had scored high on the written and oral examinations, that regular employment, a mandatory requirement to retain parole, was just days away. I was soon to be disillusioned, however. The state had instituted a freeze on hiring and what appeared to be certain employment vanished.

Looking for work was very difficult for me. Ukiah was a small town: my brother-in-law was a police officer, the family was well known, and my sister was employed at the state hospital. Everyone knew one another's business, and the main source of entertainment appeared to be gossip. No one knew about my past and neither I nor my family desired to make it public knowledge but, at age forty-one, I had never been employed, had no work references, had never cashed a check, held a credit card, maintained a savings account, or opened a checking account. I realized that my best chance for obtaining employment, at least until the state started hiring, was to look for manual labor. There would be no questions asked, I would be fulfilling my parole obligations, and would not subject my family to any ridicule or gossip.

The next day Tom let me borrow his truck (even though I did not have a driver's license) to scout the town in search for work. I located several new construction sites but, because of unions or lack of skill in the field, could not get hired. I then attempted to locate a contractor or some small independent company doing repair work or remodeling jobs. I was fortunate, as this search turned up a company that had several homes and landscapes to revise. I was asked if I was willing to break concrete with a sledge hammer for $2 per hour. I stated I was, which resulted in my being hired with no questions asked.

I was on my way, or at least had crossed the first hurdle, as I was now employed. I decided I would give one-half my earnings to Tom and Kay for room and board, thereby giving me the feeling I was at least contributing to the family, if not carrying my entire weight. They objected to taking the money, but I insisted. (Unknown to me at the time, they never used any of the money, but instead saved it for me, to help me buy a car for transportation.)

I reported to work for the contractor and was taken to the site where I was to start earning my first honest salary. It was hard physical labor breaking up concrete driveways and walks with a sixteen-pound sledge hammer and concrete chisel. It would have been much easier with a jack hammer but, as his business was new and small, it was apparent that the boss could not afford to purchase such expensive equipment. For me, it involved many blood blisters resulting in painful hands and arms, but it was also honest, productive work.

After several weeks, I was informed they had run out of work for me, but would gladly rehire me if and when they had more work. This was nice to hear, but being un-employed did not fulfill my parole obligations. I decided to go to the employment agency to try to find work of a more permanent nature.

Because it was late in the day when I arrived at the employment office, I was asked to take the employment forms home to fill out, then return them early the next morning. When I arrived home, Kay and I looked over the forms and realized there was no possible way to honestly complete the forms without revealing my past criminal history. The form contained many questions I could not answer. Many were pertinent to the time I was in prison and thus the proper answers were beyond what I knew. I knew nothing about Social Security, draft status, or military induction and assignments. After a family discussion, I decided to return the unanswered forms, cancel my appointment with an employment placement officer, and again attempt to find work on my own. For a short time I had contemplated falsifying the answers, but decided that would be a poor way to start my new future.

The next day I returned the forms to the office and cancelled my appointment. As I was leaving, I heard my name called, but continued to walk. Again I was called. I stopped and walked over to the man who had been calling my name, who introduced himself as Mr. Wallace; he said that he saw I had trouble filling out the forms and was willing to help me. Before I could respond, he walked away, motioning for me to follow. I am uncertain how it occurred, but I soon found myself revealing my past. He then understood why I had not completed the questionnaire.

He was helpful, kind, and, without my asking, started filling in the papers for me. He assured me that what I had confided to him would remain confidential and that he personally would handle my case to ensure this. After making the necessary arrangements for me to secure a Social Security card, he checked the file to see if there was any work I could do. There was nothing. He then suggested

I keep looking on my own, while he inquired into the possibility of future openings in the local hospitals, ambulance services, and other medical facilities. He assured me he was going to make my case a special cause and I would soon be hearing from him.

I returned home feeling very pleased and found additional good news awaiting me. My former employer had another small job breaking concrete and wanted me to return to work in the morning. I realized I was not making great strides in conquering the world, but I was working, earning some money, and meeting the employment requirements of my parole. Two days later, I received a call from Mr. Wallace concerning the prospect of a job at a local hospital. I was to contact the hospital administrator to set up an interview. It was too late that day, so I decided I would call during my lunch break the following day.

I made the call and Miss Munroe, the administrator, said she wished to see me immediately. I explained that I was dirty and would have to be back on the job at 1 p.m. She said to come as I was and assured me I would be back to work on time. I quickly washed up a bit and, without eating, went to the hospital to meet Miss Munroe. I was immediately impressed with her graciousness and the fact that she was undisturbed by my personal appearance. She asked me to give her a brief description of my medical experience and training. Again, within a week's time, I found myself revealing the criminal past that I had so desperately desired to keep hidden. She did not appear shocked or dismayed, but if anything, was more considerate. She told me my revelation would be held in strict confidence, with the exception of the radiologist for whom I would be working, if I was given the opening in X-ray. She said I would receive a call that evening if Dr. Baird was interested in interviewing me. I left and returned to my job, yet all afternoon I was silently praying that this opportunity would work out. It was a field of medicine that I most wanted to work in, and getting the position would be the culmination of my dream.

I hurried home after work to tell my family. They were as excited as me. During the entire evening, each of us waited impatiently for the phone to ring. When 9 p.m. came, and still no call, we felt somewhat discouraged. I can recall thinking that I had missed my chance because I had been honest in everything I had said. By 9:30 p.m. I had given up, but not my sister. She insisted we would get a call, even though it was late. When 11 p.m. came and still no call, I went to bed, as I was physically as well as mentally exhausted. My sister was not ready to quit yet, however, and waited another hour. She finally gave up and retired for the night.

The next morning as I was about ready to leave for my final day's work on my job, the phone rang. It was Miss Munroe and she had arranged a meeting for noon between Dr. Baird, herself, and me. She invited me to lunch, in her office, as soon as I could leave work. She said to come in my work clothes and not to be concerned about my appearance. I hurried off to work and, because I was supercharged with adrenaline, completed what should have been a six-hour job by noon. Just before noon, my employer came by, saw I had the job almost completed, and paid me off. I was again unemployed but had great hopes for a job with a real future.

I hurried to the hospital feeling somewhat apprehensive, but also very optimistic, as if a voice from within was saying, "This is it and you have made the grade." I tried hard to control this exuberant feeling, but could not. I knew this was my big chance and hoped this inner confidence would possibly give me a more assured attitude when I met Dr. Baird.

When I arrived at the hospital, I was immediately taken to the administrator's office, where lunch was waiting. I was introduced to Dr. Baird and we indulged in idle conversation while eating. During this time, I could feel Dr. Baird's eyes looking me over, but nothing on his face indicated what his assessment of me might be. I was suddenly conscious of how I must look, yet was somehow confident it was not that important, even though it did tend to make me feel somewhat more nervous.

After lunch, Miss Munroe suggested we go to Dr. Baird's office where he could privately interview me. Dr. Baird took me on a tour of the hospital and then of the small but adequate Radiology Department. During the tour, I had the opportunity to observe and learn more about Dr. Baird than I had during lunch. He was somewhat shy, highly intelligent, and had a tremendous physical impairment of his left arm. He was very soft spoken and it was apparent, by the greetings he received throughout the hospital, that he was well liked and respected.

After returning to his office, the interview began. He asked me many questions pertinent to the work, some of which I could answer, and others I could not. He then stopped asking questions and asked me to tell him about myself. I started from the beginning of my criminal activities and neither omitted nor glossed over any aspect of my past. He never interrupted me, nor at any time appeared critical or judgmental. After I had completed my entire story, he began asking me more questions.

It was at this point I realized I was not entirely qualified for the position for which I was being interviewed. I had done many X-rays on men, but only one time had I ever X-rayed a woman. In prison, this fact had not seemed important, but when I was confronted with terms such as *pelvic pneumograms*, *mammography*, and *pelvimetries*, I was totally lost. These were studies done exclusively on women. Other studies that were done on both sexes I was capable of doing. I told Dr. Baird of my feelings concerning my lack of experience, but now he asked the question that was to give me an occupation for the next twenty-five years. He asked if I was willing to work hard and study.

When I said I was, he told me he would teach me everything I needed to know to work in any hospital in the country. He told me I was hired on a temporary basis, depending on how hard I worked and continued to learn. At that moment my emotions knew no limits, for I knew I would work hard and learn. He told me he would be leaving the next day and would be gone one week, but because it was so close to Christmas, the department work would be limited, allowing me time to learn the X-ray equipment. I was to report to work the next morning. I was instructed to do the studies I was familiar with and the others were to be scheduled for Dr. Baird's return. As we were saying goodnight, Dr. Baird told me, "Regardless of how uncomfortable you feel in my absence, stay until I return."

The following day, I reported to work as instructed. When I entered the darkroom, I saw a large, beautifully wrapped Christmas gift addressed to me. It was a gift from Dr. Baird and his wife, Marion. It contained an expensive array of toilet articles for men. I was overwhelmed by their kindness and sign of welcome. Aside from the pleasure I received from their gift, however, the rest of the week was a nightmare.

It seemed that most of my patients were females who needed X-rays done, or to set up consultations with Dr. Baird after his return. All of this was difficult, as I was far from comfortable with women; I had not had time to adjust to being in their presence. Each instance was an experience in terror for me. I would perspire, stutter, stammer, and become so nervous I could hardly swallow. It was often difficult to think, because I felt they would resent being touched or talked to by an ex-convict. At times, this fear became so overwhelming that I felt like fleeing. The only way to get my emotions under control was to think of the efforts of my family and the promises to which I was committed.

When Dr. Baird returned, the situation improved beyond measure. He acted not only as my employer, but as my teacher and friend. His presence gave me confidence, and he was always present when I was troubled. He encouraged, counseled, and guided me through many difficult months. Never, other than with my family, had I known as much concern and kindness as from this man and his wife. Shortly after Dr. Baird's return, I was hired on as a permanent employee. We spent many days and evenings together: he taught, I learned. I soon became well versed in his requirements and how to manage the Radiology Department. After several months working together, Dr. Baird and I were very close.

During this period, my social life also improved. I lost my unreasonable fear of women and became somewhat of a party boy. In a short time, my life became a routine of work, drink, and parties, all to the consternation of my family. I now had a car and an apartment and was living life as I had envisioned it while in prison. During this period of my life, I also met and married a girl of whom everyone disapproved. It did not take long before we were full-fledged members of Ukiah's party set.

This went on for a full year, during which my family and friends told me they felt I was headed toward alcoholism and/or a return to prison. I did not take this seriously, as I was no longer a thief, was earning my way, and was married.

The seriousness of the situation finally became a reality, however, when Dr. Baird and my parole officer told me the very things I had been hearing from my family and friends. This frightened me and I began to seriously consider what I had and had not accomplished since my release. I was certain then that my family and friends were telling me the truth. I was failing in many ways. I sat down with my wife Marge that night and tried to discuss my concerns and the warnings and advice I had been given.

She was not impressed, but instead angered, and said she intended to continue living her life as she had for years past. I realized I was fighting a losing battle, but thought possibly I could slowly change our lifestyle and win her over to my way of thinking. It did not work that way, however, and in a short time she was going to bars alone while I was at work. This created some violent arguments and finally climaxed with her telling me to leave and that she wanted a divorce. I left and moved in with a married couple who were our friends. Marge continued to frequent the bars day and night, and soon she was entertaining men in our home. It was then I was certain that I, too, wanted a divorce.

During this period, Dr. Baird came to me with some special papers, verifying that I had worked under his supervision for two years and was a competent and qualified technician. These were the papers necessary for me to qualify to take an examination and become a member of the American Society of Radiological Technologists. Before giving me the signed papers, Dr. Baird extracted a promise that I would someday take this examination. I gave him my word. Less than a month after my promise to him, Dr. Baird was dead from a massive heart attack.

It was a difficult blow for me to handle. Not only had I lost a wonderful employer, but also a sincere friend. I felt saddened and also devastated in that I so depended upon this man for guidance. I felt panicked at the loss. My life once again seemed a mess. It was a relief when Marge finally filed for a divorce, as now I felt I had a better chance to once again truly get myself back on the right road. Not only did I want to prove myself to my family, I also wished to fulfill the hopes and trust placed in me by my dear departed friend. He gave too much for me to throw it all away. His inspiration helped me greatly to accomplish my position in life.

While I was awaiting the interlocutory decree of divorce, a beautiful and charming new registered nurse came to work at the hospital. I asked her for a date but she refused, saying that I was a married man. I explained my position, but in her opinion I was still legally married. She did consent to think about it when my papers were issued. When the interlocutory was granted, I again asked her out. From that day forward, this lovely lady has been the center of my world, my inspiration to achieve, and the most loved person in my life. On September 10, 1963, after a long year of waiting, Leone became my wife.

During the first year of our marriage, I devoted a great portion of my time to studying to fulfill the promise I had made Dr. Baird. When I felt I was ready to take the national examination, I filed the papers he'd signed. Shortly thereafter, however, my papers were returned and I was refused permission because I was an ex-convict and still on parole. With Leone's encouragement, I refused to accept this and started a campaign to convince the board that I deserved and had earned the opportunity to take the test. After several months and many letters, the board relented. Late in 1964, I took the examination, passed, and have since that date been a member in good standing in the registry. I also kept a promise made to a deceased, but not forgotten, friend.

On April 27, 1966 my life again changed, when Leone gave birth to a beautiful baby girl who has brought great joy and happiness into our lives.

During 1965, the hospital underwent many changes. There was considerable conflict between the physicians and board members, employees felt insecure in their positions, and morale was low. In addition to the problems of the hospital, Marge, for reasons known only to her, started revealing to all our mutual friends, as well as strangers, my criminal past. Despite the fact I had worked there many years, the instability of the situation, my new responsibilities at home, and Marge's actions convinced me it was time to leave.

On December 10, 1966 I submitted my two-week resignation notice, effective December 24. On December 28, 1966 I was hired at Rideout Memorial Hospital in Marysville, California, and started work on January 3, 1967.

Again I was confronted with another new beginning in my life.

After working at Rideout Hospital for two years, I was promoted to chief technologist and radiology supervisor. This was a position I held for fifteen years, until my retirement on October 1, 1984.

It was a good life. After three years, we bought a large home, and Leone became involved in the activities of our daughter Lori's school. When our daughter reached the junior high school level, we were financially able to send her to a private Christian school.

In September 1970, I petitioned the United States Parole Board for an early commutation of sentence to time served or release from parole. In July 1971 I was released from active parole supervision. This did not mean I was off parole, only that I did not have to send in a monthly financial statement and was free to travel to other states without first seeking permission.

On December 14, 1976 I was given a certificate of early termination of parole and was no longer under the supervision of the United States Parole Commission. It also meant I could not be picked up for an infraction of parole and returned to prison with no recourse.

After being released from parole, I started to think about the possibilities of a presidential pardon. This became very important to me for two reasons: first, it would allow my daughter, if ever confronted with my criminal past, to admit that the charges were true, but also to state that I had been pardoned after working and earning my way back into society; second, it would disprove the old adage "once a thief, always a thief."

I approached my daughter with my idea because I felt she would be the person who would bear the brunt of any ridicule when my past was exposed. After I had explained what I planned to do and why, I could see the idea frightened her. I did not press for an answer, but closed the conversation with the comment that if or when she was willing for me to proceed, she was to come and tell me.

It was never again discussed until early 1979, when she came to me and said she was sure I should try. On October 1, 1979 I petitioned the President of the United States for a full and unconditional presidential pardon. It was granted on December 23, 1980. I then started work to gain a certificate of rehabilitation from the State of California, a prerequisite before one may petition for a governor's pardon. On April 28, 1981 I was granted my certificate. In October 1981, I petitioned the governor for a pardon. At the present time, the criminal division has completed its investigation, the California Supreme Court has reviewed it, and it is now in the governor's office awaiting his approval or denial. I am very optimistic that it will be granted and I will have completed the full circle from criminal back to a respected member of our society. I believe that my life proves no man is beyond rehabilitation, regardless of how far he has fallen from respectability in the eyes of society.

He gives families to the lonely and releases prisoners from jail, singing with joy!

Psalm 68:6

Appendix

Alcatraz Escape Attempts

ESCAPE ATTEMPT 1

His name was Joseph Bowers (AZ-210), a forty-year-old inmate characterized by Warden Johnston as a weak-minded man. This man was in fact mentally unbalanced, so much so that another inmate took it upon himself to smuggle a letter out to a San Francisco newspaper, asking for an investigation into his condition.

In broad daylight on April 27, 1936, at 11 a.m., Bowers attempted to escape. It was an insane and futile attempt from its beginning. Under direct observation of not one but several armed guards, this mentally unstable man began to climb the cyclone fence that encircled the area where he was assigned to work. The alarms were sounded and he ignored two warning shots. Other guards were already alerted and stationed outside the fence, leaving him nowhere to go but into the arms of these waiting guards. And beyond them were the icy waters of San Francisco Bay. His escape was, of course, an impossibility. Yet, as he reached the top of the cyclone fence, he was shot through the lung, and he then plunged sixty feet to the jagged rocks below.

The first of the so-called escape attempts had resulted in the needless death of this incapacitated inmate. His crime? Bowers had robbed a small store that also housed the local post office. He netted approximately $16. For this he had been sentenced to twenty-five years in prison. This man was a victim of the unwritten but viciously enforced "policy of death for attempted escape." He died because he was an inmate of Alcatraz, under the regime of a system far more ruthless than himself, or many of the other prisoners.

ESCAPE ATTEMPT 2

On December 16, 1937, the second escape attempt ended in the death of two inmates, but this time at the merciless hands of the swift, icy, turbulent, racing waters of the bay.

Theodore Cole (AZ-258) was serving fifty years for kidnapping, and Ralph Roe (AZ-260) ninety-nine years for bank robbery. On this cold and extremely foggy day, with a strong 8 mph outgoing tide, Cole and Roe engaged in what they had considered their well-planned escape.

Countless hours of preparation had been poured into their plan. The bars in the mat shop, through which they would embark upon their escape to freedom, had been cut almost through in readiness, then cleverly filled in with black shoe polish to preserve the appearance of being solid and uncut. At approximately 1 p.m. on their long-awaited day, they were locked into the mat shop. The fog was rolling in. After taking the count, the guard was to then take the next group to its work area, call in the count, then return to the mat shop, where he would remain until the next count at 1:30 p.m. This absence would allow the escapees a one-half-hour head start before their absence was detected. Unknown to the guard, their escape plan was already in progress upon his return to the mat shop.

After the guard had left at 1 p.m., Roe and Cole wrenched loose the cut bars, dropped to the ground below, and proceeded to a locked gate in the fence. This particular gate was used to dump useless parts of tires from the mat shop into the bay. Here they used a wrench to break the gate lock, after which they climbed down to a ledge twenty feet below. They were now at the water's edge. Each inmate carried a sealed five-gallon can with straps attached to act as a life preserver, and a knife. Not taken into account in all their well-laid plans were the treacherous, menacing waters on which they depended for transportation to freedom.

Shortly after entering these waters, the two men were grabbed by the swiftly moving current and swept out toward the ocean. As they approached "Little Alcatraz," a tiny island off the end of Alcatraz, they were torn loose from their supportive cans. They both disappeared beneath the surface of the water—first Roe, then Cole—never to be seen again. Their cans raced away to vanish in the by-now heavy fog.

From the metal shop and clothing factory above the mat shop, those few inmates who were aware of the plan watched the attempted escape and death of their fellow inmates from the beginning to its disastrous conclusion. Not one inmate later interviewed by the FBI and administration ever admitted they knew about the plan or what happened. Their purpose was not only self-protection, but also to give continued hope to others who felt hopelessly incarcerated and to frustrate the administrative authorities. After all, the silent disappearance of these men cast the first small doubt about the feasibility of escape from the island. It also changed the routine of the prison. On days when there was a thick fog, we were kept in our cells. If we were at our workshops when the fog started to roll in, we were immediately returned to the cellhouse for lockup.

ESCAPE ATTEMPT 3

The third escape attempt from Alcatraz can best be characterized by its sheer brutality. It was a plan that was conceived, plotted, and attempted by three desperate inmates.

Thomas R. Limerick (AZ-263), Rufus Franklin (AZ-335), and James C. Lucas (AZ-224) were all long-term inmates, serving time for kidnapping, bank robbery, or both. Two of the inmates had detainers from other states: Lucas for escape from another prison, and Franklin for murder in Alabama.

The plan was simplicity itself, but certainly not fail-safe. First, kill the guard in charge of the wood shop where they worked, then climb up on the roof through the window, where they had already cut some bars. Next, attack the gun tower guard on the roof of the building, securing his weapons. This would enable them to advance on the catwalk from tower to tower, killing each of the officers as they approached and, in so doing, securing more weapons as each tower fell to their assault.

The escape proceeded as planned. Officer Royal C. Cline was assaulted, taking repeated hammer blows to the head. The climb to the roof was uneventful. After cutting several strands of barbed wire, they were on the roof undetected, even in the bright sunlight. The plan to assault the first tower was then put into action; however, here their luck began to run out.

Normally the tower guard sat in his tower with the door open and unlocked. This day, unknown to the three, a relief guard—Officer Stites—was on duty and had closed and locked the door. As the three charged the tower, they realized their plan had gone awry, yet chose to continue. Still advancing, they hoped to break the glass and obtain the guard's gun.

Officer Stites was rudely awakened to the attempted escape as a piece of iron thrown at the tower crashed through the glass and hit him in the knee. He drew his .45 automatic and shot Limerick above the right eye. Limerick continued his charge, but fell, unable to proceed any further.

Franklin was fast approaching from the right side of Limerick and again Stites fired, hitting Franklin in the left shoulder. Even as Franklin was falling into the barbed wire that edged the roof of the building, he still managed to raise the hammer he was carrying in an attempt to throw it at the tower. Stites fired again, this time with a rifle, hitting Franklin in the right shoulder. The barbed wire, from which he dangled motionless, saved him from plunging to his death below.

Lucas continued to approach the tower from the other side and finally got to the locked door. Stites again fired but missed. By then the shots had brought another guard, who converged on the tower, and Lucas, seeing his hopeless plight, surrendered.

Although he may already have been dead, it was later reported that Limerick died in the hospital from his head wound. Franklin and Lucas were tried for the murder of Officer Cline. After a three-week trial in San Francisco, they were both convicted of murder and given life sentences.

This escape attempt was futile from its beginning. Even if they had obtained the weapons in the first tower, and their plan to reach the water's edge had been accomplished, there was still no possible way to escape the island. The ultimate outcome of this desperate attempt would have been their death. However, once their plan had been initiated with the killing of Officer Cline, there was no turning back, even if they did realize the impossibility of the path before them. Simply, this is what Alcatraz did to men.

ESCAPE ATTEMPT 4

The fourth attempt at escape was to be subdued and quiet, as the five men involved planned to slip away from the island without gunfire or fanfare. Not only did their plan fall short, they failed to accomplish what they set out to do, and their escapade ended in the death of one inmate. It was certainly not quiet, but rather involved much fanfare.

The inmates involved were: Arthur (Doc) Barker (AZ-268), doing life for kidnapping; Dale Stamphill (AZ-435), serving life for kidnapping; Rufus McCain (AZ-267), doing ninety-nine years for bank robbery and kidnapping; Henry Young (AZ-244), serving twenty years for bank robbery; and William (Ty) Martin (AZ-370), doing twenty-five years for post office robbery and assault. (Rufus McCain was later stabbed to death at Alcatraz by Henry Young.) Since D Block had not been a part of the remodeling of Alcatraz "in which to hold the country's most notorious inmates," as stated earlier, the five inmates involved (who had all managed to get themselves transferred there) had found it easy to cut the bars on their cells, spread the bars on the window of D Block, and slip out of the window during the early hours of the morning on January 13, 1939. (Note: after this attempt, D Block was updated with the most modern safeguards.)

Unfortunately, as they worked frantically on their raft project, using their clothing to lash the driftwood they had gathered together to make a float that would support them in the swift, cold water, the guards were busy with their count. The cut bars and spread window bars were noticed, as was the absence of the five involved. In just a matter of minutes, the institution's full force was deployed on all roads around the island. Search parties were scouring every known cove and the beach. Towers were alerted, the escape siren was sounded, and searchlights were sweeping every inch of shoreline. The island launch with armed guards and high-powered lights was joined by a Coast Guard patrol boat in the search of the cove area just below D Block. Their planned escape was thwarted, as the men were quickly spotted—cold, naked, and bruised.

Three of the inmates dropped to the beach when ordered to surrender; however, Stamphill and Barker were said to have made a dash for the water. This seems unreasonable, in view of the fact that they were surrounded, not to mention that two boats with armed personnel were in their direct line of flight. Also unreasonable and unconceivable: both men, although naked, bruised, unarmed on a rocky beach, and completely surrounded with no possible hope for escape, were ruthlessly shot numerous times as they proceeded toward the water. Stamphill, wounded, fell to the ground, but survived. Doc Barker died on a stretcher in the prison hospital.

In my opinion, shooting down defenseless, helpless men when their capture was inevitable (considering the forces involved) senselessly verified the existence of Johnston's unwritten policy of death for attempting to escape.

ESCAPE ATTEMPT 5

This attempt was less daring than any of the previous tries. No one was injured and the unwritten death policy claimed no lives. Of the four inmates involved, all serving life terms, one was to die later in the bloody shoot-out of 1946.

The setting once again was the industrial area, but in a new and more secure shop built to replace the aging facilities that had been the scene for two of the four previous attempts. The plan was to capture the guard in the shop, use the shop's electric emery wheel to cut the bars, scale the fence, and descend to the water, where a high-powered boat was to be waiting to carry them to freedom. The boat was to be driven by a relative or friend of one of the participants.

Two of the inmates involved, Joseph Cretzer (AZ-548) and Arnold Kyle (AZ-547), were brothers-in-law and crime partners. Both Cretzer and Kyle were serving sentences for murder as a result of a prior attempted breakout at McNeil Island, a federal penitentiary in Washington state.

Sam Shockley (AZ-462) was a slow-witted individual who had neither the intelligence nor the ability to concoct or execute an escape of his own making. He was a follower of others. It was this low mentality and lack of any foresight that led to his death by execution in the gas chamber at San Quentin in another aborted escape attempt in 1946.

The last member of the foursome was Lloyd Barkdoll (AZ-423), a large, muscular individual with a formidable appearance. It was his youth and appearance that got the breakout off to a good start, as he first intimidated the shop foreman, resulting in his easy capture. After the foreman was bound and gagged, the inmates went to work with the emery wheel. They were interrupted several times during their labors by people entering the shop. As each official entered, he was overpowered, bound and gagged, and locked up with those captured before him. The list of captured guards was rather impressive, considering that the superintendent of industries, a captain, and a lieutenant of the guards were among them.

It soon became apparent to the inmates, however, that their plan was going to fail. The emery wheel, which could not cut through the tool-resistant bars, broke. The hourly count was soon due and no boat had yet arrived. Captain of the Guards Paul Madigan convinced them to surrender. Reluctantly, the hostages were untied and the inmates were taken away to C Block. It was later learned that the boat had failed to appear because the intended driver had been arrested prior to the attempted break.

ESCAPE ATTEMPT 6

John R. Bayless (AZ-466) was somewhat of a loner who rarely confided in others, although he was not antisocial as such. He was one of the first inmates I met at Alcatraz and one that I sincerely liked. He offered me considerable good advice that was very helpful in my adjustment to the environment. He warned me of many situations that could occur and suggested how to handle them if encountered.

Bayless was "con-wise," but not prone to violence unless it was for his own protection or to preserve his reputation as a solid "con," which indeed he was. I believe his escape was a spur-of-the-moment decision, one that was not plotted, but just more or less happened.

It was September (date uncertain) and Bayless was assigned to the garbage detail, which was considered an "outside the walls" assignment. This gave him more freedom than could ever be achieved within the walls. His detail was often out of sight of the gun tower, as the men made their daily pick-ups around the island. One day, while they were on rounds, an unexpected fog descended upon the island. Before the crews could all be recalled and returned inside, Bayless slipped away from his supervisor and hid in the water in an attempt to lose himself in the fog, hoping to then swim to the mainland.

His attempt was short-lived. As he began floundering around in the water, he was heard by the guards, who were already searching for him. He was ordered to surrender, which he readily did. He was found cut, bruised, and battered by the rocks, almost incapacitated from the cold, and nauseated from swallowing saltwater.

While being tried for the attempted escape from Alcatraz, Bayless tried to bolt from the courtroom, again on a whim, in still another unsuccessful attempt at escape. His efforts gained him an additional five-year sentence.

To my knowledge, Bayless is the only inmate who twice served time at Alcatraz. He returned in later years as

AZ-966, with another bank robbery charge that carried a thirty-five year sentence. It is said that Theodore (Blackie) Audett was returned in later years, but I have been unable to substantiate this fact. [Editor's note: Roughly thirty men made return trips to Alcatraz over its twenty-nine-year history; Audett was sent there three times.]

ESCAPE ATTEMPT 7

The morning of April 14, 1943 dawned as a rather gloomy day. A thin layer of fog was lying several hundred yards off shore, but the sun was slowly burning this away. The bay was alive with activity. Coast Guard cutters were patrolling the huge submarine net that stretched across the Golden Gate. Buoy tenders were checking the large metal buoys that held the net afloat, and swift naval vessels were darting here and there checking for hazards (such as mines) that might impede the movement of the large cargo and troop ships that were so important to the war effort. In this setting, I believe the unwritten policy of death for escaping Alcatraz inmates was again enforced.

The plot involved four inmates. Harold Brest (AZ-487) was a thirty-one-year-old bank robber serving a life sentence. Floyd Hamilton (AZ-523), age thirty-six, was serving twenty-five years for bank robbery. (Floyd was the brother of Raymond Hamilton, a public enemy, who was electrocuted for the death of a guard in a prison break from Huntsville Prison. Raymond was a member and partner in the infamous Clyde Barrow–Bonnie Parker gang.)

The third inmate involved, Freddie Hunter (AZ-402), age forty-two, was serving twenty-five years for postal robbery. (Hunter, like Hamilton, was a member of another notorious crime gang in the Karpis–Barker era. These two gangs, along with several others, were responsible for the conversion of Alcatraz from a military to a federal maximum-security prison and for the changes in the laws which gave jurisdiction to the federal government for certain crimes.) The last member of this ill-fated and doomed venture was James Boarman (AZ-571), age twenty-four, who was serving a twenty-year sentence for bank robbery.

Jimmy was the youngest inmate at Alcatraz until my arrival in 1942. We had much in common, including our youth. He was a friend I enjoyed spending time with, and we had a very competitive rivalry on the handball court. He was very athletic and, though slight of build, had strength and endurance. I think he was the one man who, had the fog not suddenly vanished that day, could and would have made it to freedom.

The setting again involved the old industrial building and the mat shop. The inmates were making concrete blocks. This work gave them access to the mat shop, where the bars had been cut in advance, as in the case of Roe and Cole. The action started when the officer in charge of their group returned to the work area after delivering other inmates to another assignment. When the guard walked into the mat shop to check the other inmates, who were out of sight inside, he was overpowered, bound, gagged, and put in a corner where he could not be seen.

The inmates knew Captain Weinhold was making his rounds and morning inspection of all the shops. It was imperative that he be captured and subdued quietly, or the whole plan was finished. Captain Weinhold, just as the previous guard before him, did not see enough inmates in sight, and entered the building. As he stepped inside the door, he was confronted by the four inmates. After a struggle he too was subdued, bound, and gagged.

With the capture of Captain Weinhold, the way was open for the inmates to carry out their desperate plan. Even though the thin veil of fog had lifted and visibility was very good, they felt committed to carrying out their attempt. They had gone too far—turning back would have ensured them years in isolation and additional sentences.

The men kicked out the pre-cut bars and Hamilton climbed out. A large plank was passed to him, which was used to bridge the gap between the building and the perimeter fence. One after another they exited the building, traversed the plank, and reached the water's edge. All without incident. Now, in the critical phase of the whole plan, they had to swim away from the island in such a way that they would not be seen by any of the towers—especially the tower on the roof of the building from which they had come. If they could just get out far enough, they would be difficult to see.

Unknown to the escapees, Captain Weinhold had already worked the gag loose from his mouth and was shouting for help as the men entered the water. When the captain realized his voice was being overcome by the saw running in the woodshop, he instructed Guard Smith to work his whistle out of his pocket. When this was accomplished, they maneuvered their bodies until the captain was able to get the whistle in his mouth.

While the guard and captain were trying to loosen their bonds, the tower guard had become alarmed because he had not been able to reach Guard Smith in the mat shop. He called the armory and requested that others be dispatched to investigate. This action put administration on alert.

The roof tower guard then heard the shrill, sharp, penetrating sound of the whistle above the noise of the saw. He ran to the edge of the roof and observed the four men in the water below. Instead of firing a shot into the air to alert the other towers of the escape in progress, he immediately began shooting to kill the trapped men. This act was needless, considering that a warning shot would have put the island's entire recapture mechanism into action. The escape siren would have sounded, the island launch would have proceeded to the area, joined by Coast Guard cutters and other official boats in the area. The escapees would have been cut off and the inmates captured without injury. A warning shot would also have given the inmates a chance to stop and surrender rather than face the murderous gunfire that rained down upon them.

Instead, in keeping with the death policy, the guard

opened up and attempted to kill each of the four inmates. The first shots hit Brest and Boarman. Hunter and Hamilton dove for the bottom and swam back to the protection of the cliffs. They reached the shore of the island and climbed into a cave in the cliff, where they buried themselves in a pile of old rubber from the mat shop. When the launch reached the two men still in the water, they found Brest, wounded in the elbow, supporting Boarman, who had been shot through the head. When Brest was pulled from the water, he lost his hold on Boarman. Officers managed to get a boat hook under his belt, but as they attempted to pull him into the boat, his belt broke and his body sank out of sight, never to be recovered. Before losing his body, they saw his wound and realized he was dead.

I realize I feel a certain bitterness and resentment as I write about this particular incident. I resent the fact that a friend I liked and respected had his life so callously snuffed out when he was in fact helpless and harmless in the water. His death was totally unnecessary. I will always remember that his death was an execution by those in authority, who were never held accountable for their actions. Those people lived, and convinced others of, the old philosophy that "the only good convict is a dead convict." This was the mentality of many of the early guards of Alcatraz and still exists in many prisons to this day.

After the capture of Brest and the loss of Jimmy's body, the search was concentrated in the area of the shoreline cliffs and caves that bordered the old industrial building. At the entrance to one cave, some blood was discovered. The search was intensified in this particular section. A powerful movable light was brought in and a team entered the cave. A shot was fired, and Freddie Hunter emerged from under a pile of debris and waste from the mat shop. The hunt for Hamilton continued, but with less intensity, because several guards thought they had seen Hamilton shot and then sink when the guards opened fire on the inmates. The search continued throughout the next two days and nights but was then abandoned because everyone was convinced Hamilton was dead. When the search was given up, Hamilton, who was suffering from hundreds of cuts and abrasions, emerged from the same cave that Hunter had been captured in. His condition was poor because, in addition to the cuts and bruises, he suffered from dehydration, extreme cold (after being in the chilling waters so long), and sheer physical exhaustion.

He made an attempt to swim, but realized that it would be suicidal. He found the strength to climb back over the fence and through the same window he had used to get out of the mat shop, and fell asleep in another room. He was discovered by one of the two men he had helped capture and subdue at the start of this escape. He was taken to the hospital with over five hundred cuts and bruises on his body from the rugged rocks and wire.

Another triumph for Alcatraz and administration. Another death for the inmates.

ESCAPE ATTEMPT 8

This attempt shows the power of the inmate to observe, plan, wait, and then use his ingenuity and daring to attempt an escape that no one thought possible.

On Saturday, August 7, 1943, such a plan was put into effect by Huron (Ted) Walters (AZ-536). On the surface, his plan to escape may appear rather impulsive, but in reality it was well planned and executed. It had as great a chance of success as most tried at Alcatraz. Ted had been assigned to work in the prison laundry. He had worked there for several years and had always felt its close proximity to the water and its location outside the walls offered some possibility of escape, if only he could find it.

He eventually discovered the key that he had been seeking. While sitting in the recreation yard on a Saturday with the rest of the institution's inmates, he observed that the road tower and wall guards were not as observant of the industrial area as they were during the weekdays. Their attention was centered on the yard, that being the most likely possibility for trouble. When the guards did check the industrial area, it was usually with a perfunctory glance or a casual stroll to the tower, after which they immediately returned to the yard wall.

Ted's next step was to get an assignment to work in the laundry on Saturday. This posed no real problem: there was an abundance of work and a shortage of inmates willing to give up their recreation time on a weekend; also, he was a senior worker in the laundry, whose expertise could increase production. Because Ted was not an athletic individual and it was known he did not like the cold, windy yard, it aroused no suspicion when he asked for a Saturday assignment to the laundry. Still another element that favored Ted's plan was a shortage of guards during weekends, which at times necessitated their being moved about and shifted to different stations, thus leaving some areas of the industries short of their normal complement.

Ted's plan worked well at first. He proceeded, undetected, and quite successfully, until he was foiled through the element of fate. He had successfully slipped out of the laundry, climbed the fence, and started down the outside when he lost his grip and fell, severely injuring his spine. Ted made it to the water's edge, but the injury had cost him valuable time and, before he could try to swim away, he was missed. The siren sounded and, with that, his chances vanished.

He was captured and carted off to isolation in solitary confinement. Ted served out his thirty-year sentence, and was killed in October 1971 by a Texas Ranger after a robbery and hostage situation went bad. A sharpshooter fired from what was said to be the miraculous distance of one hundred yards, hitting him directly in the head. Ted's hostages were freed uninjured.

ESCAPE ATTEMPT 9

On July 31, 1945, John K. Giles (AZ-250) shocked the entire inmate population, as well as the administration of Alcatraz, by his attempt to escape.

Giles was considered by the inmates to be a "loner." He had no special friends or close associates and was very careful and cautious in anything he said to other inmates. He was a rather frail and physically weak man, and escape was never thought of in connection with him, despite the fact that he was serving twenty-five years for assault on a postal custodian and had a life detainer from the state of Oregon. Escape was not a strange occurrence to him, however. He had escaped from Oregon State Prison after serving fifteen to sixteen years of his life sentence.

Nothing in Giles indicated that he was an escape risk. He had worked on the dock for several years and had served ten years of his twenty-five-year sentence. Because of his years on the clock and his frail health, he had special duties that often separated him from other dock workers. This separation favored the plan he had in mind.

Over a period of time, he acquired, piece by piece, the complete uniform of an Army technical sergeant. This was accomplished by stealing from the laundry that was brought to the island from nearby military posts to be laundered, pressed, and returned. As the laundry was unloaded and dumped for inspection of contraband, and before it was sent through the snitch box, Giles could pick out whatever he needed. After the clothing was passed through the snitch box, it was loaded onto trucks and taken to the laundry. As Giles acquired each individual piece, he hid it until his uniform was complete.

On the morning he chose to put his plan into action, he

took his stolen uniform from its hiding place, slipped behind a building, and put it on. He then put his coveralls back on and the uniform was hidden. He returned to his work area unobserved and went about his assigned tasks. He was now ready and waiting for the 10 a.m. run of the Army boat *Coxe* to Angel Island.

The *Coxe* appeared around the end of the island and, as she docked, the crew was lined up and counted. When the count was completed, the crew was dismissed to return to their work while the guards and deckhands unloaded the arriving cargo. All returned to their work areas except Giles, who dropped unobserved below the wharf, walked on a stringer to the freight entrance of the *Coxe*, which was below the dock level, removed his coveralls and stepped aboard the boat in the sergeant's uniform.

Stories differ as to how his absence was discovered. Some say that as he was stepping from the stringer into the *Coxe*, a swell caused the boat to rock away from the dock and he was observed by two soldiers leaning on the rail. The soldiers were undecided as to whether he was an escapee or a sergeant doing some work from the boat. Before they could come to a conclusion, the boat cast off and was on its way to Angel Island. They decided to inform the captain of their observation before the boat could dock. The captain of the boat radioed Alcatraz and Angel Island of the possibility he had an escapee on board.

A quick count was called on Alcatraz, and Giles' absence was confirmation that he was on the boat. A speedboat was dispatched to Angel Island and it arrived before the *Coxe*. Associate Warden Miller was waiting there to take Giles into custody.

The other version of the incident gives credit to an alert guard, who noticed that Giles was absent from the departure count. When he was not located, it was decided he had gotten on the *Coxe* and was headed for Angel Island. The speedboat was sent to overtake the *Coxe* and apprehend Giles. The latter version is what the island administration chose to release. This explanation, however, leaves unanswered the question of why Giles would get on a boat that would take at least fifteen minutes to dock if he knew a count would be taken as soon as the boat left the dock. He was not stupid.

ESCAPE ATTEMPT 10

May 2 to May 4, 1946. Coy, Cretzer, Hubbard, Thompson, Carnes, Shockley.

Covered in detail in this book, this was the bloodiest escape attempt ever made at Alcatraz and the last attempt to do so by force and violence. The four following attempts were made after my transfer to McNeil Island.

ESCAPE ATTEMPT 11

This escape, like the attempt made by John K. Giles on July 31, 1945, was of longer duration but as unsuccessful as its predecessor.

On July 23, 1956, Floyd P. Wilson (AZ-956) disappeared

from the dock. He, like Giles, was quickly missed, but managed to elude capture for approximately twelve hours before being recaptured.

ESCAPE ATTEMPT 12

On September 29, 1958, Clyde Johnson (AZ-864) and Aaron Burgett (AZ-991) were working on the outside garbage detail. They grabbed their guard, bound and gagged him, then slipped into the frigid waters with the intention of swimming to freedom. Shortly after the pair slipped into the water, the trussed officer was missed. He was quickly located and the escape was in serious trouble. Clyde Johnson was found in a short time, clinging desperately to a rock to avoid being swept out to sea. Aaron Burgett could not be located. Approximately two weeks later, his body was located in the bay near the island. It was the first time the treacherous waters had given up the body of a dead Alcatraz escapee.

ESCAPE ATTEMPT 13

This escape involved several inmates, but only three made it to the water. An elaborate plot that utilized dummy heads, it consisted of digging into the utility corridor and then, by removing the roof ventilators, crossing the roof and descending to the ground. This gave the men free access to the water at any area outside the view of the towers. The three inmates, brothers John and Clarence Anglin (AZ-1476, AZ-1485), and Frank Lee Morris (AZ-1441), disappeared into the cold, life-taking waters of the bay, never to be seen or heard of again. This escape was possible because the prison was rapidly deteriorating, was soon to close, and security was far more lax than it had been in prior years.

ESCAPE ATTEMPT 14

The last and final escape from Alcatraz was attempted just three months and one week prior to closure. It was again accomplished because of the relaxed attitude that had taken over the security of the prison. On December 14, 1962, John Paul Scott (AZ-1403) and Darl Parker (AZ-1413) made their way from the kitchen basement to the water. Darl Parker was only able to swim to Little Alcatraz before the cold water made it impossible for him to go any further. John Paul Scott, possibly in better physical condition, reached the mainland but, because of the severe coldness of the water, was unable to make good his escape and subsequently was soon back in captivity. The irony of the situation lies in the fact that the final attempt was a success in the physical ability of the inmate, yet Alcatraz and the cold, turbulent waters of the bay were the eventual winners.

From its opening as a federal maximum-security prison on August 22, 1934, until its closure on March 21, 1963, there were fourteen escape attempts and many deaths as a result. During these attempts, seven men were shot to death and six drowned. Of the six that drowned, only one body was recovered. Alcatraz did its work well. It was never beaten, except by John Paul Scott, and the Fates decreed that even though he was successful in one respect, he failed in the end.

Acknowledgments

I would like to express my sincerest thanks and appreciation to the following persons who were so generous with their time and talents in the preparation of this book.

To Marilyn McCarthy, for her endless hours of typing, correcting my grammatical and phrasing errors, and her sincere belief this would someday be a readable book.

To Wilbur (Will) Hoffman, for his untiring reviews, advice, and efforts to see this book published. It was often his encouragement that kept the book alive. As a successful and published author (of *Sagas of Old Western Travel and Transport*) he was aware of the frustrations that face a first-time author.

To Ruth Hoffman, for her gracious hospitality and concern that everything be done correctly. And for her willingness to tolerate the hours of time I took from their family life. My gratitude to the Hoffmans is beyond my ability to express.

To Kay and Tom Stacey for their willingness to take into their home a person just released from prison, and their willingness to provide a home, encouragement, and financial support. They gave me a home and all the support possible in addition to raising their own children. It is difficult to envisage the courage this action took, especially in view of the fact that Tom was a police officer and any unlawful action I might have taken could have ruined his livelihood and his career.

To Shirley Ann Munroe, who gave me my first opportunity after release from prison to earn an honest living and to contribute to others by using the skills I learned as an X-ray technologist.

To Harold Lawson, M.D., a man who became my friend despite my sordid past. He, along with Shirley Ann Munroe, was always there to defend, protect, and guide me during the first and most difficult years after release from prison. He and Shirley Ann Munroe were friends to be cherished and loved.

To Dr. Bernard Baird, a true friend, who asked nothing but the best you were able to give. It was he who taught me X-ray technology. It was his unselfish giving of himself, his time, and his knowledge that prepared and equipped me to enter into a profession that gave me a very wonderful and fulfilling life while being of service to others.

To Dr. Robert Wankmuller, a friend who gave me spiritual guidance when I was at an impasse in life and my writing. His advice to "Put it in the hands of the Lord" was the best I could have received.

To Lori Marie Quillen, my daughter, for her courage and willingness to face the stigma of an ex-convict father in order that I might apply for presidential and gubernatorial pardons.

To my friends at Rideout Hospital, especially Amon Fairey and Mike Burke, as well as my staff, who were understanding and supportive when my writing was not going well.

To John Martini, Lee Shenk, Rich Weideman, Donna Middlemist, Donald M. Scott, and Nancy Bernard, for taking the time to critique my manuscript. They were very kind and offered many helpful suggestions.

And to Mr. Charley Money, for his interest, advice, and help in getting this book published.

God bless you one and all.